The Shallow End of War

The Shallow End of War
Accounts of the Royal Navy in the 'Sideshow' Theatres of the First World War, 1914-18

Conrad Cato

The Shallow End of War
Accounts of the Royal Navy in the 'Sideshow' Theatres of the First World War,
1914-18
by Conrad Cato

FIRST EDITION

First published under the titles
The Navy in Mesopotamia 1914 to 1917 (extract)
and
The Navy Everywhere

Leonaur is an imprint
of Oakpast Ltd

Copyright in this form © 2013 Oakpast Ltd

ISBN: 978-1-78282-166-3 (hardcover)
ISBN: 978-1-78282-167-0 (softcover)

http://www.leonaur.com

Publisher's Notes
The views expressed in this book are not necessarily
those of the publisher.

Contents

Preface to the Navy in Mesopotamia, 1914–17	13
THE NAVY IN MESOPOTAMIA	
"Wilkey"	15
Children of Kanee	17
An Amphibious Engagement	29
The Taking of Nasiriyah	40
The Man and the Axe	49
The Retreat From Ctesiphon	57
A Forlorn Hope	65
The Dawn of a New Era	73
Preface to the Navy Everywhere	82
THE NAVY IN EAST AFRICA	
The White Flag at Dar-Es-Salaam	87
Bottling up the "Königsberg"	95
Destruction of the "Königsberg"	106
An Airman's Adventures	114
THE NAVY IN THE CAMEROONS	
The Story of "King Bell"	128
Some Incidents of the Earlier Operations	136

Amphibious Operations 147

THE NAVY IN SERBIA

The "Terror of the Danube" 159

The Fall of Belgrade 164

The Great Retreat 174

THE FIRST KITE-BALLOON SHIP

1. H.M.S. "Manica" at Gallipoli 186

2. H.M.S. "Manica" in East Africa 193

THE NAVY IN THE PERSIAN GULF

The Tangistani Raids 209

THE NAVY IN ROUMANIA

The Battle Near Topalul 221

The Retreat from the Dobrudsha 234

The Battle of Vizirul 245

THE ADEN PATROL

An Outpost of Empire in Somaliland 255

Scotching the Wolf's Cub 274

THE RED SEA PATROL

The Taking of Salif 285

To
Captain Cathcart R Wason, R.N., C.M.G.
This Book is Dedicated,
In Memory of the Two Happy Years
During Which the Author was Privileged to
Serve Under His Command

Preface to the Navy in Mesopotamia, 1914-17

In writing these historical sketches of naval work in Mesopotamia, I have been guided by the evidence of naval officers who took part in the events narrated, and in some instances I have myself been an eyewitness. In every case I have checked these unofficial accounts by referring to the official despatches, and I hope that in this way I have succeeded in guarding against inaccuracy. It must be understood that my object has been to give some slight indication of the work which has been done by the navy in the course of the campaign; and though I have necessarily alluded to the military operations, I have made no attempt to give a complete account of any of the engagements so far as the army was concerned in them. The sketch entitled *The Children of Kanee* was originally written as a yarn, but, inasmuch as it records an incident which actually befell one of H.M. sloops on the Tigris, I have included it.

Conrad Cato.

London,
July, 1917

The Navy in Mesopotamia

Chapter 1

"Wilkey"

(Lieutenant-Commander Frederick J. G. M. Elkes, R.N.R., killed in action on December 7, 1914, at the taking of Kurnah.)

I think he was the only incurable optimist I have ever met. When he went sick we all used to throng into his cabin (it was the captain's deck cabin, to which he was removed for the sake of fresh air), and the sick man used to cheer us up in his own inimitable way. It was like a bracing tonic to see his funny old face and hear him talk broad Lancashire. There was a photograph in his cabin of two bonny little girls with twinkling eyes, and he used to tell me about them; and when I told him that it was easy to see whence they inherited those eyes, his own would give just that identical twinkle. Like all brave men, Wilkey was very simple and very human.

We all called him Wilkey, but whether the name was merely an amplification of his real name, or whether it referred to a well-known popular comedian, is more than I can say. He held two medals for lifesaving, as I found out by accident (for Wilkey never said much about himself); also he was a remarkably good shot with a Service revolver. If there was any kind of sport or fun to be had anywhere, Wilkey was always right on the spot. Above all, he was an incurable optimist. I believe that if he had fallen from a royal-yard he would have thrown a smile to anyone who happened to be in the foretop as he passed, and would have sung out, "Ah'm all right so far."

At Gib. the doctors declared that he had appendicitis, and insisted on sending him to hospital; but three or four weeks later he fetched up at Aden in a P. and O., and found us there tinkering up some engine-room trouble. When at last we reached the bar of the Shatt-al-Arab, and learned that we were to start a campaign in Mesopotamia, Wilkey was in a state of gleeful excitement, especially on hearing that he was to take command of an armed launch. Of course we called it H.M.S. *Wilkey*, but it turned out to be a clumsy little craft, and its engines were constantly refusing duty.

Wilkey, nothing daunted, declared that "if the bally old pa-acket wouldn't steam by herself, he would get somebody to tow him into action." He got her into the river somehow or other, but it so happened that there was no action just then, because one of our sloops silenced the guns of the Turkish battery and put all the Turks to flight, so that our troops were landed without a casualty or scrap of any kind. The capture of Busrah followed shortly afterwards., and Wilkey was transferred to the command of another armed launch called the *Shaitan*, and the original H.M.S. *Wilkey* was put out of commission. He came back to the old ship at the bar for a day or two during the transfer, and before he left again for the river he called me into his cabin, handed me his keys, and asked me to take charge of his possessions. "If anything should ha-appen to me," he said, "joost send them all to the missus." And so I said goodbye to Wilkey.

It was on December 3, 1914, that the sloops and armed launches left Busrah and steamed upstream to a position about ten miles below Kurnah. Next morning early they proceeded as far as the junction of the Shwaib and Shatt-al-Arab, about three miles south of Kurnah, and found the Turks entrenched in a long line from the village of Mazeerah to the left bank of the river. Our troops landed north of the Shwaib, and under cover of the naval artillery and two R.F.A. guns mounted in stern-wheelers they advanced towards the enemy's trenches. It was a slow business, for there was not an inch of cover on that flat open plain, and the Turk was sticking like a leech to his trenches; but at last he found it was getting too hot for him, and by one o'clock in the afternoon he had skipped back out of it. Then came the turn of the armed launches.

There were only three of them—*Lewis Pelly*, *Miner*, and *Shaitan*—but when they received the order to go upstream and shell the enemy's positions at Kurnah, the joy of battle entered their souls, and they went forging on until they got within 800 yards of the Turkish guns. Now, the Turk has a little way of pretending that he is not there, and of letting you come up quite close to him, and of then informing you, without any preliminary, that he is very much there all the time. If his gunnery in those days had been anything to write home about, there would have been no armed launches left; and as it was, they found their position quite uncomfortably warm. The sloops were round a bend of the river and could not see the Turkish guns, so the gallant little trio had to face the music all by themselves.

It was not long before the *Miner* got a shell into her engine-room at the water-line, and the water followed it through the hole. Stoker Petty Officer Arthur Jones stopped one piece of shell with his back and another with his head, and Stoker Douglas Lacey, R.N.R., became troubled in his mind about him and about the cascade which was flooding the engine-room deck. But Jones just said: "Never you mind about me. We're here to keep steam in this bloomin' boiler. That's our job. And we just carry on with it as long as the blankety old packet stops afloat. See, mate?" So they carried on. That is why the captain of the *Miner* was able to take his packet downriver and run her on the mud, so saving her from sinking. That night the engineers from the sloops patched up the hole, and next day the *Miner*,[1] serene and smiling, said she was ready for some more whenever they liked.

Meanwhile the other two went on plugging away until the general sent word that he must wait for reinforcements before he could proceed any farther, and then the armed launches were recalled. Wilkey appeared that evening in the *Odin's* mess with a face like a map of Polynesia. It was peppered all over with little bits of shell, which had just penetrated the skin and lodged beneath it. The doctor was for digging them out at once, but Wilkey was for a whisky-and-soda. "My fa-ace," he explained, "was never very mooch to look at. So ah'm not worrying about it." That was on the evening of the 4th, and for the next two days there was a lull in the operations while reinforcements were being brought up from Busrah.

On Monday, December 7, 1914, the programme opened with an overture by the sloops and armed launches, which advanced upstream about a mile, . and shelled the enemy's guns at Kurnah and his trenches on the left bank of the river. Under cover of this bombardment our troops began to advance, the plan being to clear the Turks from the left bank, cross the Tigris about three miles above Kurnah, which lies on the right bank, and then attack from north and south simultaneously. By two o'clock in the afternoon the first part of the programme was completed; the trenches were carried and the Turks driven back to their second line. It was at this juncture that the armed launches were sent up to assist the troops, and to cover their left flank from snipers or any hostile force, which might be lurking in the palm groves on the right bank below Kurnah.

---
1. Lieutenant Cuthbert E. Heath-Caldwell, R.N., in command.

Now, things that float differ from things that crawl in that they cannot hide themselves in a hole. While Tommy was making himself fairly comfortable in the abandoned Turkish trenches, Jack afloat on the water was thinking to himself that no gunner could ever hope for a better target than he presented. As for the Turk, he played his old game of Brer Rabbit, laying low, until the three launches came nicely round the bend into a direct line of fire. And then he let drive.

Wilkey was standing on the bridge of the *Shaitan*; beside him at the wheel was Chief Petty Officer Thomas Trenwith, and beside Trenwith stood Mr. George Pysey, who was the skipper of the *Shatian* in the palmy days of peace before ever the white ensign flew from her masthead. "Let them ha-ave it properly," Wilkey was saying to his gun's crew below. "Keep on plooging away." He watched the spurts of flame from the Turkish guns flash out with every round, and in his ears was the shrill music of their shells shrieking all round him.

But he was not thinking of the Turkish shells. His eyes were glued to his binoculars as he spotted the fall of each one of the *Shaitan's* shells, and directed the gun-layer as to his range and direction. "Eh, but that was a beauty!" he said; "you've got her joost right now. Carry on. Let them ha-ave it . . ." The sentence was unfinished A shell hit the *Shaitan's* wheel, ricocheted off it, and passed clean through his body. He died with the joy of battle on his lips and in his heart. Chief Petty Officer Trenwith was badly wounded; Mr Pysey was stunned, and knew no more until he recovered consciousness enough to be aware of something which lay huddled up on the deck beside him, and dreamily wondered what it was. Meanwhile Petty Officer Walter Vale, who had been below with the gun's crew, had realised at once that he was face to face with one of those moments in a man's life when action must follow thought as thunder follows lightning.

In half a dozen strides he was on the bridge, in a fraction of a second he understood that for the moment he was in command of the ship, another fraction told him that the steering gear was hopelessly smashed, and a flash of memory brought back to him an axiom of seamanship which he had learned many years ago: When the steering gear is out of action, you can steer by the engines, if she has twin screws. So he grasped the engine-room telegraph, signalled "Starboard ahead and port astern," swung the ship round, brought her downstream, and fetched her up alongside the senior naval officer's ship. There he stepped on board, saluted the S.N.O., and made his report in the same sort of tone as if he were coxswain of a steam-pinnace reporting to the Officer of the Watch that he had brought off the liberty men from the shore. The cultivation of the emotions is one of the things we neglect in the service.

Of the further events of that day and the day following a brief summary will suffice to complete the story. By the evening of the 7th our troops had cleared the left bank of the enemy, and next morning they were seeking a favourable spot to cross the Tigris. Meanwhile there was silence in the village of Kurnah, and the belief gained ground that the Turks had fled up the river during the night, The *Lewis Pelly*[2] proceeded towards the village to reconnoitre, and reached within 400 yards of it before she was greeted with a heavy fire, which made her skip back in haste according to her orders. There followed a mighty bombardment by the sloops, and in the afternoon the *Lewis Pelly* tried her luck again.

But the Turk had not got tired of the Brer Rabbit trick, and the ships had to shell the enemy heavily in order to cover her return. In the evening the General announced that the crossing of the Tigris had been effected, and that the troops on the other side were bivouacking for the night, and would attack at daybreak next morning. About midnight a small steam-launch was seen coming down from Kurnah with lights ablazing brilliantly, and doing her best to attract attention. In her were found three Turkish officers, who came under a flag of truce to offer the formal surrender of Kurnah. On December 9, 1914, the Union Jack was hoisted in the village, and Subhi Bey, formerly Vali of Busrah, with 35 officers and 95S men, became prisoners of war.

Wilkey lies in the cemetery at Margill, about five miles upriver from Busrah, and a monument has been erected by his shipmates to him and to Ordinary Seaman Edward Gibson, who died of wounds received in the same engagement. Of Wilkey the official record says:

> This officer behaved with conspicuous gallantry throughout the operations. He was an able officer, and is a distinct loss.

The unofficial record must add that he was one who, keenly revelling in the joy of life, had no fear of death. He was an incurable optimist, and, if ever he turned his thoughts to the mysteries beyond the grave, I know he must have found there a land full of hope and promise. In Shelley's *Adonais* we may find the epitaph which best befits him:

---

2. Commanded by Lieutenant John F. B. Carslake, R.N.

He is not dead, he does not sleep;
He has awakened from the dream of life:
'Tis we who, lost in stormy visions, keep
With phantoms an unprofitable strife.

CHAPTER 2

Children of Kanee

It happened at the village of Kurnah, which lies at the junction of the Tigris and Euphrates. Kurnah is never mentioned nowadays without reference to the fact that local tradition has acclaimed it as the site of the Garden of Eden, and the reputation of the garden has consequently been dragged through the mud by all the makers of mirth from *Punch* downwards. A more uninspiring spot it would be difficult to conceive. On every side a flat expanse of delta, which becomes a marsh in the flood season, and in the dry season is little more than a desert with a fringe of palm-trees near the river's edge, a scorching sun, plenty of dust, and plenty of mosquitoes.

Such is Kurnah, and whether or not it ever was the Garden of Eden, at all events it was once an outpost of the British Empire; for at the beginning of 1915 it was the northernmost limit of the British advance, and was being held by a small garrison of English and Indian troops supported by the guns of H.M.S. *Thora*. Some six miles higher up the Tigris the Turks and their Arab allies were encamped with a fairly considerable force, and were busily entrenching themselves and constructing gun emplacements wherever they could find a dry stretch of ground. All the surrounding country was in flood, and the work of the artillery, both British and Turkish, was severely handicapped. The British, however, had an important advantage in the possession of a flotilla of sloops and armed launches, whose artillery could be moved up or down the rivers to any spot where it was required. This advantage proved to be a determining factor in the early stages of the Mesopotamian campaign.

Against this naval force the Turks had nothing more formidable to oppose than a river gunboat which carried nine-pounder guns, and had always shown a remarkable agility in skipping up the river whenever the British sloops hove in sight. If the Turks could have found a-means of supplementing their very inadequate naval strength, the history of the Mesopotamian campaign would have been very different reading, but the transportation of men-of-war from Constantinople to Baghdad is no easy matter when all the sea-routes are held by the enemy. Constantinople was forced to the conclusion that even in an inland campaign sea-power has an uncomfortable way of asserting itself, and that when rivers and floods wash out all the ordinary rules of military tactics, and drive the belligerents to a form of warfare that can only be described as amphibious, sea-power represents the ace of trumps in the game. The Turks were not slow to realize this, and were embarrassingly persistent in the little attentions they paid to the British sloops. Having no guns to outrange the *Thora's* guns, they tried other devices.

The earliest and most ridiculous entertainment was to creep downstream at night in native canoes and bombard the ship with rifles at close range. This was obviously futile, but it served to amuse the Arabs in the Turkish camp; for the Arabs used to have a theory that if you hit a ship on the funnel you may pierce its most vital organs, and make it an invalid for life. The next effort was the kerosene tin filled with explosives, suspended from a plank and floated down the river—an ingenious device as far as it goes, but rather primitive for twentieth century warfare. The main defect in it is that there is no guarantee that the plank will float in the right direction, and, as a matter of fact, the strong current invariably carries it to the bank within a very short distance. Two attempts were made, and both failed; but as a result of them a boom defence was constructed across the river, and by way of additional security the *Thora* used to drop downstream every night below the pontoon bridge at Kurnah. There followed a distinct lull in the proceedings, and we had to wait patiently for the next effort.

One evening in March, 1915, there was a "kag" going on in the *Thora's* wardroom mess, where some half-dozen officers were indulging in that most innocent of short drinks, the "*Pow de Souza*." Let me explain that a "*Pow de Souza*" is a slice of sour lime in a claret glass of soda-water, with a suspicion of gin to flavour it, and a "kag" is a form of discussion peculiar to the navy, where everybody speaks at once, and no one pays the least attention to what anyone else is saying. The theorem propounded by the navigator was that a certain well-known flag-officer belonged to the bulldog breed. He did not lay it down as a theorem, of course, but as an axiom, which is the orthodox way of initiating a "kag."

And, of course, he did not trouble himself with definitions, so that no one was quite clear as to the meaning of "bulldog breed" as applied to an admiral, and the "kag" very nearly fell flat in consequence. But, fortunately, the Paymaster came to the rescue by propounding another theorem all on his own. He boldly stated that the bulldog breed had had its day, and that in twentieth-century warfare brains were worth ten times as much as breed, bulldog or otherwise. It is impossible to say what course the discussion took, because, when five or six people are all talking simultaneously, the resultant sound is about as intelligible as that of a bluebottle in a biscuit tin.

During a temporal lull in the turmoil a private of marines, told off as wardroom officer's servant, announced that the soup was down from the galley, and all the disputants disappeared into their cabins to clean themselves. This was the usual procedure in the *Thora*; nobody ever thought of getting ready for dinner until dinner was waiting to be eaten.

At the dinner-table there were certain rules to be observed. "Kags" were allowed, but they were conducted with a decorum and self-restraint almost worthy of the House of Lords, and anything which savoured of "shop" was interdicted. The mess rather prided itself on its conversational powers, which could cope with such subjects as shoes, and sealing-wax, and cabbages, and kings. (Ships were usually barred under the classification of "shop.")

The navigator could always speak fluently on any subject under the sun, whether he knew anything about it or not; the first lieutenant had an extensive knowledge of history, ancient and modern, a catholic taste in English literature, ranging from *Chambers's Encyclopaedia* to the latest guidebooks of English counties, and a passionate devotion to the works of Rudyard Kipling, Nathaniel Hawthorne, and the author of *Gals' Gossip*. The sub was also of a literary turn of mind, and dabbled in verse-making; while the paymaster could quote long passages from the English poets as well as from the Odes of Horace (until he was smothered with a sofa cushion). The doctor, although he was by nature somewhat taciturn, used to stimulate the conversation with a few well-selected interjections, such as, "Just think!" or "By Gosh!"

The claims of Kurnah as the site of the Garden of Eden were under discussion, and the Book of Genesis had been consulted as to the identity of the four rivers which flowed from the garden; and when the translation of the authorised version was challenged the revised version was produced, and everyone had become satisfied that the garden was at the junction of the Tigris and Euphrates. The possibility that either or both of the rivers might have been diverted from the courses which they followed in the days of Adam had just been mooted, when the paymaster was heard to be gently muttering to himself. The First Lieutenant instinctively stretched out for a sofa cushion, but it so happened that the paymaster was not quoting Horace, but Kipling's *Conundrum of the Workshop*. He was saying:

Now, if we could win to the Eden Tree where the Four Great Rivers flow,
And the wreath of Eve is red on the turf as she left it long ago,
And if we could come while the sentries slept and softly scurry through,
By the favour of God we might know as much as our father Adam knew.

"Well, that wasn't much," said the navigator.

"On the contrary," said the paymaster, "I believe that Adam was quite a sagacious old boy."

"But he knew absolutely nix until he had eaten of the Tree of Knowledge."

"He lived a hundred and thirty years," said the paymaster impressively.

"Well, *you* must be getting on that way, and you—"

"Now you're condescending to personalities," said the paymaster.

"Well, what did he know?" asked the navigator with the air of one who has put a real poser.

"He knew the name of every beast of the field and every fowl of the air."

"How d'you know he did?"

"Because he named them himself."

"But I bet you he didn't remember them all after he'd done it."

The paymaster was not prepared to make a definite assertion on tins point, so he let the navigator rattle on with a string of statements which would appear absolutely irrelevant and disconnected, unless you happen to know the navigator. The only thing which checked the flow of his eloquence was the fact that the dead-lights were screwed down in order to darken ship, and in spite of two electric fans the atmosphere in the wardroom was not conducive to protracted efforts in oratory. So the navigator paused to gasp, and the first lieutenant struck in with:

"Now then, old pay, let's have it. What did our father Adam know besides the names of the birds and beasts?"

The paymaster cleared his throat ominously.

"Once upon a time," he began, "in the days of long ago, when the earth was inhabited by a race of giants—"

"Is this Teutonic mythology?" asked the sub-lieutenant suspiciously.

"No, it is not," said the paymaster.

"What is it, then?" asked the navigator.

The paymaster paused, and his eye kindled with the light of cherished memories.

"I once knew a man," he said, "who had a blazer specially made for him with all the crudest and most startling colours he could think of, and across it he had emblazoned four letters—M.O.B.C."

"What does that stand for?" asked the navigator.

"That's just what everybody wanted to know. For days he kept them guessing, and they tried every variety of boating club, bicycling club, Badminton club, and bowling club. When they tired of guessing, he told them M.O.B.C. stood for 'My Own Bally Colours.'"

"Excuse me, pay," said the first lieutenant, "but can you explain to me what this has to do with the race of giants?"

"Nothing, except that the race of giants belongs to my own bally mythology."

"And now we have it. Go on."

"One of the giants was called Kanee, and he took a long journey to this very land of Mesopotamia."

"Where from?" asked the navigator.

"Now, look here," interposed the first lieutenant, "give the pay a chance. You know that he never gets through a yarn in less than half an hour under the most favourable conditions, and by that time he has invariably forgotten the point."

"If there ever was one," added the sub.

"Go on, pay . . . he took a long journey to Mesopotamia."

"And there he found the Eden Tree," said the paymaster.

"So he knew as much as old Adam," suggested the navigator.

"What did you say was the name of this worthy gentleman?" asked the first lieutenant.

"Kanee was his name, and after he had found the Eden Tree he gained a sixth sense. People now call it common sense, on account of its rarity; but of course they don't know that it is a sixth sense, or that Kanee was the first to possess it. After this he returned to his native land, where he begat many children."

"By Gosh! Just think!" said the doctor, who always liked to contribute his quota to the conversation. The paymaster was encouraged to conclude his narrative.

"And the children of Kanee settled in many parts of the world, but mostly in the land to the north of the Tweed, and in Yorkshire and in Kent."

"How about Middlesex?" asked the sub, who was born there.

"There may be some even in Middlesex. Anyhow, all the children of Kanee inherited this sixth sense, and they alone possess it."

"What a bit of luck!" said the doctor, suddenly remembering another phrase in his repertoire.

"Well?" said the navigator. "Is that all?"

"That's all," said the paymaster.

"What a rotten yarn!"

A distant thunder broke through the still night air—the sound of artillery firing. A signalman presented himself at the wardroom door.

"Turks firing at Snipe Camp, sir."

"Where are they firing from?"

"Can't say exactly where it is, sir."

"Can you see the flashes of the guns?"

"I saw one, sir, on the port bow."

"Towards Birbeck Ridge?"

"Out in that direction, sir."

"Can you see where the shells are falling?"

"No, sir; I think they must be falling short—somewhere the other side of the trees."

"Have you reported to the captain?"

"Yes; sir; he's on the bridge now."

The signalman withdrew. His report created a mystery, for between Snipe Camp and Birbeck Ridge there was a wide stretch of flooded land, and so far as was known the Turks had no guns with long enough range to bridge the distance. It was hardly conceivable that they would drag their guns all the way from their camp to Birbeck Ridge to blaze at Snipe Camp, knowing that it was beyond their range. The obvious inference was that they had procured some new guns of larger calibre.

There was a little desultory conversation on the subject, but it was too nearly akin to "shop" to arouse much enthusiasm at that hour of the evening; and the navigator seized an early opportunity of changing the subject.

"Well, pay," he said, "you haven't explained the point of that yarn yet."

"It isn't a yarn," said the paymaster. "It's my own bally mythology."

"Just think!" said the doctor.

"Perhaps it's allegorical," suggested the sub.

"Fancy the sub being able to say a word like that at this hour of the evening," commented the first lieutenant.

"Quite a good effort," said the sub complacently.

"Well, just explain the allegory, then," said the navigator.

"You were talking just now," said the paymaster, "about the bulldog breed, and I was talking about the man who can think."

"But you aren't going to start it all over again, are you?" asked the first lieutenant apprehensively. Just at this moment the captain came into the wardroom.

"Number One," he said, "'I'm going up the river tomorrow to have a makey-look-see. I fancy the Turks must have got hold of some new guns, or else they have managed somehow to bring the old ones a good deal nearer than they have ever been before."

"The signalman says their shells are falling a good deal short, sir."

"Yes, but what can their little game be? They wouldn't be such fools as to drag those old guns—of course they may be merely trying to shake us up a bit."

"It would be interesting to see what sort of guns they have brought down there."

"I don't suppose they'll leave them there; but, anyhow, I'm going to make a reconnaissance tomorrow."

"Have the Staff heard of any fresh guns arriving?"

"No, I was talking to them only this morning, and they hadn't heard of anything then. It's rather mysterious. . . . Anybody on for a rubber?"

It was a queer coincidence that someone during the evening asked how an observation mine is worked. The explanation was refreshingly devoid of technical terms.

"There's a road, or a river, or a railway, or something, and you know that the enemy is coming along it sooner or later, so you shove a mine under it. On one side of the road is a tree or something conspicuous.

You draw an imaginary line from the tree to the place where your mine is, and continue it to the other side of the road. Then you dig a hole in the ground, and connect your mine to it by electric cable. The tree, the mine, and the hole, are all in the same straight line. When you see the bloke you want to scupper coming along the road, you hide in the hole and wait until he is between you and the tree. Then you press the key, and up he goes. Only you must be quite sure that you are looking at the right tree. . . . Did I deal these? One no-trump."

At an early hour next morning the bugle sounded off general quarters, and the ship proceeded cautiously up the winding river to the accompaniment of the leadsman's monotonous chant, "By the mark, three," "And a half, three." It was a morning of glorious sunshine in the days of spring, before the land becomes a steaming caldron and the sun a pitiless furnace. Beyond the floods on the starboard beam was a stretch of sand where wild boars could be seen roaming in search of their day's rations; nearer at hand a jackal was picking his way through the flood and casting furtive glances in the direction of the ship, possibly wondering whether some lucky chance might yield him a feast before the day was out. A signalman on the bridge was sweeping the horizon with his glass. Presently his attention became riveted upon some object in the distant reaches of the river, and he watched it carefully for a few moments before turning to the captain who stood beside him.

"She's coming down, sir," he said.

"What is?"

"The Turkish gunboat, sir."

The captain raised his binoculars. There was no doubt about it; the gunboat was steaming slowly down the river. A wave of excitement swept through the ship. The *Marmaris* coming down to engage us! What a chance! It seemed almost too good to be true. It was the first opportunity since the beginning of the war for a scrap with something which floated. All the guns' crews beamed expectantly, and the order to load with common shell was carried out with an alacrity which, for the East Indies Station, seemed positively undignified. But the captain was thinking—thinking hard. Why should a gunboat with only nine-pounders come down to engage a sloop with—— He signalled to the engine-room to reduce speed. Still the little Turkish gunboat continued her course downstream until she came to a bend in the river, where she stopped and waited, a daring challenger inviting the British Lion to come on if he dared. Was she within range? The question was eagerly canvassed. Not quite; another thousand yards would do it. Suddenly the captain's voice rang out from the bridge, "Let go anchor!" Soppitt, able seaman, addressed another member of the foremost starboard gun's crew in subdued but voluble tones:

"'Oly of 'Olies! what does 'e want to stop 'ere for? Does 'e think we're a bloomin' *Queen Elizabeth* with a range of umteen miles? Another thousand yards and we've got the blessed angels—got 'em as snug and comfy as a bloomin' weevil in a bloomin biscuit. Of all the darnation shows—what does 'e want to stop for?"

"Will you try a shot at them, Number One?" came from the bridge through the megaphone.

"Ay, ay, sir."

The first lieutenant was in the foretop, spying out the land with a pair of binoculars. He leaned over the railing and gave his orders. "Close up, starboard gun's crew. Extreme elevation. Deflection five right. Fire as soon as you're ready." The starboard gun fired, and the first lieutenant raised his glasses to spot the fall of the shell. Soppitt was quite right: it needed another thousand yards; possibly another five hundred would have made it uncomfortable for the Turk. Would he come down farther and try his luck? What was the range of his guns? Was he going to return our fire? These and a hundred other questions were being eagerly discussed on the fo'c'sle, but the prevailing question was, Why did the skipper drop the hook just at the moment when he had the chance of sending the Turk to glory?

"What's the matter with the bloke?" asked Forest, a corpulent shipwright.

"'E's afraid of 'urtin' 'em," said Soppitt, waxing sarcastic.

"'Ow would you like to 'ave one of them nasty shells come at your 'ead? You wouldn't 'alf like it, you wouldn't. And you didn't ought to want to send 'em at a bloomin' Turk's 'ead. Poor innocent, misguided Turk, what don't know no better!"

The criticisms were getting dangerously pointed, when the appearance of the sub-lieutenant coming up the fo'c'sle ladder enjoined silence. As the sub usually did duty as cable officer, everyone waited expectantly for the order "Up anchor." But the order was not given. The starboard gun tried a few more rounds, and succeeded in eliciting a reply from one of the Turk's nine-pounders. It was some slight consolation to see the Turkish shell fall a good two thousand yards short. Presently a shot from the starboard after-gun appeared to fall fairly close to the enemy, and as a result he was seen to be getting under

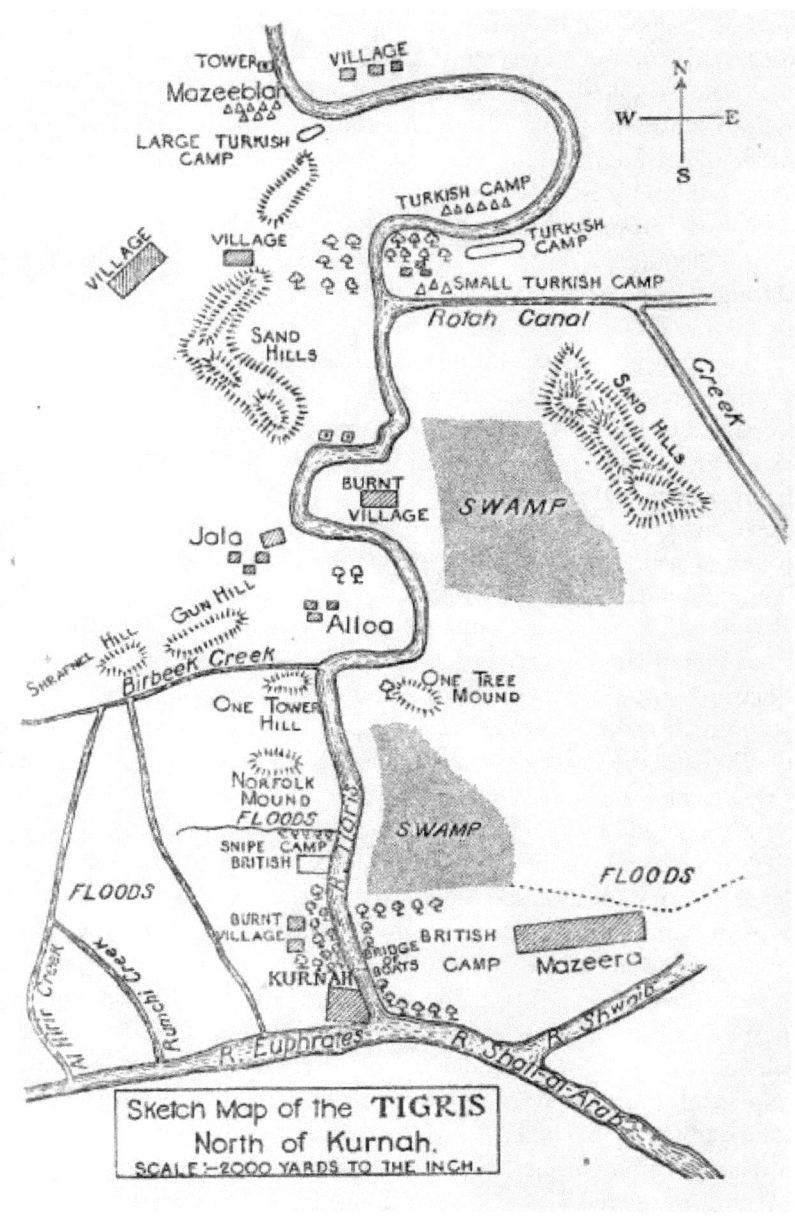

way. Many eyes were turned to the *Thora's* bridge to see if there were any sign or portent that the order would be given to proceed, but the captain stood there with an expression on his face as inscrutable as the Sphinx's.

Slowly and cautiously—for there was none too much room in the river—the Turkish gunboat turned round, and began to creep back up the river. Her deliberate movements seemed to say in tones of infinite regret: "If you're afraid to fight me, there's no use in my waiting any longer." The indignation of Able Seaman Soppitt grew beyond his own jurisdiction, and, after some futile efforts to find words capable of expressing it, he relapsed into a sullen silence, liberally punctuated by vigorous expectoration. But still H.M.S. *Thora* lay at anchor, and showed no intention of advancing another inch.

And then something happened. It is hard to explain why it happened. Perhaps the observation-station was badly placed, or perhaps the observer was over-enthusiastic, or perhaps he was looking at the wrong palm-tree. Anyhow, he pressed the key—the key which was intended to send a British ship and a hundred odd officers and men to kingdom come. A few yards in front of the *Thora* a column of water shot up and towered high above her masts. It was a magnificent sight, reminiscent of the Crystal Palace fireworks on a Brock's Benefit night. The ship's company watched it with respectful appreciation, but they did not cheer, possibly because they had a queer kind of feeling that, according to all the rules of chance and probability they should have been performers in the entertainment instead of mere spectators of it.

They gazed in silence, and when the fountain had subsided they gazed at the dead fish floating down the stream. Soppitt was the first to find his voice, but his observations relating to the enemy and their methods of warfare would suffer so much in translation that it is better to imagine them in the original. The most eloquent passage in his speech was devoted to certain German engineers who were known to be operating with the Turks. To them he ascribed the conception of the whole plot, and it is probable that he was right in his surmise. For the scheme was elaborate and worked out with Teutonic thoroughness, from the firing by night on Birbeck Ridge, to decoy us into a reconnaissance, to the final manoeuvres of the *Marmaris* which served to bait the trap. The only fault to be found with it was that it presupposed that no captain of a British man-o'-war would ever ask himself the question, "Why does a gunboat with nine-pounder guns advance to attack a sloop with four-inch guns?"

A few hours later the navigator, replete with a substantial lunch, was reclining on the wardroom sofa.

"How did the skipper know that that blankety mine was there?" he asked.

"I don't suppose he did," said the first lieutenant.

"D'you think it was just a fluke that he stopped?"

"No," said the paymaster; "there was no fluke about it. The skipper just happens to be one of the children of Kanee."

But the navigator has no faith in the paymaster's mythology. Probably he objects on principle to all private mythologies. Moreover, he inclines to a faith in the bulldog breed.

At the beginning of June, 1915, the *Marmaris*, with many holes in her side, was lying a half-sunken wreck in the Tigris, five miles above Ezra's Tomb. But that is another story. It is only worth mentioning here because, among the books and papers in the possession of her crew, the ship's log was found.

A staff officer sent us the translation of an entry in the month of March, 1915, which read:

> Proceeded down-river as far as Rota Creek in order to entice the British sloop *Thora* over the mine-field above Kurnah.

CHAPTER 3

An Amphibious Engagement

In the early days of the war, Lord Crewe, speaking in the House of Lords about the campaign in Mesopotamia, described it as an amphibious campaign. And the expression was remarkably apt. When you are waging war in a country which is under water for six months of the year, you gradually acquire the habit of thinking amphibiously. This does not mean, of course, that you become amphibious in your mode of life, or that you learn to waddle like a walrus or make a noise like a hippopotamus. But, being forced to fight in two elements simultaneously, you adjust your notions about fighting accordingly. When a third element—the air—is added to the other two, a further adjustment has to be made, and you learn among other things that supremacy in the air may give eyes to your own artillery and blindness to that of the enemy.

This is a simple proposition compared with the problem which arises when there is no dry land on which your artillery can move about, or your infantry advance to attack, or your cavalry maintain a pursuit if the enemy retreats. These problems can only be solved by learning to think amphibiously. Towards the end of May, 1915, it was decided to attack the Turkish force above Kurnah, which lies at the junction of the Tigris and Euphrates, with a view to a further advance up the Tigris.

This force was estimated to be a little over three thousand strong, and it was entrenched upon various sand-hills and dry patches of ground in the midst of the floods. In these days, when we reckon the strength of armies by the million and casualties by the thousand, no one could be expected to take much interest in so small an affair; and when the London newspapers published the bare news that our forces had advanced from Kurnah to Amarah, the only noteworthy comment of the Press was a petulant outcry by one of the weekly journals, wanting to know, "When is this picnic in Mesopotamia going to cease?" For at that time Mesopotamia was regarded as only a small side-show, bearing no obvious relation to the rest of the war, and it was felt that all the Empire's energies ought to be devoted to the serious work in France and Gallipoli. At that time, too, the name of General Townshend was unfamiliar to the public, and the fact that it was his division which made the big advance from Kurnah to Amarah failed to stir the popular imagination.

The engagement above Kurnah was remarkable for two things— the unique conditions under which it was fought, and the startling success of the British arms. The ground on which the village stands was a few feet above the level of the flood, but all around it, as far as the eye could see, was flooded marshland, dotted here and there to the northward with the small sand-hills in the occupation of the Turks. These hills had been christened with such names as Norfolk Hill, One Tree Hill, One Tower Hill, Shrapnel Hill, and Gun Hill. So inconspicuous are they in the dry season that a casual observer would imagine that the whole countryside was a dead-level plain; but in the summer of 1915 their barren soil stood out clearly amidst an ocean of green reeds, which grew to a height of five or six feet above the level of the water. The depth of the flood varied considerably, but the average was probably about two feet, and it would have been quite possible for the infantry to wade through it, if the ground had not been intersected by numerous *nullahs*, or dykes, cut at right angles to the river for irrigation purposes. Most of these were too deep to be fordable, and so it was necessary to devise other means of enabling the infantry to advance.

The Arab has invented a long narrow boat, which is eminently suited to navigate the swift current of the Tigris. He calls it a *"bellum,"* and propels it in deep water with one oar and one paddle, and in shallow water with two punt poles. The bellum played a very conspicuous part in the engagement above Kurnah. For weeks beforehand Tommy had been patiently learning the gentle art of punting, and studying how to avoid that distressing situation where the punter has to make up his mind whether he will say goodbye to his punt or to his pole. The *sepoy* also had been an assiduous student of the art; it was all part of the process of learning to think amphibiously. Then steel plates arrived from Busrah, and a new weapon of war was called into being— the armoured *bellum*.

Here was an ideal method for infantry to advance across No Man's Land. Comfortably seated on the thwarts or in the bottom of the *bellum* under the lee of steel plating, they were to be punted through a forest of green reeds, and could dream that they were spending a summer's day on the upper reaches of the Thames, until suddenly they would wake up with a bump to find that they had emerged from the forest, and had run aground on the sand-hill which was their objective. Then they must dream no longer, for a few yards in front of them the Turks in their trenches would be busy with their rifles, and the job of an attacking infantry is one of those which is all the better for being done quickly.

So the problem of creating an amphibious infantry had been solved. Next came the problem of the artillery, and it is not an easy matter to make a 4.7 gun into an amphibious monster. The best we can do with it is to mount it in a barge, and get a paddle-steamer to tow it upstream to wherever it is needed. It can then tie itself up to the bank and get to work. This sounds all right in theory, but in practice there are one or two serious obstacles. In the first place, a barge is a low-lying craft, and the gunner cannot see his objective over the top of the reeds. In the second place, when the aeroplanes have helped him to find his range, he cannot be sure of keeping it with any exactness, because his barge has a trick of recoiling after every round. The artillery did not take at all kindly to amphibiousness.

Then there were the mountain guns, which scorned anything so commonplace as a barge, and invented a craft all their own. They got the idea from the children in the kindergartens, who fold bits of paper and make all sorts of wonderful things out of them; the most wonderful of all is the double canoe, consisting of two very angular boats joined together along the beam like a pair of Siamese Twins. Take two *bellums* and place them alongside each other; then fix a wooden platform athwart the pair of them amidships; on this platform mount your gun, and, in order to protect the gunners from a blazing sun, build over them a pergola with frame of wood and roof of matted reeds; and there you have the recipe for the amphibious mountain gun. It is artistic if it is nothing else. In the stern-sheets of each bellum stands the gondolier with his punt pole, and by dint of much practice the two gondoliers learn to punt in blissful harmony. The troubles of the mountain gunner, however, are the same as those of his big brother the 47. In a forest of reeds, his fire is indirect, and his platform as unstable as a wayward minx.

Fortunately, the tale of the artillery is not yet completed. We have yet to reckon with the naval guns. Three sloops and a small flotilla of armed launches took part in the engagement above Kurnah and to them, at any rate, the presence of water everywhere brought no difficulties or embarrassments. They had bridges and foretops from which their gunnery could be controlled, and in the case of the sloops the guns were at a sufficient height from the water to enable the gun-layers to see what they were aiming at.

Their gun platforms, compared with those of the 4.7's and the mountain guns, were the essence of stability. It is true that their masts and funnels afforded the enemy a splendid mark for range-finding, but, fortunately, the Turkish gunnery at that time was poor; and although the ships were hit occasionally, there were no casualties and no material damage. It was one of the naval guns which at a range of something over 8,000 yards sent a shell right into the embrasure of a Turkish gun, which had commanded the village of Kurnah and the straight reach of river running past it. The gun was silenced, for all its crew were knocked out, and so an unmolested advance up the river was secured as far as Snipe Camp, about two miles above the village. This was the naval programme—to concentrate on each battery singly, and so silence them one after another.

Meanwhile the infantry were to advance through the reeds in their armoured *bellums*, and at the appointed times were to land on the various sand-hills and rush the enemy's trenches. The only thing which went wrong with the programme was that, except on Norfolk Hill, the Turk would not wait to be rushed. The deadly accuracy of the artillery upset his nerves badly, and, if he saw no chance of skipping back out of harm's way, he resorted to the white flag. This was not like the Turk, for usually he hangs on to his trench with the tenacity of a badger in a hole. But the naval guns, after they had silenced all his batteries, got the range of his trenches and adjusted the time fuses to a nicety, so that life was really not worth living in those trenches. The battle started soon after five in the morning, and by noon some half-dozen of the Turkish positions were in our hands, together with a fair number of prisoners and quite a useful haul of material. This completed the general's programme for the day, and the afternoon was spent in burying the dead beneath a blazing sun, while the shade temperature registered 110° F.

There was one feature in our equipment which deserves special mention, if only on account of its picturesqueness. This was the amphibious field hospital. The Arab has a form of river craft larger than the *bellum*; it is called the "*maheilah*," and is fitted with a mast and a sail. In its pristine form it is not unlike a fishing smack, but its two ends curl upwards like a Viking's ship, and its prow is adorned with paintings in the style of an illuminated manuscript. Now picture it after its conversion into a field hospital. The mast has been unshipped, and the well has been boarded over to make a continuous deck from prow to stern. Again we must revert to childhood's days, and study the design of Noah's Ark. The frame is of wood and the roof and sides of matted reeds, and on the roof is painted a large red cross.

Inside are neatly arrayed cots and all the appurtenances of the medical branch, including the hospital orderlies, whose brows are as wet as the village blacksmith's, and whose scanty attire is wetter still, for 110° F. in the shade is not far removed from a Turkish bath. Still, they are prepared for 350 casualties, and it was not their fault that they only had 23 to deal with. The total cost of the operations (apart from heatstroke cases which come into every day's work in peace as well as war-time) was three men killed and twenty wounded; and so it was really quite natural that the worthy gentleman in his armchair in Fleet Street should tell his readers that Mesopotamia was a picnic.

Next day the aeroplanes brought word that the Turks had abandoned the rest of their positions, and were in full retreat up the river in steamers, barges, and *maheilahs*, and then the whole British force began to move forward in pursuit. Now watch the procession as it files up the Tigris. First two armed launches doing duty as minesweepers, with a wire hawser towed between them; then the sloops, which look like giants amidst this motley assembly of river craft; after them more armed launches. Then come the stern-wheelers carrying the infantry, who have now abandoned their armoured *bellums*. It is a queer-looking craft, this stern-wheeler, something like a two-storied wooden house with an old hay-making machine at the stern, kicking up the water high into the air with as much grunting and groaning as though a spavined horse was setting the wheel in motion.

Besides the stern-wheeler there are the Irrawaddy paddlers, and the Indus tugs, and the steel barges of the Supply and Transport Corps; but all these are prosaic compared with the hospital *maheilahs* and the mountain guns with their double canoes and pergolas of green reeds. Darting in and out among the fleet are the motor-boats which carry about the staff officers and other important persons. There is something about the whole scene which brings back memories of Henley

Regatta, with its house-boats, its river steamers, its motor-launches, and its decorated pleasure craft.

But the enemy is in retreat, and where are the cavalry? Now, it is useless to argue with the cavalry. When they say that they cannot learn to think amphibiously, they mean it, and there is nothing more to be said about it. Their argument is, of course, that the horse is not an amphibious animal, and there is a good deal of truth in it. But the general is never nonplussed by these trifling limitations. If the horse is not amphibious, at all events the Navy is versatile, and when it has finished playing the role of artillery it will turn joyfully to the role of cavalry without requiring any rehearsals. All the rest of the story of the advance from Kurnah to Amarah is purely naval history; for the navy now leaves the army behind—all except the staff officers who find accommodation in the sloops—and goes pounding up the Tigris, past Bahran with its mud forts, past the attempted obstruction near Rotah Canal, past the remains of the Turkish camp at Mazeebla, round the Peardrop Bend, and into the then unknown reaches of the river.

The enemy had a long start, but his steamers were heavily laden and were towing barges full of infantry, and his *maheilahs* stood no chance in a race with steam. Bit by bit the distance between pursuers and pursued grew narrower, and just before sunset the enemy came within range of our guns. As the sun dipped below the horizon and the sky was suffused in a soft glow, the guns began to bark from the leading armed launch, which had been ordered to proceed to the head of the flotilla and to look out for mines. Soon after, the thunder and flame burst from the senior naval officer's ship, which followed a mile or so behind. In a wilderness of green marshes the silver windings of the Tigris showed up clearly in the evening light, and the pursuing ships forged ahead at a steady pace, ever mindful of the chant which came from the leadsman in the chains.

In the distance were the white sails of the fugitive *maheilahs*, like the wings of frightened swans, and in front of them the desperate little steamers were struggling to tow their barges laden with Turkish infantry. Ahead of them all was the Turkish gunboat *Marmaris*, bound on her last run for safety, and knowing in her sorrowful heart that she could never reach it. When the brief twilight had faded away, and darkness enveloped the whole scene, our guns still went on spitting fire, although their targets were fast becoming invisible. But it was needless, for the fugitives had realized that the game was up. The *maheilahs* lowered their sails, and those of the steamers which had not been sunk by gunfire drew sullenly to the bank, and waited for their captors to come up.

Only a very few of the men tried to escape into the marshes; most of them were too familiar with the habits of the Marsh Arab to make so hazardous an attempt. Among these few were three of the German engineers who had been employed at Busrah in connection with the Baghdad Railway, and had joined the Turkish Army at the beginning of the campaign. They in the innocence of their hearts thought that they could make their way in an Arab *mashoof* (canoe) across the marshes, and find a road which would take them to Baghdad, but they knew not the Marsh Arab. Two days later three naked German corpses were found near the river.

The last to abandon hope of flight was the *Marmaris*. She had left all her companions behind and disappeared into the darkness. But we knew what water she drew, and we knew roughly the depth of the river, so we did not worry about her. We also knew that she had some holes through her side, and probably some wounded men aboard her, and that probably her captain would have only one thought in his mind—how to render his ship beyond repair, so that she could be of no service to her captors. Presently a flickering light shot up from across the marshes, and as it grew it revealed the dark outline of a ship some five miles away round a bend of the river. The *Marmaris* had found salvation in *harakiri*; her crew had set her on fire, and encamped on the river-bank until such time as H.M. Navy should offer its hospitality to them. Her guns, however, were afterwards found to be in excellent order, and for some strange reason the ammunition in her magazine was not affected by the fire.

The pursuers had forgathered in the gloom of a clump of palm-trees, which had appeared as a conspicuous landmark in the midst of the marshes. Nestling in the palm-trees, a blue-domed temple marks the spot where the prophet Ezra is said to have died on his way from Palestine to Persia. It was an inconvenient spot to select, because it is a long way from everywhere, and necessitates a tedious journey for the Jewish pilgrims from Baghdad, who, in the days before the war, came every year to visit the tomb. It would seem that Ezra was mindful of the maxim that a prophet must be buried a long way from his own country if he would be honoured by his own people; but even he could not foretell that some day a British man-of-war would come along with an ordinary signalman who knew not Ezra, and insisted on referring to the noble edifice as "Eliza's Tomb." Let the prophet rest in peace.

He at any rate is untroubled by the voracious swarms of mosquitoes which haunt his resting-place, or by thoughts of malaria, or of a thermometer which refuses to drop to a respectable position even after nightfall, but keeps a tightly packed medley of naval and military officers gasping for breath beneath their mosquito-nets, and steadily dripping all night long on mats of woven reeds, which have the merit of allowing the drops to soak through, and so leave a fairly dry surface beneath the restless sleepers.

Next day saw the innings of the armed launches, for they alone can now continue the pursuit up the river. One Turkish steamer laden with troops has yet to be accounted for. All the rest of the Turkish force is at Ezra's Tomb under the custody of the sloops, until such time as the army can come up and take charge of the prisoners. At daybreak the armed launches get under way, the most commodious of them finding accommodation for the senior naval officer and the general, with a small personal staff. They go pounding on through the Narrows, past the village of Kulat Salih and into the broader waters above, until the general begins to grow nervous. "We really don't know what we are up against," he reminds the S.N.O.; but the S.N.O. is a born optimist, and all he says is: "I think we will just go round the next bend."

By steadily continuing the process of going round the next bend, they find themselves waltzing into the town of Amarah. Ahead of them is the launch *Shaitan*, but she is too intent on retrieving the lost lamb to feel any curiosity about this quaint-looking town; so she goes on plugging away at her best speed right through Amarah into unknown regions beyond, until in due course she overhauls the runaway, and induces it without much argument to return with her downstream. Some hours later she re-enters Amarah in triumph, and hands over another big batch of prisoners.

Meanwhile the rest of the flotilla have come to anchor, and are admiring the picturesque features of the town, including the Arab ladies drawing water from the river in kerosene tins. The S.N.O. is saying affably to the general, "So this is Amarah," but the general is busy thinking. The total British force at the moment, counting in all the crews of the launches, the general, his staff, and a dozen privates, amounts to eighty-eight officers and men. So the General says the time has come to find out what they are up against. A naval lieutenant is sent ashore in a skiff with six Tommies, and he makes straight for the Turkish barracks, where he finds quite a lot of soldiers, such as one often does find in barracks. He seeks out the commanding officer and asks him how many men he has there. The number was between 400 and 500.

"Is that all?" asks the naval lieutenant. "Then tell them to pile arms and fall in on the river-bank. They will be stowed in barges and sent down the river at the first opportunity." Now, the commanding officer does not know that the total British force at Amarah is only eighty-eight, nor that the British Army is at least twenty-four hours behind the navy. All he knows is that he has seen a steamer-load of discomfited infantry tearing up the river with an armed launch in chase, and that armed launches have guns. So he deems it wise not to argue the point. His men are told to pile arms and in due course are comfortably stowed away in barges. And that is the story of the taking of Amarah.

The, sub-lieutenant of the *Thora* was temporarily in command of one of the launches, and was ordered to take a barge-load of prisoners alongside him, and to mount guard over them. His launch had a crew of *lascars*, and the only white man besides himself was a private in the Royal Marine Light Infantry, who constituted a small but dauntless bodyguard. The sub also had a revolver and a deck-chair, both of them useful articles in an emergency. The night was divided into watches of one hour each; while the sub paced the deck, revolver in hand, the private slept peacefully in the deck-chair, and then after an hour the positions were reversed. But, if the truth must be told, they were mighty glad the next day to see the first of the river steamers bringing up the army. So was the general, and so were all the officers of H.M. Amphibious Cavalry; for those Turks were beginning to think, and among other things were beginning to think that they had been bluffed in a most ungentlemanly way. Moreover, embarrassing problems of commissariat were looming ahead, as must inevitably happen when the cavalry makes a big haul of prisoners some eighty miles beyond their nearest base.

So ended the amphibious engagement, and, turning to the profit and loss account, we must estimate the enemy's casualties in killed and prisoners at between 3,000 and 4,000, and we must add to these a substantial haul of steamers, barges, *maheilahs*, guns, ammunition, and stores.

On the other side we have to place three men killed and twenty wounded. The result of the operations has been an advance of nearly eighty miles into the enemy's country, and the capture of a garrison town. The general, who conceived the whole scheme and carried it out according to timetable, with amazing punctuality, was then un-

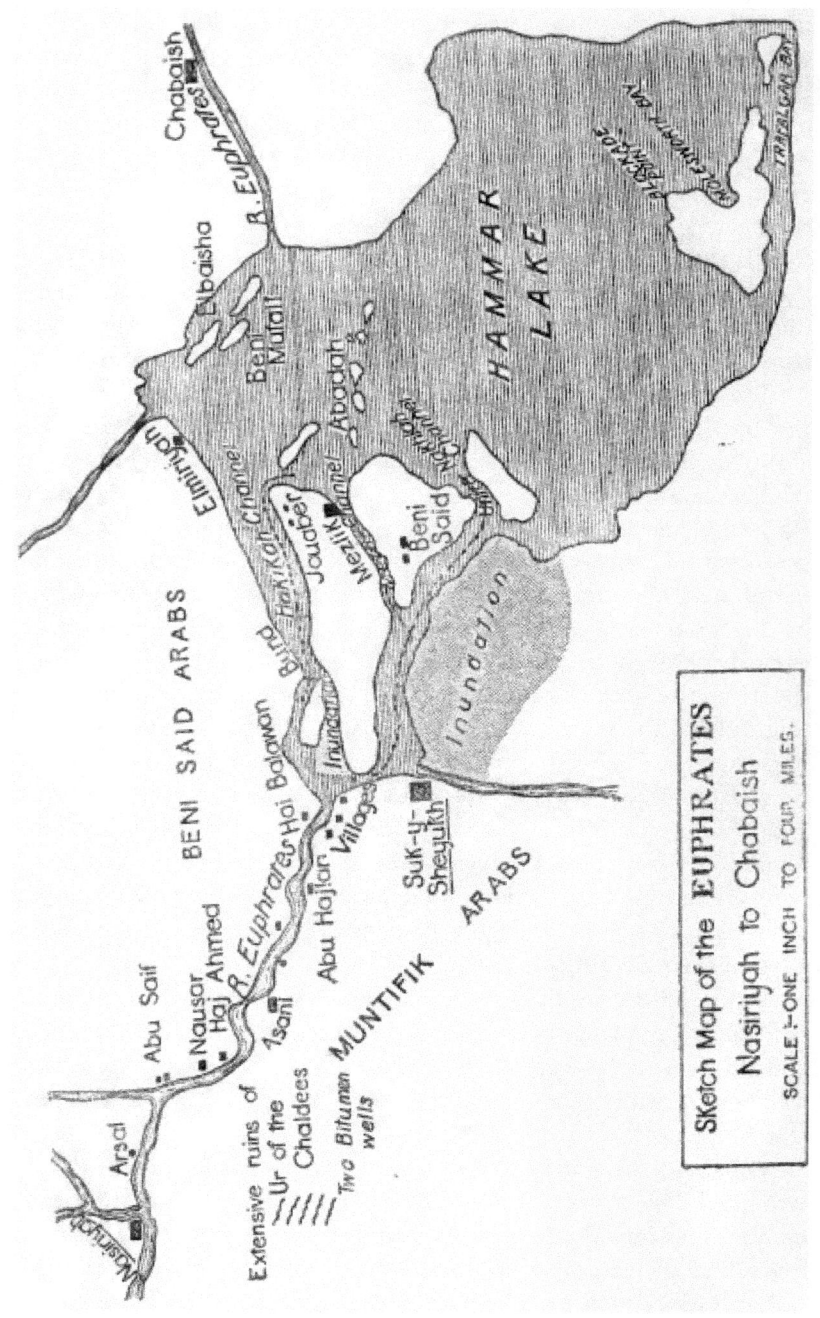

known to fame. He was destined to find it later by becoming the victim of the first disaster in the campaign. That was many miles farther up the river, where the land is dry, and the British genius for thinking amphibiously could find no scope.

CHAPTER 4

The Taking of Nasiriyah

There are two main essentials for amphibious warfare; one is land, and the other is water. In the engagement above Kurnah which resulted in the capture of Amarah, there was not very much land, but there was plenty of water. In the advance to Nasiriyah[1] up the Euphrates, which commenced about a month later, there was a moderate supply of land, but of water there was usually too little, and occasionally too much. There was too little to get over the Hammar Lake anything drawing more than five feet, but when we blew up the obstruction across the Hakeekah Channel the water came through like a cataract, and there was a great deal too much of it. The expedition to Nasiriyah taught us that in amphibious warfare the parts played by the navy and army respectively must vary according to the proportion of water to land, and according to the general condition of each of them.

The reason that we decided to go to Nasiriyah was that the Turks had used it as a base, from which in their optimistic minds they had once hoped to recapture Busrah. That dream was settled forever when our forces operating from the fort of Shaiba defeated a considerably larger Turkish force concentrated at Berjitsiyah Wood. The story of the Battle of Shaiba is as thrilling as a battle story can be, and the only thing that restrains me from telling it is the recollection that I am writing about the Navy in Mesopotamia, and the Navy had nothing whatever to do with it. When the Turks retreated from Berjitsiyah, they returned to their base at Nasiriyah; and as this base lies on the flank of our advance up the Tigris, it was decided that their presence there was a dangerous embarrassment.

If further reasons are required for the Euphrates expedition, it may

---
1. Pronounced Naz-i-reeah.

be mentioned that Nasiriyah is the centre of influence over the powerful Arab tribes in those parts, and that it has some strategic importance because it stands at the south end of the Shatt-al-Hai, the river which joins the Tigris and the Euphrates, flowing out of the former river at a point just above Kut.[2] It was also the headquarters of the Turkish civil administration of the western portion of the Busrah *villayet*.

Having decided to go to Nasiriyah, we had only one other question to settle—how to get there. A crow or an aeroplane would go in a straight line of about 100 miles from Busrah; but things that float could not go by that route because there was not enough water to float in, and things that walk could not go by that route because there was too much water to walk in. So they had to go nearly due north for about fifty miles, and then nearly due west for about eighty-five miles, while the crow and the aeroplane were taking their leisure along the hypotenuse of the triangle. But the troubles of the things that float and walk did not end here. The first eighty miles of the journey was comfortable enough, for any of the river craft could take them up the Shatt-al-Arab from Busrah to Kurnah, and then up the Euphrates from Kurnah to the village of Chabaish.

It was beyond Chabaish that the troubles began. The first of them was the Hammar Lake, a large expanse of shallow water with a tortuous channel running through it. When the expedition started on June 26 the channel was five feet deep; when reinforcements were sent up about the middle of July it was only three feet deep; and when stores and ammunition were required at the end of July for the newly installed garrison, they had to be dragged in *bellums* over a stodgy mixture of mud and water.

The Hammar Lake at the best of times is not a delectable health-resort. For scenery it has an unlimited expanse of reed-growing marshes, occasionally varied with island villages and a few clusters of date-palms. For climate it has the alternatives of a biting blast in winter and an intense humid heat in the summer. Its human population is small and by no means affluent; its insect population consists of voracious hordes of mosquitoes, which are as numberless as the sands on the seashore, and appear to thrive exceedingly.

Having crossed the Hammar Lake, the expedition entered the Hakeekah Channel, which joins the lake to the broad waters of the Euphrates. Here they had their first intimation that the enemy was ready and waiting for them. Two motor-launches, built by Thornycrofts

---

2. The *u* pronounced like double *o*, as in "foot."

for the Turkish Government, and armed with pom-poms, opened fire on the advancing river steamers. The naval flotilla returned the fire, and the motor-launches retired gracefully. The procession of river steamers then entered the channel without further interference, and after about half a mile of it they came to their next difficulty. This was an obstruction (known in local parlance as a "*bund*") which the Turks had built right across the channel.

As a rule the Turks have been singularly unfortunate over their obstructions. They tried one between Busrah and the Persian Gulf, another just below Kurnah, and yet another near the Rotah Creek, a few miles above Kurnah; but in every case we found that by means of careful navigation we could circumvent the obstacles. The Hakeekah *bund*, however, was quite a different affair. They had plenty of time in which to prepare it, and for once they managed to do the job thoroughly. They filled *maheilahs* (river sailing craft) with mud, and sank them across the channel, and then they piled more mud on top of them, so that a first-class dam was constructed; and it held back the waters of the Euphrates until they spread far and wide over the land, and were forced to find other passages into the lake.

But all things human are transitory, and the Turkish *bund* is no exception to the rule. It takes time, however, to blow up a *bund* with dynamite, and it is not a pleasant job when there is a tropical sun beating down on the workers all day long, when the night temperature seldom falls much below 100° F., and when two impudent little motor-boats, skulking round the corner, persist in irritating the workers by dropping pom-pom shells at frequent intervals. Still, it is only a question of time, and when the firing of the fuse has been followed by a mighty bang, there is a channel through the *bund* 4 feet deep and about 150 feet wide, and through it the water comes pouring in an avalanche.

How can an unwieldy stern-wheeler plough her way against such a cataract? There is only one possible solution of the problem—to haul her through with a wire hawser. Picture a long line of struggling humanity, streaming with perspiration, backs bowed and sinews at the stretch, as they tug for dear life to get the steamers one by one through the channel. The naval flotilla goes first, and as soon as it reaches calmer waters it proceeds to reconnoitre the enemy's position. Meanwhile the work of hauling the transports through goes on wearily, and at the end of five days all the craft are safely anchored at a spot near Ati's Tower.

The enemy's first position was at the junction of a small tributary, called the Gurmat Safah, with the Euphrates. Here he had guns which commanded the Hakeekah Channel, and was craftily entrenched on either side of it. On July 5, at daybreak our troops advanced to the attack, and the naval flotilla supported them with gunfire. And here is a convenient opportunity to point out the inward meaning of the axiom that in amphibious warfare the respective roles of Navy and Army must always vary with the respective conditions of water and land. The naval flotilla consisted of three sternwheelers,—a small armed launch called the *Sumana*, and two horse-boats with a 4.7 inch gun in each. All these craft were palpably makeshifts, commandeered for the purpose of this expedition, because they had a small enough draught to pass through the Hammar Lake.

The senior naval officer was in one of these stern-wheelers (the *Shushan*), and he expressed himself quite candidly upon her merits as a fighting ship. He referred to her as the "ancient *Shushan*," but I think it would have sounded better if he had said "venerable," for there is a persistent rumour that she was once the royal yacht of Nebuchadnezzar, King of Babylon. He also described the troubles of the gun's crew of the twelve-pounder which had been temporarily mounted in her. After every round they examined the deck carefully to see how much of it had carried away; and when they found that on the port side the deck could stand the strain no more, they shifted the gun over to the starboard side, and went on gaily firing until a violent recoil very nearly sent the gun, the mounting, and the remainder of the deck, through the bulkhead of the fore-cabin.

This, as the S.N.O. remarked, made good shooting very difficult. The horse-boats with their 4.7 inch guns suffered mainly from their lack of elevation. Indirect fire over the tops of the reeds was the only possible method; and although this was checked by an officer with a telephone from an advanced observing-station, it could never be as effective as direct fire from a stable platform at a suitable elevation. The Army had howitzers and mountain batteries, but their troubles were much the same as those of the horse-boats. On the other hand, the Turks had a good supply of guns mounted in well-constructed emplacements, so as to command the various reaches of the river.

It is not surprising that Major-General Gorringe during the course of the operations sent a message to the army commander at Busrah: "I do not appear to have the superiority in artillery, which the calibre and range would reasonably lead me to expect." Perhaps he had in mind the achievement of General Townshend's division above Kurnah, when the artillery of three sloops-of-war and a flotilla of armed launches swamped the enemy's guns, and enabled the army to gain a decisive victory at a cost of only twenty-three casualties.

In spite, however, of the difficulties with which the gun-layers had to contend, the enemy's first position at Gurmat Safah did not give much trouble. His guns were silenced after about four hours' bombardment; and when his small force of infantry tried to skip back, they were outflanked by the 24th Punjabis, advancing in *bellums* in the approved amphibious style, and were made prisoners. The result of this first scrap was that the Hakeekah Channel was open to us, subject only to the possibility of mines, for which two of the sternwheelers proceeded to sweep. In this they received unexpected assistance, for they were hailed from the bank by a party of Arabs bringing a little present with them in the shape of a Turkish officer. They explained that he had been sent down from Nasiriyah to raise the Arab tribes into a state of active resistance against the invaders; but the tribes did not feel that they wanted to be raised, and they really did not know what to do with the officer, so they handed him over for disposal.

He turned out to be an amiable kind of Turk, and he was so much overjoyed at finding himself still alive that he proceeded to guide the mine-sweepers to the most likely places. All the same they found only one mine; presumably the Turks had run short of mines. On emerging from the Hakeekah Channel we found a river some 200 yards broad, and along its bank were several small villages with gardens and patches of cultivated soil, usually surrounded with mud walls. On the left bank were occasional palm groves and fringes of willow-trees, but the right bank was almost entirely devoid of trees. The banks themselves were nothing more than causeways a few hundred yards wide between river and flood, and beyond them the whole country at this time of year was completely under water. Here was a magnificent terrain for a defending force, for there was no way of getting round them, and no alternative to plain, ungarnished, brutally expensive frontal attack. To make matters worse, the dry land was intersected at frequent intervals by dykes which had been cut at right angles to the river for purposes of irrigation.

The first item in the programme was the occupation of Suk-y-Sheyukh,[3] which lies a little south of the head of the Hakeekah Channel. This was entrusted to the naval flotilla and the chief political of-

---
3. Pronounced Sook-y-Shook (the Market of the Sheikhs).

ficer, who hoisted the Union Jack in the presence of a representative gathering of local *sheikhs* and villagers. The flotilla then led the way up the Euphrates until they reached Asani and located the enemy's main position near a place called Mejinineh, about four miles below Nasiriyah. Three thousand yards lower downstream another had attempt had been made at an obstruction by sinking two steamers and a Thornycroft launch in the river; but it was a complete waste of good material, for there was very little difficulty in getting through it.

On July 7 a reconnaissance told us that we were up against a strong position, and that the enemy was well supplied with guns; so there was nothing to do but to wait for reinforcements and more howitzers to come up from Busrah. At the same time the *Sumana* was sent down for repairs necessitated by a shell which hit her when she was in the Hakeekah Channel, and punctured a steam-pipe. Both she and the transports had plenty of trouble in getting through the Hammar Lake on their way back, and it was now becoming an urgent question whether the operations could be completed before the fall of the river made the line of communications inadequate.

On the night of July 13 we attacked on both banks, the 12th Brigade on the left bank and the 30th Brigade on the right bank making frontal attacks, while the 24th Punjabis crept round through the floods to make a turning movement and capture some sand-hills behind the enemy's position. If this turning movement had succeeded, the Turk would not have been able to hold his ground; but, unfortunately, our native troops found a stiffer opposition than they could tackle, and when a tribe of Arabs attacked them in the rear they had no alternative but to get back as best they could. The general came to the conclusion that the reports were true of the Turks having received considerable reinforcements, and that he could do nothing further until more forces were sent up from Busrah, so he asked for more infantry, more artillery, more ambulance, and more aeroplanes.

His message even suggested that the operations were assuming the character of trench warfare, which up to that time had been unknown in Mesopotamia in the modern sense of the word. It did not sound like a pleasant prospect at a time of year when the heat is most intense and the mosquitoes at their most virulent stage of activity, and it is not altogether surprising that the temper of the expedition was suffering severely. The commanding officer of one of the sternwheelers wrote to say that "it would need three or four nights from 9 p.m. till 1.30 a.m., and several large glasses of lime-juice and soda, to express my moans and general opinion of the way this show is run." He had been spending many nights towing strings of *bellums* up to the front trenches to supply our troops with food, and he had been greeted regularly with a hail of shells and rifle-shot from the enemy.

It was a monotonous kind of entertainment, and he was beginning to grow weary of it. He had to carry on, however, for another ten nights before the reinforcements from Busrah had been ferried, punted, dragged, or pushed, through the mud and water of the Hammar Lake, and brought up to the front. Meanwhile gun positions had been moved forward, trenches extended, and various other preparations for attack completed; and all the time the workers were painfully conscious of three things—that the thermometer stood high, that there were plenty of mosquitoes in the world, and that the Turks had some very pretty shots among their snipers.

At daybreak on July 24 the great attack was launched, and on the left bank the 12th Infantry Brigade soon met with success, occupying the enemy's advanced trenches after about two hours' fighting. The real trouble, however, was on the right bank. Here the 30th Infantry Brigade found that a branch channel of the river, known as the Mejinineh Channel, formed a serious obstacle between themselves and the enemy. It was too wide to jump and too deep to ford, so they appealed to the Sappers and Miners for assistance. The Sappers and Miners said that they would be happy to throw a bridge across, if only they could get there with their materials. It was then that some staff officer had a splendid brainwave, and remembered a rule set forth in an unofficial and unpublished treatise on the art of amphibious warfare.

"When in doubt, apply to the Royal Navy." So the Royal Navy's aid was invoked, and the little *Sumana* (commanded by Lieutenant W. V, Harris) was told off to tow a barge with a consignment of sappers, miners, and bridging materials, up to the Mejinineh Channel, while the rest of the naval flotilla did their best to cover the operation by their gunfire. The barge itself was to form part of the bridge, and the *Sumana* was to deliver it safely and in a suitable position in the channel. As soon as the Turks saw what the game was, they let drive at the *Sumana* with everything they could bring to bear on her. The marks of the rifle bullets made her look as though she had the chicken-pox, and the shells—aimed, fortunately, too high to do vital damage—punctured her luckless steam-pipe once more.

But she got the barge into the channel and stood by while the Sappers and Miners completed the bridge. Then the 30th Brigade

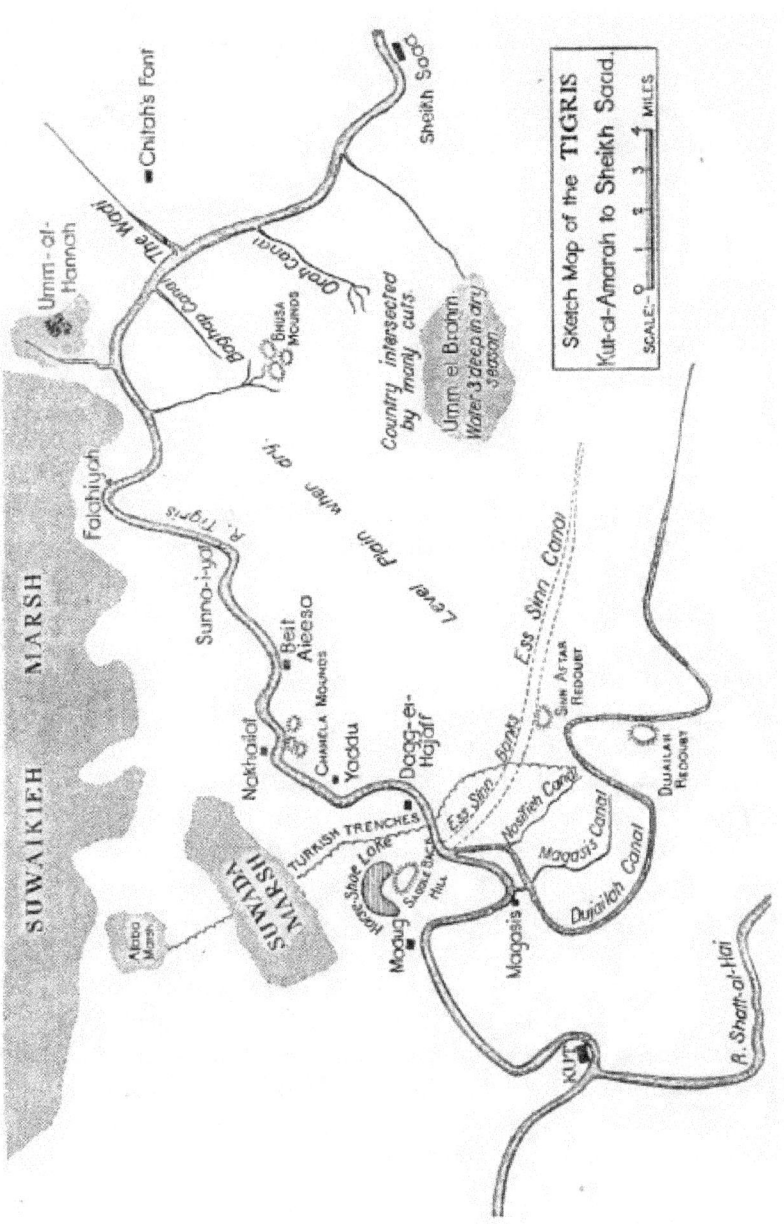

came pounding over it, and, though the Turk still clung like a leech to his trench, he knew in his inmost heart that he could not hold it. By noon the main position was captured, and there remained only a forlorn hope of a position at Sadanawiyah. Whatever might have been its powers of resistance, they were nipped in the bud by the S.N.O., who brought his ship abreast of the foremost trench, laid it alongside the bank, and blazed at the Turks with everything that the little *Shushan* could boast in the way of armament. Then our troops charged the trenches, and the Turks decided that it was not worth their while to stay there. By six o'clock in the evening they were in full retreat, but the work of the day was not even yet completed as far as the navy was concerned.

The flotilla immediately proceeded up towards Nasiriyah, and, before they had gone far, what should they meet but their old friend, the Thornycroft motor-launch with the pom-pom! (There were originally two of these, but the Turks sank one when they tried to obstruct the channel.) She did not linger long, but as she departed she kept her pom-pom going busily. Now, it was annoying to think that a little thing like that, after making itself highly objectionable, should get off scot-free. Lieutenant Commander Seymour in the *Shushan* realized this, and he strode up to the twelve-pounder in the bows, and announced that he was going to have three shots if the gun-mounting and the deck would stand it. He laid the gun himself and fired. The first shot was a bit short, the second was a bit over, the third hit her plump and set her on fire. Her crew ran her into the bank and jumped ashore; and that was the end of the Thornycroft motor-boat.

At Nasiriyah the naval flotilla found white flags flying, but when they got abreast of the Turkish barracks some soldiers on the roof opened fire with their rifles. The navy replied with shells and Maxims, but it was getting too dark to see, so they dropped back and anchored below the town. Next morning a deputation of Arab citizens came off to report that the Turks had evacuated the town, and to invite their kind friends, the British, to occupy it. Major-General Melliss, of the 30th Brigade, had accompanied the naval flotilla, and a hundred Gurkhas had also managed to find accommodation in the little stern-wheelers. The party landed in state on the morning of July 26, and hoisted the Union Jack at Nasiriyah.

CHAPTER 5

The Man and the Axe

If simplicity of language be a virtue in a general's despatches, the best part of them will be found in those rare passages towards the end when a hero is recommended for the Victoria Cross. A deed of heroism needs no embellishment of the pen, no mellifluous recital, no *pæan* of praise; the briefest statement of fact and circumstance is enough to present it to the imagination and proclaim its worth. It was in the simplest of words that Major-General Townshend told the story of the death of Lieutenant-Commander Edgar C. Cookson, R.N., and recommended him for the posthumous award of the Victoria Cross. And the story in itself is a simple one, but as it involves the story of the first capture of Kut-al-Amarah in September, 1915, of which very little has ever appeared in the public Press, I propose to tell it in detail.

It was not until nearly three months after the occurrence of the events I am about to relate, that the attention of the people of England was turned to Mesopotamia by a series of disasters, which culminated in the surrender of Kut by General Townshend's division after a siege lasting 145 days. During that anxious period a good deal was heard about the strong Turkish positions between marsh and river, which the relieving forces tried in vain to pierce, and such names as Sanna-i-yat, Beit Aieessa, and Ess Sinn became quite familiar to newspaper readers for a short while. But now I want to go back a few pages in the campaign, and show how the same division, blessedly unconscious of the fate in store for it, turned the Turks out of that very stronghold at Ess Sinn, drove them back in full retreat, and marched triumphantly into the town. No more striking illustration could be found of the vicissitudes of war than is afforded by these two periods in the history of the Mesopotamian campaign—the first twelve months up to the autumn of 1915, and the next five months from December, 1915, to

April, 1916.

The causes which brought about the transformation are not for discussion here, nor can any comparison be drawn between the two days' engagement, which resulted in the first capture of Kut, and the long series of operations by means of which we tried our utmost to relieve the beleaguered garrison. The conditions were entirely different from alpha to omega. In the first place, in September, 1915, the forces engaged on both sides were comparatively small; in the second place, there was then dry weather and dry ground; in the third place, although the scene of operations was the same, the Turks then relied on only one position—at the Ess Sinn Banks—and made no attempt to hold any positions to the east of it. Nevertheless, the first capture of Kut-al-Amarah was in itself a performance of sufficient merit to deserve more recognition than the few lines in which the newspapers recorded it.

The main item in the plan of attack was the device of deceiving the enemy as to where the real blow was to be delivered. Our Army was divided into two columns, of which Column A was a formidable force consisting of all three arms, and was placed on the right bank of the river. Column B, which was placed on the left bank, consisted only of infantry and a small supply of artillery. With this disposition of troops the battle opened on September 27, and Column A gave every semblance of a lively attack, while its cavalry stood ready to make a vigorous pursuit if the Turks gave way. But as a matter of fact all this was merely play-acting. At nightfall the Sappers and Miners constructed a pontoon bridge across the river, and during the dark hours the greater part of Column A crossed to the left bank, where the real offensive was to take place, only two battalions being left behind to cover the bridgehead.

The field of operations on the left bank may be described as a channel of land between marsh and river, subdivided by swamps into four narrow passes. On the extreme north the Suwaikieh Marsh, about eight miles from the river at Ess Sinn, extended east and west for many miles, and formed an impassable boundary. In between were three smaller marshes in a straight line running northwards from the river, which were known as Horseshoe Swamp, Suwaida Marsh, and Ataba Marsh. The Turks made use of these to protect their flanks, and had dug their trenches in between them. Before daybreak on September 28 Column A had not only reached its position of deployment, but had divided itself into three portions—No. 1 to make a frontal attack between Horseshoe and Suwaida, No. 2 to turn the Turkish flank by advancing between Suwaida and Ataba, and No. 3, consisting of cavalry and armoured cars, to go right up between Ataba and the northern boundary, in order to prevent a possible attempt on the part of the enemy to turn our right flank.

Meanwhile Column B, at the south end of the line, was to attack the Turkish trenches between Horseshoe and the river. If we could succeed in getting past this line of swamps, we should have no further obstacle to bar our advance upon Kut, which lies on the same side of the river. If, however, we had attempted to press our attack on the right bank, we should no doubt have succeeded in it; but there would still be the river between us and our object, and that it would have proved a serious obstacle the history of the subsequent operations has conclusively shown.

It is rather surprising that the Turks were deceived by our ruse, and it is still more surprising that on September 28 they took so long to realise that we did not intend to make any serious attack on the right bank. It was half-past five in the evening before they managed to get their troops across the river, and start to bring relief to those which had borne the brunt of the day's fighting. By this time our No. 2 force, having fulfilled its mission, was advancing westwards between Horseshoe and Suwaida. But on seeing the Turkish reinforcement advancing from the river, our force turned southwards, swooped down on the enemy, and completely routed them. By night we held the greater part of the enemy's trenches and had inflicted heavy casualties, with the result that he decided to retire, and before daybreak was in full retreat along the road to Baghdad.

The part played in the operations by the naval flotilla was necessarily that of a floating artillery. The flotilla consisted of three armed launches—*Shaitan*, *Comet*, and *Sumana*—four horse-boats, and two small motor-boats. The horse-boats had each a 47 inch gun, but the launches were too flimsily constructed to carry anything larger than a twelve-pounder. In addition to these craft there was the Royal Naval Air Service, with their seaplanes, who did invaluable work in reconnaissance, in observation of artillery fire, and in carrying important messages. It cannot be said that they enjoyed their job, for the truth of the matter is that most of them were in the throes of malaria. Major Gordon, of the Royal Marines, who was their chief, says very plaintively that in a hot climate he does not like a machine whose slipstream blows directly through the radiator on to the pilot's face. On one occasion he collided with a *bellum* as he was getting off the water, and damaged his chassis, and he explains in his best official language that:

> This accident was due to the pilot not being in a fit condition to fly, as he had been sick with malaria the day before.

But it was simply a case of necessity's compulsion, for we were short of aeroplanes at the time. Three days later he managed to get through the ordeal of a flight of 240 miles without accident. He was splendidly backed up by his men, of whom he says:

> Out of twenty ratings, eighteen have been attacked by malaria, some on more than one occasion since leaving East Africa. This illness is hampering the work to a great extent, as the majority of the men are not fit for a long day's work. They all, however, insist on working, and will not say when they feel ill.

A dose of Mesopotamia on top of a dose of East Africa without a sugar-plum of leave in between is rather strenuous even for the R.N.A.S., and it is comforting to know that they were all sent home shortly afterwards for a rest and change of climate. To return to the three armed launches. Their job the first day was to keep up a bombardment of the enemy on the right bank, in pursuance of the scheme of creating the impression that the main attack was to be made there. On the second day they still confined their chief attentions to the right bank, with the idea of keeping down the enemy's fire from that quarter against our brigades operating on the left bank. As soon as an aeroplane brought them word that the operations far inland to the north had been successful, they moved upstream, and engaged the enemy at close range.

Here they found the enemy's shells and rifle-fire made things rather warm for them, and the general sent word that they were not to advance any farther. So they hung on where they were, and secured themselves to the bank. At six o'clock in the evening another message came through from the general. It told them that our attack at the north end of the line on the enemy's left wing had been completely successful, and that the Turks were retreating. The message went on to refer to an obstruction across the river near Kut. Unless this could be removed, it would be impossible for the flotilla to aid the cavalry in pursuing the enemy. The general therefore requested the senior naval officer to proceed upstream, examine the obstruction, and, if possible, destroy it.

Lieutenant-Commander Edgar C. Cookson was acting S.N.O. at the time, in the absence of three officers senior to him, of whom two had taken their ships to Ceylon for health-recruiting purposes, and the third was in hospital. He ordered the flotilla to darken ship, and about seven o'clock the three launches crept upstream, followed by one of the motor-boats. As they approached the obstruction they were detected, and a heavy fire with rifles and machine guns was opened on them from the trenches on both banks of the river. They found that the obstruction consisted of a *maheilah* in the middle, and two iron lighters, one each side. These were placed across stream in a line and joined together by wire hawsers. The first idea was that, if the *maheilah* could be sunk by gunfire, there would be plenty of room for the ships to pass between the two iron lighters. Whether this theory would have proved correct, or whether the sunken *maheilah* would have been a worse obstruction than the floating *maheilah*, was never determined, because it is not such an easy thing as it looks to sink a *maheilah* by gunfire.

It became clear that the only satisfactory way of removing the obstruction was to cut the moorings by which the craft were held together, and send the *maheilah* floating downstream with the current. The S.N.O. ordered the *Comet*, from which he was directing the operations, to proceed upstream and place herself actually alongside the *maheilah*.

No mere words can convey an adequate idea of the inferno of rifle-fire which greeted the vessel as she carried out this manoeuvre. To the Turks it was of vital importance that the obstruction should remain intact until they had time to get their army away; for their line of retreat for the first few miles lay within easy range of the river, and if the armed launches were able to go upstream at once, they would probably make the difference between an orderly retreat and a rout. Fortunately, all three of the launches were fitted with bullet-proof plating, and so long as a man's duties allowed him to keep under cover he was fairly safe. But it was not always possible to keep under cover.

For instance, there was Leading Signalman Gilbert Wallis, who had to get into an exposed position in order to make his signals visible. He was wounded at a very critical moment, and was unable to stand up; but he managed to prop himself against something and carry on with his signal. It was fortunate that he could do so, for without that signal there would have been worse calamities. Then there was Private

A. G. May, R.M.L.I., who was working the *Comet's* six-pounder from behind its gun-shield. He was working it single-handed, and was feeling quite happy at his job until his gun-shield carried away—and then he went on working it without feeling happy. The *Comet's* guns were decidedly unfortunate, for the three-pounder on the port side was always in trouble. The bolts which were meant to hold the mounting to the deck got so loose that they threatened to draw out altogether. Leading Seaman Ernest Sparks, however, continued to fire the gun and to hope for the best, but it was rather like riding a thoroughbred with two broken reins patched up with a bit of cotton.

The *Comet* was brought alongside the *maheilah* to the musical accompaniment of bullets pattering on the steel plating like raindrops on a window-pane. They came in a thick shower from both sides of the river, and those which missed the ship went shrieking overhead like a swarm of harpies. Lieutenant-Commander Cookson peered through the darkness at the wire hawsers which held the *maheilah* in its place, and in a moment his mind was made up.

The captain of the *Comet* (Lieutenant W.V. Harris) heard him shout for an axe; but was too busy manoeuvring the ship to attend to him, and it was too dark to see from the bridge what actually happened. The eyewitnesses were the gun's crew on the fo'c'sle. They saw the S.N.O., axe in hand, leaning over the *Comet's* steel plating in an endeavour to reach the wire hawser. Then they saw him get over the plating and step on to the *maheilah* itself. Immediately afterwards they saw him fall between the ship and the *maheilah*, and they hastened to extricate him and bring him back into the ship. There were more bullet holes in him than they cared to count; he died within ten minutes.

The captain of the *Comet* found that no less than twelve men in the little ship were wounded, and wisely decided that it was impossible to do anything more under such a heavy fire at point-blank range, so he signalled to the other launches his intention of retiring. This was the signal which Leading Signalman Wallis managed to get through, although he was unable to stand up on account of his wound. All the flotilla got back safely, and anchored for the night in the Nakhailah Reach.

Next morning early they went upstream again, and found that the enemy had fled from their trenches abreast of the obstruction, leaving only two men with an old muzzle-loading cannon, which they fired off in the true comic-opera style. By ten o'clock the ships were at Kut; but they had no time to dally there if they were to overtake the enemy. Unfortunately, the Tigris itself proved an enemy, and they found many obstructions of which the hand of man was quite innocent. The *Sumana* ran aground and broke both her rudders; the *Shaitan* was hit by a shell from one of the Turk's rearguard guns, but, fortunately, the mishap did no more than delay her progress, and she was able later on to come up with the *Comet* again. They sighted two of the enemy's steamers ahead of them, and managed to send a shell into the Busrah, causing her to drop two maheilahs full of ammunition which she had been towing, and so find safety in "her superior speed. But the *Shaitan* and *Comet* still pressed forward, until they suddenly found another contretemps to deal with.

The Turks had detached a small force of infantry and some mountain guns to make a detour inland, rejoining the river some way below our forces, there to harass our line of communications. This force was now on its way back, and, seeing British steamers in front of it, opened fire on them with the mountain guns. So the two armed launches were in the uncomfortable position of having the enemy both ahead and astern of them. At this critical juncture the *Shaitan* ran aground again; she soon got off, however, and Lieutenant Mark Singleton, who was now acting S.N.O., decided that the pursuit must be abandoned, as there was grave risk that the ships might be cut off altogether. So they turned round and made their way back to Kut.

When General Townshend heard the story of Lieutenant-Commander Cookson's death, he sent a special despatch to General Headquarters detailing the facts. Having described the situation in which the *Comet* was placed, with a heavy fire at point-blank range from both sides of the river pouring into her, the despatch concludes with these simple words: "He found that he could not send a man over the ship's side to cut away the obstruction, because it meant certain death, so he took an axe and went himself."

That is all. No laudatory phrases; no embellishments; just a plain recital of a plain story. But was finer tribute ever penned? As senior naval officer he had been entrusted with an important task, but when he arrived on the scene he found that to order a man to execute it would be to send him to certain death, and so—"he took an axe and went himself." When the children of the centuries to come take up the burden of their marvellous heritage as citizens of the British Empire; when they turn to the pages of history and learn about the strange transformations which the land of Mesopotamia has seen; when they trace the records from the days of Babylon's glory, which endured for two thousand years, through the ages of pomp and magnificence which marked the reign of Haroun-al-Raschid, Caliph of Baghdad, through the years of poverty when, under the thraldom of Constantinople, industries were abandoned, waterways were left to flood the country at their will, and peasants taxed into a state of starvation to fill the pockets of *valis* and *mudirs*; when at last they come to the Great War, which brought the British flag into this realm of mighty rivers, and with it the dawn of a new era: then let us hope they may find a breath of inspiration, giving them strength to bear the burden they have inherited, in the simple story of the sailor who "took an axe and went himself."

CHAPTER 6

The Retreat From Ctesiphon

By one of the ironies of Fate, the big disaster of the Mesopotamian campaign synchronized with the debut of the most important accession to the naval forces in the country—the specially constructed gunboats, which were sent out in sections and put together at Abadan. On October 23, 1915, H.M.S. *Firefly*, the first of the new craft, was launched; and ten days later she arrived at Busrah, where she shipped her guns and ammunition, carried out her gun trials, and proceeded the same day up-river, to play her part in the famous push towards Baghdad.

Needless to say, she was an object of great interest to soldiers and sailors alike, for she was the very latest thing in Mesopotamian novelties; and while the experts were talking learnedly about her armament, her engines, her draught, her searchlight, her wireless equipment, and all else connected with her fighting efficiency, the ordinary mind was content to admire her domestic fittings—the bunks, the lockers, the telescopic wash-handstands, the flap-tables, the wicker chairs, wicker mess-tables, and all the rest of her furniture and appointments. She had little opportunity, however, of showing herself off, for she was born in stirring times, and her baptism of champagne was shortly to be followed by her baptism of fire.

Under the command of Lieutenant-Commander C. J. F. Eddis she proceeded to Aziziyeh, where she found the three armed launches *Comet*, *Shaitan*, and *Sumana*, the stern-wheelers *Shushan* and *Massoudieh*, and four horse-boats, each carrying a 4.7 inch gun. This was the whole of the naval flotilla at that time capable of getting up the river. Other gunboats were on the stocks and were nearing completion, but the Great Push could not wait for them. It is not to be supposed, however, that the fortunes of this luckless attempt to rush through to

Baghdad could in any way have been affected by an increase of naval strength. A great change had come over the character of the campaign since the summer of 1915, and it could no longer be described as amphibious warfare. The floods had subsided with the fall of the rivers, and the fighting had receded northwards beyond the flood area.

The first taking of Kut-al-Amarah at the end of September, 1915, may be said to close the first chapter in the history of the campaign. Thenceforth the operations approximated in character to normal military operations, and the functions of the navy were reduced to supplementing as well as they could the army's artillery, patrolling the long line of communications, and standing by to take up the role of cavalry in the event of the enemy being put to flight. So far as artillery work is concerned the navy were at a big disadvantage, in that the masts and funnel of a gunboat offer an ideal mark on which the enemy's gunners can take their range; and while land artillery can take advantage of irregularities in the ground to conceal itself, the gunboat must always present a conspicuous target.

Moreover, the river-banks were high, and for guns with a flat trajectory it was impossible to get under the lee of them, and at the same time command the appropriate range; the only way of firing the projectile over the bank was to keep at a sufficient distance from it, by taking advantage of the river bends, and this, of course, exposed the ships to the full view of the hostile gunners. A further difficulty confronting the navy was the low level of the river, which is full of shoals and shifting sand-banks, and is very difficult to navigate. This explanation is necessary to a full comprehension of what befell the navy during the retreat from Ctesiphon.

On November 22, 1915, the naval flotilla was lying at the village of Bustan, about two miles east of Ctesiphon; and as soon as our attack began the flotilla became heavily engaged with the Turkish guns on the right bank of the river, and at the same time was bombarding the Turkish trenches. Their main trouble was the difficulty of locating the enemy's guns, which were very cleverly hidden. The enemy, on the other hand, had been able to prepare for the attack, and had evidently made careful calculations of the exact ranges of various points on the river. Their position was an enviable one, for they were firing all the time at exposed targets while they themselves were well concealed, and could seek protection in trenches or dugouts whenever our shells began to fall uncomfortably close to them. None the less the flotilla carried on with the work for four days, although the *Comet* had been badly hit on the first day; fortunately, she was not compelled to withdraw, as it was found possible to repair the damage on the spot.

It is not my purpose to write the story of what was happening on land during these four days, except in so far as the record is necessary to explain the fortunes of the naval flotilla. I have heard General Townshend's attack at Ctesiphon described as a masterpiece; and I have heard it said that he achieved exactly what he predicted—no more and no less. He is reported to have said, when he had arrived at Ctesiphon and had made a reconnaissance of the enemy's position, that by engaging the enemy he could win the battle, at a price, but that his force would be so much depleted that further progress would be impossible. His orders were to engage the enemy, and he carried them out, completely defeating one Turkish division and capturing 1,300 prisoners and several guns. At the end of three days' hard fighting he had driven the enemy back to their second line of trenches; and then came the ominous report that large Turkish reinforcements were arriving.

So there was the general, several hundred miles from the base, on a barren plain swept by bitter cold winds, with over 4,000 casualties on his hands, a badly equipped medical service, and a fleet of river transport so inadequate that supplies had broken down, and some of the troops had been without food for three days. The order to retire came from headquarters only just in time; in another day or two it would have become impossible for him to extricate his division. On the night of November 25 the field of Ctesiphon was abandoned, and the army retired to their previous camp at Lajj, about six miles downriver.

Next day the retreat continued towards Aziziyeh, and it soon became apparent that there were still further difficulties to be overcome. The problems connected with the navigation of a winding river, with sharp bends at frequent intervals, a strong current, and shifting sandbanks, have already been mentioned; it must now be explained that all the food, ammunition, and stores of the army were loaded in barges, which were towed in pairs on either side of paddle-wheel steamers. Only those who have had experience of river navigation can appreciate the full significance of this. To manoeuvre a paddler, with a couple of heavy barges tied alongside her, round one of those bends was a feat in itself, and this feat had to be repeated at very frequent intervals.

It has been said by Napoleon that an army marches on its stomach, and, remembering this maxim, we may find a silent but eloquent expression of the military faith in the efficiency of the navy and the Merchant Service. For the army from Ctesiphon marched on in a straight line, trusting to the skippers of the river craft to bring the food and stores round all the tortuous windings of the river, and to come up with them when required.

As it turned out, nearly all the transports got stuck about four miles below Lajj, and a new function for the navy in Mesopotamia was revealed—the rescue of stranded army rations. Throughout the whole of November 26 the naval flotilla was busily engaged in towing transport barges off the mud, and throughout the next day they were occupied in the same way a little lower down the river. One of the tugs had taken a wrong channel near Zoeur, had run aground, and been abandoned by her crew on the approach of some Arab cavalry. So the *Comet* and *Shushan* went in search of the straying tug, found her, and extricated her, meanwhile carrying on a hot argument with the Arab cavalry. The work of rescuing stranded barges went on all that night and during most of the next day; and when all the transports were at last cleared, the *Comet* and the *Shaitan* themselves ran aground about eight miles above Aziziyeh.

They remained aground all night, while the enemy's advanced troops carried on a heavy sniping from the right bank, and next day from the left bank as well. But the *Comet* got clear, crossed the river, and kept the sniping parties at a respectable distance, while the *Firefly* and *Shushan* were busy attending to the *Shaitan*. But the poor old packet was past praying for; she had bumped the mud so often in the course of her long career that she had lost heart for her job. She was leaking like a sieve, and there was nothing for it but to salve her guns and stores and abandon her. This was not an easy operation to carry out, with energetic snipers on both banks of the river; so the senior naval officer had to send an appeal to the general for help, and in the afternoon some cavalry came out from Aziziyeh and eased the situation.

When the rest of the flotilla arrived at Aziziyeh, the S.N.O., feeling that the entertainment of the past few days had been too strenuous for real enjoyment, suggested to the general the advisability of sending the transport barges in advance of the army, instead of leaving them in the rear to be shepherded home by the navy. He pointed out to the staff the difficulties of navigation under the existing conditions, and the fact that the transport had to cover a much longer route than the army owing to the tortuous course of the river, the distance by road from Lajj to Kut being about 75 miles, and the distance by river 210 miles; and he warned them that, if the barges were not sent ahead, it was probable that many of them would be lost, should the Turks continue the pursuit. He then despatched the *Shushan, Massoudieh* and the horse-boats down-river to make all speed to Kut, leaving only the *Firefly, Comet,* and *Sumana,* behind with him.

It is impossible at this date to ascertain the reason why it was not found possible to act upon the S.N.O.'s advice, but the fact remains that on November 30 the transport barges left Aziziyeh about the same time as the troops recommenced their march, and anchored that night in the Ummal-Tubal reach, abreast of our camp. Here occurred the most dramatic incident of the retreat. At daylight on December 1 large enemy forces were seen to the north-west, at a distance of about two miles; and all round the horizon were still larger forces, which appeared to encircle the British camp on three sides. This was not the awakening vision that the leader of an army would covet, and it came with the greater unexpectedness because this was the first occasion in the campaign that the Turk had been in the position of the pursuer. His extraordinary mobility in retreat was well known to us, but now we learned for the first time that he could be equally mobile in pursuit.

There was no leisure, however, to spend in moralizing, for with the first streak of dawn the enemy launched a vigorous attack. The naval flotilla was in action immediately, and, spotting a large body of Turks massed together not more than 3,000 yards away, the *Firefly* and *Comet* proceeded to pour lyddite into them with methodical rapidity. Meanwhile the army was hastening its retreat, burning all the food and stores which it was found impossible to transport. The air was filled with a blue haze and the penetrating smell of sizzling hams combined with the gentle odours of petrol and burning sacks of flour. How ardently must the beleaguered garrison at Kut, a few weeks later, have wished that all those good things, which were destroyed on that eventful morning, had remained to them!

But the great object was to get the army safely away, and in an incredibly short space of time it melted like a cloud on the horizon. There remained the little gunboat and the two armed launches, still plugging away with lyddite shells—*Horatius Cocles, Spurius Lartius,* and *Herminius,* barring the way of the advancing army. They were aided at the outset by the cavalry brigade, which prevented a Turkish column from enveloping our right flank, and by our land artillery, which fought a desultory rearguard action as it retreated.

The three little craft carried on with their job, heedless of whether they were receiving support or not, until a Turkish shell hit the *Firefly* amidships and penetrated her boiler. Lieutenant-Commander Eddis was badly wounded, and one of the stokers was killed; the engines were put out of action completely and the ship began to drift helplessly downstream. Then the *Comet* took her in tow, but in trying to negotiate a narrow bend in the river both ships stuck on the mud, the *Comet* being firmly wedged against the bank. The *Firefly*, however, managed to get afloat again, and was sent drifting downstream, but it was not long before she grounded on another shoal.

Meanwhile the *Sumana* had come up, and was making desperate efforts to drag the *Comet* off the mud; but by this time our troops had all retreated eastwards, and large bodies of Turkish troops had entered our camp. The enemy had also brought up several field guns to short range, and were subjecting all three of the ships to an accurate and heavy fire. Finally the enemy's infantry came running up to the river and completely surrounded the ships, pouring a hail of rifle-shot into them.

The S.N.O. decided that it was useless to make any further attempt to save either the *Comet* or the *Firefly*, and, having called up the *Sumana* to come alongside the *Comet*, he climbed aboard her, and sent a skiff to fetch off the officers and men of the *Firefly*. The S.N.O. was one of those cheery optimists whose optimism is merely stimulated by being in a tight corner. It is recorded of him that, as he was leaving the *Comet* with bullets pattering against the ship's side and singing in his ears, and shells shrieking over his head, he turned to the officers standing beside him, and said, with his inimitable chuckle of glee, "A champagne supper if we get out of this—what?"

So the little *Sumana* took aboard her the two stranded ship's companies, and staggered downstream, so heavily laden that her deck was almost awash. The last she saw of her two lamented sisters was that they were both on fire, with large bodies of Turkish troops surrounding them. But their crews were safe for the time being, their guns and engines had been disabled, and the S.N.O. had got his confidential books tucked under his arm—all except an obsolete signal book, which had to be left in the *Firefly's* safe, because the fire had made the safe too hot to open. I have heard a yarn that in that selfsame safe was a plan of Baghdad drawn up by the general, showing the houses where the British troops were to be billeted when they entered the city.

General Townshend was always very thorough, and prepared for every contingency, even when he had very little faith in the possibility of its occurrence. Von der Goltz and Khalil Pasha must have smiled sardonic smiles when that plan of Baghdad was brought to their notice.

In the hurry of our army's retreat two barges filled with stores had been left behind, and the *Sumana* had taken charge of them, intending to bring them down to Kut. But now they were surrounded by the Turks, and it was impossible to rescue them. So the little *Sumana* went struggling on, with an abnormal draught which caused her many a bump on the mud, and attended by a constant risk of taking a list and rolling on to her beam ends. It was not long before she came to more evidence of the troubles of a retreating army. One of the transport steamers, towing a lighter on either side of her, had run aground at a difficult bend near Shidhaif. Now, one lighter contained a few stores and some sick and wounded Indian ranks, and the other lighter contained a very large supply of military ammunition for guns of all calibres and for rifles.

There was no time to lose, for the Turks were hot on the pursuit and their field guns were within range. The only question to be decided was, Which of the two lighters ought to be salved first? and the S.N.O. made up his mind in a moment—the one which would be of more value to the enemy. It was dragged off the mud, and so was the transport tug, and the pair were sent on their way downstream. This left the problem of the sick and wounded in the other lighter. To take them aboard the *Sumana* was impossible, for it needed little more than an extra featherweight to make her founder. There happened to be a small steam-launch within hail, and the S.N.O. told her captain to go alongside the lighter and take off as many of the sick men as he could accommodate, without jeopardizing the safety of his craft.

As it turned out, this solution of the problem was no solution at all, for in some unaccountable way—possibly because the captain attempted to take too many people aboard, and so made the launch unwieldy—the rescuer got aground in the shallows, and had to be abandoned. The *Sumana* could not possibly attempt to give assistance, for with the load she had to carry she could not even return upstream against the current. Moreover, matters had become urgent, for between her and Kut were many big bends of the river; and if the Turks with their field guns took a straight line across the plain, they would be able to reach one of these, and so cut off the possibility of further retreat.

When darkness fell, the difficulties of navigation increased threefold—in fact, it is nothing short of a miracle that a small overladen craft should have been able to find her way through those tortuous channels of the river at its very lowest season, round hairpin bends, and over treacherous shoals. Sub-Lieutenant C. P. Tudway, who handled her, deserved a better fate than to be among the garrison which surrendered at Kut some five months later. When at last the *Sumana* reached Kut on December 2, she found that she had outpaced the troops after all, and was two or three hours in front of them. They arrived that same evening thoroughly exhausted, and perhaps the most cheering sight which greeted the careworn staff was the smiling face of the S.N.O. One of them gave vent to his feelings by exclaiming: "Well now! we never expected to see you again."

So ended the famous retreat from Ctesiphon, and it is no exaggeration to say that the navy in Mesopotamia never had more difficult duties to perform than during those unfortunate days. The loss of the *Comet* and *Shaitan* was bad enough, but the loss of the *Firefly* was a disaster. She was the first-born of the new brood, and the navy regarded her with eyes of pride, as every mother regards every firstborn child. She had been snatched away from her parent, and become a captive in alien hands, which knew not how to heal her sores nor soothe her afflictions. For more than a year she bore her sorrow patiently, and then came the day of her deliverance, when the tragedies of Ctesiphon and Kut were overlayed by the brilliant record of General Maude's advance and the capture of Baghdad. But that is another story.

Chapter 7

A Forlorn Hope

The month of April, 1916, was full of dramatic incidents in the Mesopotamian campaign, and ended with one of the most dramatic events of the war—the surrender of Kut-al-Amarah. To everyone engaged in the campaign it was a month of long and terrible suspense, and the psychological barometer of the whole British force was going up and down like a piston-rod, as each scrap of news came through from the front. On the 5th of the month we captured the El Hannah position, and it was reported in Busrah that our casualties had been remarkably small, that the Turks had retreated to a lightly held position, some miles to the rear, that we might confidently expect to clear them out of that on the morrow, and that we should then be up against their last and main defence at the Ess Sinn Banks.

Next day we heard details of the operations: There were five lines of trenches to be taken before El Hannah became ours; the Turks first retreated to a position at Falahiyah, which we attacked at nightfall and captured; meanwhile on the right bank of the river we had driven the Turks out of their position, and when they counterattacked we completely outmanoeuvred them and caused them very heavy casualties. All this sounded such excellent news that our spirits soared into the clouds, and we began discussing what would be the most appropriate way to celebrate the relief of Kut. Blowing off sirens and hooters and sending up rockets seemed somehow inadequate for such an occasion, and a searchlight display by the assembled squadron, even if it could be arranged, would be a commonplace method of expressing our emotions.

For the next day or two nobody dared to cast any shadow of a doubt upon the universal confidence that Kut would be relieved; the only latitude allowed to the pessimists was the expression of the view that it would take longer than was generally anticipated. And then there followed a week of ominous silence from the front. The barometer began to fall slowly but steadily, for we knew that, when a big push is in progress, no news must inevitably mean bad news. The Turks were holding us up at Sanna-i-yat, the position which early reports had declared to be only lightly held, but which had evidently been much strengthened by the enemy. A few days later came news that the floods had entered both the Turkish trenches and our own, and that, while we had managed to pump the water out of ours, the Turks had been forced to move back to higher ground, and had lost heavily in doing so.

We also heard that we had advanced on the right bank of the river, and that arrangements had been made to supply food to Kut by means of aircraft. This was about the 15th of the month, and the barometer began to rise again, but not very rapidly. The precise effect which the floods were likely to have upon the operations was at first an uncertain quantity; but when we learned a few days later that our troops were engaged in making a causeway through the floods as an essential preliminary to further advance, we realized that Fate was against us, and that the advent of the flood season had taken place at a most unfortunate moment. And all the time there were small driblets of intelligence trickling through to us about the desperate straits to which the Kut garrison was reduced. We were all busily engaged upon efforts in mental arithmetic. Given that the aeroplanes at our disposal were so many, that each aeroplane was capable of carrying so many pounds of food per day, and that the garrison of Kut was so many thousand, how much food would be received by each man, and how long could they hold out upon such scanty supplies?

Up to this time not a word had been spoken in H.M. ships about the *Julnar*. Some of our artisan ratings had been sent upriver to Amarah, and most of us knew that they were to fit up steel plates round her steering positions and engines, and make her as secure as was possible against gun and rifle fire; but none of us spoke of it. In the wardroom of one of the sloops an officer remarked that the moon was not rising until past eleven o'clock, and the remark was received by an ominous silence and severe scowls. Ashore, however, the importance of secrecy was not so fully appreciated. The various messes were openly canvassing the chances of the vessel getting through the blockade, and I have heard that even the Arabs in Busrah bazaar were making it a subject of speculation.

The difficulties of keeping the matter secret were obvious. The vessel had been loaded up at Busrah with some 250 tons of food, and had then gone up to Amarah, where she was specially fitted for the great ordeal. However assiduously false reports were spread as to her purpose and aim, the most simple-minded person must have made a shrewd guess as to the real nature of her mission. I happened to go up to Amarah shortly after she had left there for Sheikh Saad, and walking along the bank I met one of the river-transport skippers. He had just brought down some sick and wounded and a few Turkish prisoners, and told me that he had passed the *Julnar* the previous evening. I suppose the expression on my face indicated my surprise at his referring to the subject. "You can't put the cat back in the bag when she's once out of it," he said. "Why, I overheard some of my prisoners exchanging bets on the possibility of her getting through."

The voyage of the *Julnar* was never anything more than a forlorn hope. She was a twin-screw steamer, and faster than most of the river craft, and if any vessel at all could slip through the blockade she was that vessel. In order to gauge her chances we must appreciate the nature of the task in front of her. First of all, she had to face the ordinary difficulties of navigation—a winding river with hairpin bends and occasional shoals, which even in the flood season were capable of pulling up a heavily laden vessel. Secondly, she had to face these difficulties in the dark, for to make the attempt by daylight was, of course, out of the question. Thirdly, she had to run the gauntlet of the Turkish guns on both banks from Sanna-i-yat to Kut—a distance of over twenty miles by river—to say nothing of a possible fusillade by rifles and machine guns. Fourthly, there was the possibility that the Turks might have sown a minefield, or, what was more probable, have stretched a wire hawser or some such obstruction across the river, in anticipation of the attempt being made.

Aeroplane reconnaissances were made, and the airmen reported that they could see no signs of minefields or obstructions; but the waters of the Tigris are muddy, and it was more than possible that objects beneath the surface would escape detection. Turkish prisoners, however, were unanimous in declaring that no obstructions had been prepared. This information, however, if it could be relied on, only served to emphasize the first two difficulties—the negotiation of the sharp bends in the river and the ticklish job of navigating in the dark. The admiral himself said that he had very little hope of the success of the undertaking, for the odds against it were too great.

I believe that it was first suggested some weeks previously by a member of the army commander's staff, and was referred to the senior naval officer: that it was debated at some length between the army commander, the staff, and the S.N.O.; and that it was in the first instance abandoned as being beyond the range of practical politics. When, however, the position of the beleaguered garrison became critical, the proposal was again brought up, and was referred to Vice-Admiral Sir Rosslyn Wemyss, the Commander-in-Chief of the East Indies Station, who had arrived at Busrah on April 10, 1916, in the yacht *Imogene*, in the course of his tour round the naval ports of his station.

He had at once proceeded upriver, in one of the gunboats, to the scene of the operations, and the most important question upon which he had to decide was this question of whether or not the attempt should be made to send a ship through to Kut. Without pretending to know what considerations influenced the admiral's mind, I feel that the problem, although a momentous one, was simple enough in its elements. The beleaguered garrison were nearing the end of their tether; the fate of some 9,000 officers and men was in the balance; the army had appealed to the navy for help. So long as there was the smallest grain of a chance, so long as it could be said that with the aid of extraordinarily good luck there was a remote possibility of success, that appeal must not be made in vain.

The admiral sent out private letters to the officers of the Mesopotamian squadron asking for volunteers for the command of the *Julnar*. There was no need to point out to them the dangers of the enterprise, or the slender hopes upon which it had been sanctioned; they all knew that the chances of success were practically negligible. But most of them sent in their names, and the admiral's next problem was that of making the selection. His choice fell upon Lieutenant Humphrey O. B. Firman, R.N., and to accompany him he selected Lieutenant-Commander Charles H. Cowley, R.N.V.R., whose intimate knowledge of the river, gained in the service of Messrs. Lynch Brothers, was likely to be most valuable. Mr. Reed, who was given a temporary commission as Engineer Sub-Lieutenant, R.N.R., also volunteered to accompany the expedition. The crew consisted of one engine-room artificer, one leading stoker, three stokers, one leading seaman, and six able seamen. All these were volunteers drawn from the men of the gunboat flotilla. The admiral says of them:

They were under no misapprehensions as to the dangers they

ran, and they knew that I considered it most unlikely that they would reach their destination and fulfil their task; and had it not been that I realized that it was the one and only chance of saving the garrison, I would not have given my consent to such an undertaking.

At eight o'clock on the evening of April 24 the *Julnar* started from Falahiyah on her perilous voyage, and, as though to give her an enthusiastic send-off, our artillery at once opened a terrific bombardment of the enemy's lines. The object of this was, of course, to keep the Turks in their trenches, and so reduce their chances of detecting the blockade-runner; and at first it really looked as if the ruse had been successful, for there was no indication that she had been detected. We began to make calculations as to her probable progress; but in so doing we were obliged to guess her speed, for there had been no opportunity for testing it after she had been armour-plated and loaded.

The moon was due to rise at 1.15 a.m., which gave her just over five hours to cover the twenty odd miles; and taking into account a strong adverse current of about four knots, the allowance was not excessive. After Sanna-i-yat her course would be fairly straight for the first two miles or so, as far as Beit Aieesa; but after that there would be several nasty bends, including a specially difficult one at the end of the Nakhaila reach. Then came the Ess Sinn position, where it was reasonable to suppose that the Turks would be on the look-out, and some four miles farther on was the hairpin bend of Magasis Ferry, which is eight and a half miles from Kut by river, but only four miles as the crow flies. Our only hope lay in the darkness of the night, which was intensified by the high banks of the river; if she had really managed to pass through the front enemy position at Sanna-i-yat without being seen, it was just conceivable that the Turks in the back positions might be caught napping.

While we were in the midst of these anxious speculations, a report came from H.M.S. *Mantis* that a red light had been seen at some distance up the river, and we were told that this was the recognized Turkish signal that a vessel was passing up the river. The futility of further speculation became painfully obvious; there was nothing for it but to sit down and wait patiently for the issue, whatever it might be.

The full story of the voyage of the *Julnar* will never be known until the war is over, and our prisoners in Turkey have been released; the only glimpse we can get through the veil which shrouds that heroic endeavour is to be found in the chronicle of one of the beleaguered garrison. We will therefore change the scene to Kut itself, and see what was happening among those who for nearly five months had kept the flag flying in the face of grim starvation. The quotations are from the report written by Lieutenant H. S. D. McNeal, R.F.A.; and though his account of the death of Lieutenant-Commander Cowley is no more than hearsay, there are circumstantial details about it which serve to lend corroboration to it. But first of all I will quote two short extracts, which in themselves afford an awful revelation of the sufferings endured by those brave men:

> Esmeralda, my charger, was killed and eaten on April 18. Poor thing! she died in harness all right.

For a long time before that date the issue of horseflesh as part of the daily rations had become the normal routine; the trouble was that even this form of food had come to an end.

> On April 23 we drew as rations four ounces of bread, one ounce of sugar, and half an ounce of cheese.

How well I remember seeing the arrival at Busrah of some of the exchanged prisoners, those who were too far emaciated to stand the smallest chance of surviving the long journey which would have been before them had they been carried into captivity. I saw a batch of human skeletons with a thin covering of skin over their bones, and I shuddered and turned my head away. About a year later I returned to the heart of the Empire, and found the walls placarded with appeals to the people to eat less bread, and a Food Controller spending his days in trying to persuade the citizens of England not to waste food. Truly we are an unimaginative race. But let me pass on to the entry in Lieutenant McNeal's report, which relates the occurrences of the eventful night of April 24.

> Great excitement prevailed in Kut when it was heard that the relieving force would attempt to send the steamboat *Julnar* through with rations. It was decided that if the boat got through undisabled it was to come up to Kut itself and be unloaded, but that if it was hit it was to be beached at the fort. The artillery made special preparations to cover its arrival, and everyone was on edge with expectation. Shortly after midnight heavy rifle, fire was heard down-river, and we knew that the attempt had begun. For fifteen minutes the firing was very rapid; then it

died down, and our spirits with it. Another burst of firing came, and our spirits rose accordingly; but this also died away into silence, and we knew that the attempt had failed.

Oh the anguish of it! After five months of hardship and struggle against the pangs of hunger, after five months of alternating hope and despair as each item of news from the relieving force trickled through to the defenders, after five months of grim determination upheld by the traditions of the Empire to which they belonged—by the memory of Lucknow, where "*ever upon the topmost roof the banner of England blew*"; of Delhi, of Khartoum, of Ladysmith, and of Mafeking—after five months of unfaltering loyalty to their beloved General and of unflinching faith in his leadership, those sons of Britain and of Britain's Indian Empire realized that the last hope had gone, and that nothing now remained to them but to surrender. The silence after the second burst of rifle-fire told them that the attempt had failed.

Lieutenant McNeal says:

Afterwards we heard that every member of the crew was killed by rifle-fire.

(Hearsay was at fault in this, for it has been ascertained that only the two officers—Lieutenant Firman and Lieutenant-Commander Cowley—were killed. All the rest were taken prisoner, but among them five were wounded.)

The journal continues:

The navigator, Captain Cowley, had dropped at the wheel with a bullet through his groin, just as he was steering the ship through the most critical place in the whole river, a hairpin bend. While consciousness lasted he hung on, but the boat was swept into the bank and grounded.... When the Turkish officers boarded the boat, they found him unconscious, with his hands still gripping the steering-wheel, and, in spite of all the efforts of the Turkish doctors to save him, he died without regaining consciousness.

Whether or not this account of Lieutenant-Commander Cowley's death is accurate in its details, all who knew him will feel confident that he died at his post. His loss was a severe one to the expedition; for apart from his universal popularity, and his knowledge of the natives, among whom that popularity extended, his familiarity with every reach of the river between Busrah and Baghdad made him a very valuable asset in the British forces. Both he and Lieutenant Firman received the posthumous award of the Victoria Cross.

Aeroplanes next day reported that the *Julnar* was in the hands of the Turks at Magasis Ferry.

The rest of the story is soon told. On April 26 the garrison at Kut gave up all hope, and proceeded to destroy the remainder of their store of ammunition, by decapping it and dropping it into the river. Negotiations were opened with Khalil Pasha as to the terms of surrender, and at first there was some expectation that the garrison would be allowed to return to India on parole. When, however, word was passed that, in exchange for this concession, the Turkish Commander demanded that all the guns should be handed over to him intact, the officers and men of the garrison unanimously declared that, rather than surrender the guns to be used against their own comrades by the enemy, they would go as prisoners of war to Turkey.

On April 29 General Townshend gave orders that the guns were to be destroyed, and sent round word that all, except the extreme cases in the hospitals, would be made prisoners. The last act of the garrison was to destroy the wireless installation. On that eventful morning we at Busrah were taking in the farewell words of the men with whom we had worked and fought. In a pathetically brave message General Townshend expressed his thanks to the army commander, to General Gorringe, and to the officers and men of the relief force, for the efforts they had made. There followed a long pause; then came the simple word "Goodbye"—and then ... silence! So ended the most disastrous chapter in the history of the Mesopotamian campaign.

CHAPTER 8

The Dawn of a New Era

The Babylonian Empire endured for over two thousand years—from 2700 B.C., when Ur-bahu combined all the city kingdoms into one empire, until 538 B.C., when Cyrus invaded the land and annexed it as a province of his Persian kingdom. For over two thousand years this country was pre-eminent in the world as the home of art and commerce, famed for its carpets, its cloths, its embroideries, its schools, its libraries, its poets, its astronomers, for all that is comprised in the word "civilisation." The walls of Babylon, we are told, were 200 cubits high, 50 cubits thick, and 60 miles in circumference; and when the city had been laid low by the Persian conquest, Alexander the Great promised to rebuild the ruined temples, but after employing 10,000 workmen for two months he was not even able to clear away the rubbish. So the city which once was queen of all the world remains to this day a mass of broken bricks and rubbish.

But the prosperity of the land could not vanish in a day; the fertile soil of Mesopotamia, and the great rivers which then irrigated it and provided the natural highways of commerce, still endured; and Babylonia still remained a rich prize, for which Syrians, Parthians, and Romans, in turn competed. And finally it fell into the hands of the *caliphs*, the successors of Mohammed, who founded a new city farther to the north, and called it Baghdad. Here the wealth and pomp and luxury, which had once been Babylon's, were transferred; here Haroun-al-Raschid reigned in the ninth century in a palace with vaulted ceilings, rich mouldings, inlaid mirrors, and massive gilding; here was the home of Sindbad the Sailor, from which he set out upon his wonderful travels, always calling at Busrah to charter his ship and load her with his merchandise.

Then came the ravagers from the Ottoman Empire, followed by

centuries of strife between Turkey and Persia, fighting for this land of wealth like dogs over a fat bone. But still, in spite of all, the prosperity of the country remained to it, until in 1638 the Sultan of Turkey finally prevailed, and from that time forward Mesopotamia became a Turkish province—and a scene of desolation.

Where is its wealth now? Who can believe that this wilderness of marsh and desert was once a thriving land; that where now we see half-naked nomad tribes living the lives of animals, there once dwelt the foremost agents of the world's civilisation? Where are the vaulted ceilings and inlaid mirrors to be found in the evil-smelling, narrow, unsaved, dirty, garbage-strewn streets of modern Baghdad? I am told that a few of these relics of the glorious past survive, but they look like the tawdry trappings of a yesternight's feast. Where are the richly laden vessels which once sailed from the port of Busrah to carry their wares to the limits of the then known world? Where are the poets, the astronomers, the bankers, the merchants, who spread the fame of Babylonia far and wide?

All have been swept away by that magic wand—the sceptre of the Turkish Government. It would take too long to tell how this conjuring feat has been accomplished, to describe the methods by which Constantinople essayed to govern Irak. It must suffice to indicate them in a few words. First we have the principle of *divide et impera*, which meant keeping each Arab tribe in a state of perpetual hostility against its neighbour; then we have the *valis* of Baghdad and Busrah— the governors—whose personal income was derived from the taxation of the country, and was supplemented by "saying their prayers at Kerbela" (a euphemism for raiding the Mohammedan shrine at that place); then we have the *mudirs*, or local governors, whose salaries the government carelessly forgot to pay, so that they had to raise their income by levying fines on the peasantry and tolls upon the river-craft which pass through the pontoon bridges across the rivers (built solely for this purpose, for nobody ever used them as bridges); and then we have the minor officials, such as the quarantine officer at Busrah, who charged a fee for disinfecting you before you went ashore, and another fee of an indeterminate amount for giving you a permit to land.

The conservancy of the waterways was absolutely neglected, and this was the worst crime of all, for the whole vitality of the country depends on them. It is true that in 1911 Sir William Willcocks was engaged by the Turkish Government under a five years' contract to survey the rivers and carry out such irrigation works as were found necessary; but after struggling with the Turkish officials for two and a half years he threw his hand in, and was requested by the Minister of Public Works, as a favour, to state that he resigned on account of ill-health.

In the report which he wrote immediately after his return, he contrasts Mesopotamia with Egypt; for he had travelled some years previously up the Nile from Khartoum to the equatorial lakes, and had seen the wonderful work which his own countrymen had done in that inhospitable waste of waters, to introduce new forest trees and new agricultural products, and ameliorate in some degree the conditions of life of the miserable inhabitants. His next voyages were up the Tigris and Euphrates, traversing those deserts and swamps, which today, (as at time of first publication), represent what was in antiquity the richest and most famous tract in the world, and this is what he says:

> How should I have felt if I had belonged to a race in whose hands God had placed for hundreds of years the destinies of this great country, and that my countrymen could give no better account of their stewardship than the exhibition of two mighty rivers flowing between deserts, to waste themselves in the sea for nine months of the year, and desolating everything in their way during the remaining three? No effort that Turkey can make can be too great to roll away the reproach of these parched and weary lands, whose cry ascends to heaven.

Fortunately, Turkey is no longer called upon to make the effort, for the country has passed into other hands, and the dawn of a new era has come. It broke on March 11, 1917, when the British flag was hoisted at Baghdad. The story of that wonderful advance of the Expeditionary Force from Falahiyah to Baghdad, and from Baghdad to the railhead at Samara, affords a fitting climax to the vicissitudes of the two and a half years' campaign. The part played in it by H.M. Navy was by no means insignificant; in fact, it may fairly be said that the action of the Navy in pressing the pursuit of the enemy resulted in such disastrous consequences to the Turks that it determined the fate of Baghdad. The naval force had been considerably augmented during 1916, and a large flotilla of gunboats was now on the two rivers.

Three of the large twin-funnelled vessels and five of the *Fly* class took part in the operations, and just before the final advance into Baghdad the force was increased by the *Gnat*, a fourth vessel of the *Mantis* class, as well as the recaptured *Firefly*. The actual beginning of the operations, which had such a triumphant conclusion, dates back as far as December 13, 1916, when we opened the ball with a heavy bombardment of the Turkish position at Sanna-i-yat on the left bank of the Tigris, and at the same time made an advance on the right bank as far as the Shatt-al-Hai, which we succeeded in crossing. Next day we extended our advance up both banks of this tributary stream, and so by degrees we crept closer to the Tigris at the point where the Shatt-al-Hai diverges from it.

Our object undoubtedly was to clear the right bank of the Tigris, effect a crossing on the west side of Kut, and so cut the Turkish line of communications with Baghdad. I believe it is one of the elementary axioms of military tactics that the most advantageous point for crossing a river in the face of a hostile force is at the end of a big loop; for if you have possession of the bank, you can bring up your artillery on either side of the loop, enfilade the enemy, and so force him to evacuate the loop and leave you to build your pontoon bridge without being molested. The Turks fought hard to prevent us from occupying the right bank of the Tigris on either side of that loop, which holds the town of Kut, and they were forced to defend with equal vigilance the loop farther west known as the Shumran Bend. The ding-dong struggle went on for weeks, but at last we succeeded in clearing the enemy from the right bank.

Our frontal attack on the Sanna-i-yat position was at first merely a blind to distract the enemy, but later on we made it so much of a reality that the Turks were at a loss to know where the main attack was to be launched. On February 17 a surprise attack on Sanna-i-yat gained us the first two lines of trenches on a front of some 400 yards, but, unfortunately, we were unable to hold them in face of a strong counter-attack. Five days later the Seaforths and one of the Punjabi regiments did splendid work in a repetition of the same attack, and in spite of six successive counter-attacks we managed this time to hold the first two lines of trenches. We then made feints of attempting to cross the Tigris at Magasis Ferry and opposite to Kut, with the result that the Turkish forces were dispersed over a large area, and his artillery was concentrated at points where we had no real intention of attacking.

Finally, on February 23 we effected a crossing at the apex of the Shumran Bend, first by means of ferries, which took over four battalions to cover the bridgehead, and then a pontoon bridge was constructed; the infantry of one division had crossed before nightfall, and another division was ready to follow. Meanwhile we were attacking the third and fourth lines of trenches at Sanna-i-yat, and during the day these also were captured by our troops. This was the beginning of the end for the Turks, and their sole object now was to prevent us from cutting off their line of retreat.

On the morning of February 24 the gunboat flotilla was ordered to move up from Falahiyah, and in the evening they entered Kut. Once more the Union Jack floated over the town, after an interval of nearly ten months; and if only General Townshend's division had been there to share the rejoicing, the memory of those dark days of the campaign in the spring of 1916 would have been blotted out for ever. Next day the pursuit of the retreating enemy began in earnest, and, as usual, the navy was asked to co-operate with the cavalry. At Imam Mahdi we came across the enemy's rearguard in a prepared position, and a fierce artillery duel opened up between the gunboats and the Turkish howitzers and field batteries. After a few hours some of our own field artillery came up, and later on our infantry stormed the Turkish trenches. The battle lasted all day, but by nightfall the Turk had either had enough of it, or he thought that his main army had been given sufficient time to make good its retreat; for during the hours of darkness he evacuated the position, and next morning the flotilla continued the pursuit.

I imagine that no army in the world can beat the Turkish Army in mobility. The Turkish soldier can live for days together on the food which he can carry on his back—a hard cake made of compressed dates was his usual diet—and consequently his officers have no need to worry themselves to any great extent about such prosaic problems as those connected with the commissariat and the transport of food-supplies. Their main concern, when the army is in retreat, is to get away the guns and munitions, and throughout the Mesopotamian campaign they have been singularly successful in achieving this object.

By way of illustration, it may be mentioned that on February 26 one of our columns tried to accomplish a big stroke by cutting straight across a bend of the river, fully anticipating that they would thus overtake the enemy. They made a forced march of eighteen miles over dry desert, but at the end of it they found that the Turk had been too quick for them, and their only consolation was the capture of a few guns which had been left behind. It is probable that the enemy would have succeeded, in spite of all our efforts, in effecting an orderly retreat had it not been for a daring exploit on the part of the gunboats.

At Nahr Kellak the flotilla came across the rearguard for a second time, and found them well entrenched. Our cavalry, together with the naval guns, shelled them hotly; but there was no moving them, and it became obvious that the performance at Imam Mahdi was to be repeated. It was then that the senior naval officer decided to try and run the gauntlet of the Turkish guns, and make a bold bid to slip past their rearguard. In arriving at this decision he had several circumstances to take into consideration. The Tigris at the Nahr Kellak Bend is fairly wide; and though there are always shifting sand-banks to be found in every part of the river, he had reason to believe that at this point there was plenty of water.

This was an important factor in the situation, because if the foremost ship of the line had been sunk there might have been some danger of the channel becoming blocked, and in this case the rest of the flotilla would have been in an awkward predicament. It must be realized that the enemy's trenches and gun emplacements were situated all round the bend, so that as the ships passed an inferno of shot and shell came at them from three directions. Moreover, the Turks had heavy calibre guns as well as field guns within a few hundred yards of the river, all blazing away at point-blank range; and from the trenches there came a strident accompaniment of machine gun and rifle fire to supplement the roar of the big guns.

Five gunboats took part in this wild dash round the Nahr Kellak Bend, the *Mantis* leading, and as they swept past up the river every gun they had of England used to open an engagement with muzzle-loading guns and red-hot cannon balls. The fury and deadliness of an artillery duel with modern guns at such a range almost baffles the imagination. Every ship was hit several times, but still they held their course; and Fortune smiled on them, for not one of them was disabled. The *Moth*, which was last in the line, came in for the worst punishment; two of her men were killed outright, and of her small complement more than half were wounded, including her three officers.

She was hit eight times by shells, and her after-compartment was holed below the water-line, but still she managed to keep on forging ahead. The *Mantis* also had a heavy casualty list; her quartermaster and her pilot were killed in the conning tower, and her captain (Commander Bernard Buxton, R.N.) received a nasty wound. But in spite of this he took charge of the wheel, just in time to save his ship from running ashore; and though he had never seen that part of the river before, he managed skilfully to steer his ship through the shallows.

So the enemy's rearguard was passed, and before long our flotilla came up with the main army, and opened fire on them with everything they could bring to bear—heavy guns, secondary armament, pom-poms, Maxims, and rifles. The scene that ensued is indescribable; gun's crews were shot down, and their guns abandoned, to be picked up later by our advancing troops; munitions and stores were scattered wholesale; rifles were thrown down, and even haversacks and water-bottles; and the greatest wonder of all was that the Turkish soldier was seen to run, for in normal circumstances nothing could ever make him do more than slouch along, either in advance or retreat. To quote the words of Mr. Edmund Candler, the "Eyewitness" in Mesopotamia:

> So far the enemy had conducted an orderly retirement. It was the action of the gunboats on February 26 that introduced panic and converted the retreat into a rout.

It was not long before the flotilla found something else than the Turkish Army to engage their attention. This was the Turkish Fleet, and the first vessel to come within range was our little friend the *Sumana*, one of the unfortunate garrison forced to surrender at Kut. She surrendered again now, and was restored to her rightful owners. Several transport steamers also hove to and gave themselves up, and about five o'clock in the evening the large steamer *Busrah* was brought to by a shell from the *Tarantula* and surrendered. She was full of Turkish troops, and was carrying some German machine-gunners, of whom some were found killed and the rest wounded. But the prize on which the S.N.O. had most set his heart was the *Firefly*, which the Turks had rechristened *Firicloss*—the first of the brood of Mesopotamian gunboats, which was lost to us during the retreat from Ctesiphon. She was within range, and in company with her was the steamer *Pioneer*.

Both were hit several times, but the *Firicloss* continued gamely to return our fire with her new-pattern British-made gun. At last, soon after six o'clock, she ran into the bank in the Zaljah reach, to the west of Umm-al-Tubal, and within a mile or two of the spot where she had been lost in December, 1915. We overhauled her, and found that the Turks were trying to set fire to her magazine; but we stopped it just in time, and the *Firicloss* became the *Firefly* once more. Her term of tribulation was over, and she returned again to the bosom of her family, heartily welcomed by all her younger sisters. We had to remove her to a safe distance from the *Pioneer*, which was badly afire. Later on the command of the *Firefly* was taken over by Lieutenant-Commander Eddis, who had charge of her at Ctesiphon in November, 1915. He was delighted to find in his cabin that his books and many of his papers remained intact. Our other captures included ten barges, some bridging material and pontoons, and large quantities of rifles, ammunition, and equipment.

Most of the next day we kept the enemy in sight, and together with the cavalry we helped to speed him on his way. On March 1 we reached Aziziyah, which is fifty miles by road from Kut, but about twice as far by river; and here we called a halt, while the army was reorganizing their line of communications and preparing for a further advance. The Turks had been streaming through the village—no longer an army, but a distracted rabble—casting aside their rifles and accoutrements as though they had no other thought than to get away from the sound of the British guns.

Five days later the pursuit was continued, and at Lajj the enemy's rearguard was found; but a blinding sand-storm rendered artillery work impossible, and it was left to the cavalry to force them to retire. Next day the flotilla arrived at the famous Ctesiphon position, and found it absolutely deserted. It had been strongly entrenched, and there was ample evidence that the Turks had fully intended to make a big effort here; but apparently it had been found impossible to rally them, and the great Ctesiphon stronghold was relegated to the lumber-room of past history.

The final stand in front of Baghdad was made by the Turks on the banks of the Dialah River, which joins the Tigris about eight miles below the famous city; and though the enemy's forces were so much depleted that the line was not held in very great strength, they yet managed to offer serious resistance when our infantry tried to cross the Dialah by ferry. In fact, they subjected our troops to such heavy rifle and machine-gun fire that the first attempt had to be abandoned, and we deemed it wise to adopt other methods. We sent a detachment over to the right bank of the Tigris to enfilade the Turks across the river, and incidentally to deal with enemy forces to the south and south-west of Baghdad.

This detachment gradually made its way up the right bank, and on March 10 put the enemy's rearguard to flight, occupying Baghdad railway-station early next morning. Meanwhile the struggle on the banks of the Dialah continued, and during the early hours of the morning of March 9 the North Lancashires crossed the river, and seventy of them heroically stood their ground for twenty-two hours until next morning, when the East Lancashires and the Wiltshires joined them, and drove the enemy out of the river-side villages back to the Tel Mohammed Ridge, his last position, which was occupied that night. Some motor-lighters carrying infantry across the Dialah got stuck in the mud, and had to be rescued by the *Tarantula*.

In the afternoon of March 11 the flotilla arrived at the Citadel in company with Paddler 53, carrying the army commander, and for the first time in history the Union Jack was hoisted over the City of the Caliphs. For some hours previously a state of anarchy had prevailed, and, as in the case of Busrah when our naval forces first arrived there in November, 1914, Arabs and Kurds were looting wholesale and setting fire to the houses.

Order was soon restored, however, and an inventory was commenced of the booty left in our hands. Guns, machine guns, rifles, ammunition, machinery, railway materials, rolling stock, telegraph equipment, hospital accessories—all the paraphernalia of a big army—were there. But perhaps the most interesting of all was a collection of disabled guns which had been rendered useless by the garrison of Kut on the eve of its capitulation—neglected victims of a melancholy disaster, abandoned to the inroads of rust and decay; their very uselessness bore testimony to the pathos of the tragedy in which they were involved. But a new era has dawned for Mesopotamia with the hoisting of the British flag over Baghdad Citadel; a future full of hope and promise has been opened up for this mournful land, debased from her proud estate by corruption and misrule. The brightest dawn, however, does not always disperse the clouds of yesterday, nor the golden promise of the future lighten the darkness of the past.

There are those among us whose private sorrows still rouse them to a bitter questioning of the why and wherefore of the blunders that have been made, who cannot forget that a heavy toll in the lives of Britain's sons has been levied for the lack of foresight and the errors of judgment, committed by some of those responsible for the conduct of the campaign. Such errors, alas! form the staple of the Empire's history. We Britons spend our lives in making blunders, and give our lives to retrieve them. But though the clouds remain, they are no longer dark and threatening; the dawn has come, and with it the confident assurance that in this new burden of Empire—the task of restoring Mesopotamia to her former prosperity—the generations to come will gain inspiration from the long chronicle of heroic deeds which make up the story of her deliverance. The lives of Britain's sons have not been sacrificed in vain.

Preface to the Navy Everywhere

The welcome accorded to the *Navy in Mesopotamia* has tempted me to offer to the public another book on naval work in foreign waters. The title I have chosen must not be taken to imply that I have attempted to describe the activities of the British Navy in every part of the world where they have been in progress. I have done no more than collect a few samples of naval operations in those theatres of war which fare sufficiently remote to have escaped almost entirely the notice of the war correspondents of the Press. These samples exclude altogether the ordinary routine work of the navy—the watching for the German High Seas Fleet, the hunting and destroying of enemy submarines, the sweeping up of mines, the patrolling of many thousand square miles of sea to maintain a blockade of the enemy's coast, the convoying of merchant ships, and the transporting of the army to any part of the world it happened to fancy.

All these tasks are part of the never-ending toil which falls to the lot of the navy in war-time, and, though the successful performance of them is the first essential of our national existence, no literary effort should be needed to impress this fact on the minds of the British public. I have chosen, therefore, to confine myself to those naval performances which are quite outside the ordinary sphere, and about which the public, have received comparatively little information.

The accounts I have given of these performances are based upon official reports, and, in the case of those scenes and incidents of which I was not myself an eye-witness, I am indebted for descriptive details to various officers who took part in them, and to whom I wish to express my cordial thanks. With their assistance I hope I may have succeeded in presenting a readable reminder to the public that the navy during the war was engaged on many and diverse tasks, altogether apart from that of securing to the people of these islands their daily bread.

London, May 1919.   Conrad Cato.

CHAPTER 9

The White Flag at Dar-Es-Salaam

The harbour of Dar-es-Salaam lies somewhere near the middle of the coast of what was once known as German East Africa—about a hundred miles north of the Rufigi River, where the *Königsberg* was found. When war broke out between England and Germany, the Governor of Dar-es-Salaam, probably acting upon instructions, had a floating dock towed to the entrance of the harbour, and there sunk, in order to block the channel. Whether or not it actually did block the channel was not decided at the time, but the intention of it was obvious, and the question that arose was, why did not the Germans take their ships out of the harbour first before they blocked, or attempted to block, the fairway? There were four or five ships inside, and any one of them could have been of great service as a tender to a German raider, such as the *Königsberg*, but yet they were all left inside when the obstruction was sunk at the harbour entrance. Of course it might be put down as one of Germany's blunders, but, on the other hand, it might be possible for those ships to circumvent the obstruction, or again, the sunken dock might be refloated to allow them to pass out when required.

Dar-es-Salaam was ostensibly an undefended port at the beginning of the war, and when H.M.S. *Astræa* called there on 8th August 1914 she took it upon herself to treat the place as such. She destroyed the wireless installation as a necessary precaution, and then opened negotiations with the governor. In return for his immunity from hostile operations he made a pledge that the sunken dock should not be raised, that all vessels in the harbour should be regarded as British prizes, and that no attempt should be made to take any of them out to sea. In those days we regarded the pledge of a German as being at least of some value, though we may have been a little hazy as to how much value we ought to put on it.

A few weeks later the *Pegasus*, lying up for repairs in Zanzibar Harbour, was destroyed by the *Königsberg*, and it was ascertained for a fact that this German raider had been using Dar-es-Salaam Harbour. This completely changed the situation, for it showed that a ship could get in and out of the harbour in spite of the obstruction, and, this being the case, it was more than likely that our prizes there would make their escape sooner or later, and one or more of them would take coal and provisions to the raider. So on 21st October the *Chatham* called at Dar-es-Salaam to see what was going on.

There were two ships lying behind the thick belt of palm trees, their masts visible to the *Chatham*, who thought at first that they were the *Königsberg* and one of her consorts. So she took the range, and fired two or three shells, taking care not to hit the town. The senior naval officer, however, soon discovered that he had been mistaken as to the identity of the ships, and, having insisted upon the removal of their wireless telegraphy aerials, he left them to their own devices, for he had more important work on hand. Nine days later he found the *Königsberg* herself, hiding up the Rufigi River.

Dar-es-Salaam was left alone for over a month, but the senior naval officer was never satisfied that the obstruction really blocked the fairway, and he had even less faith in the pledge of the governor that the ships would not try to escape. On 28th November H.M.S. *Fox* and *Goliath*, with two small vessels in company, anchored off Makatumbe Island, which lies a few miles out to sea from Dar-es-Salaam, and hoisted the international signal to the people ashore to send off a boat. It must be explained that the situation had changed completely, since those early war days, when the *Astræa* paid her visit there. The exploits of the *Königsberg* had clearly indicated that East Africa was not to be excluded from the war zone, whatever might be the pledges of the local governors; and then came our military disaster at Tanga, when we altogether underestimated the resistance likely to be offered by the enemy, with the result that we came off with 800 casualties—and some valuable experience. Moreover, the navy had been busy in the Rufigi River, bottling up the *Königsberg*, so that when they arrived off Dar-es-Salaam they were there for business, and in no mood for anything else.

At the same time it must be remembered that Dar-es-Salaam purported to be an undefended harbour, and was entitled to be treated as such, until there was evidence of hostile intentions on the part of

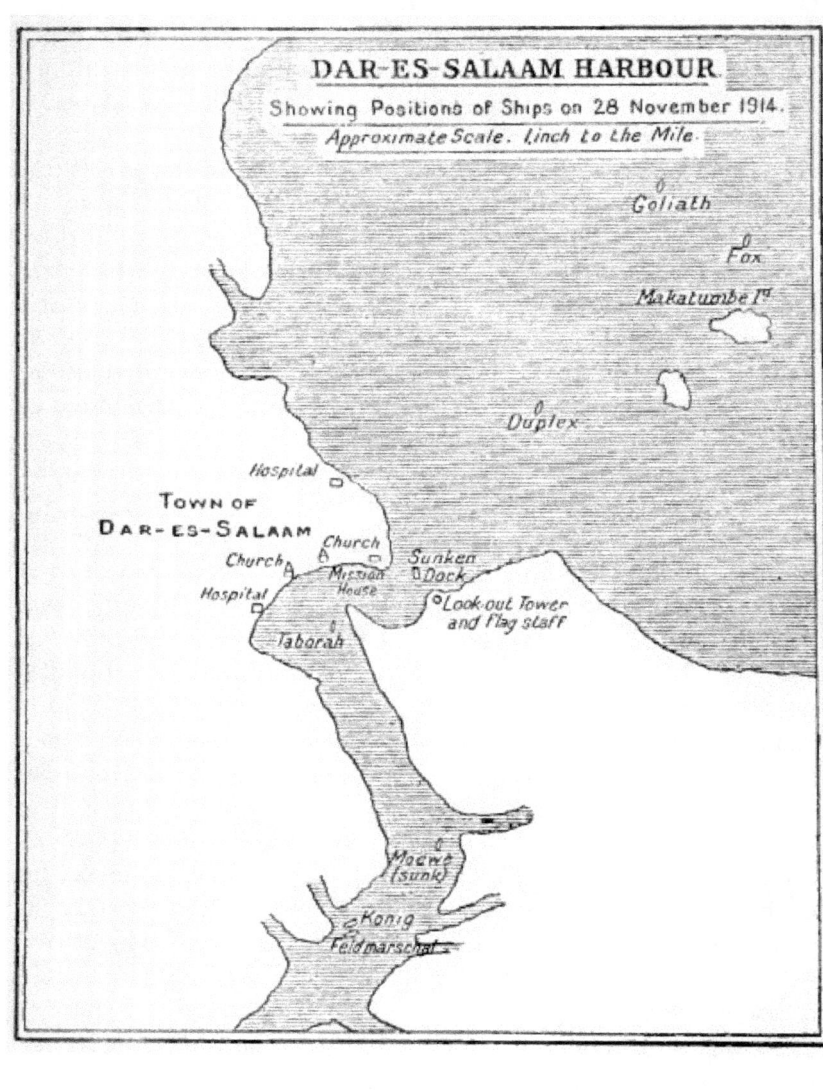

its inhabitants. So the senior naval officer hoisted the signal for a boat and waited on events. After an hour or so a motor-boat came out of harbour, flying a flag of truce, and brought up alongside H.M.S. *Fox*. In it were the acting governor, the district commissioner, and the captain of the port, who all came aboard, and were conducted to the senior naval officer's cabin. Mr. King, formerly British Consul at Dar-es-Salaam, acted as interpreter.

The senior naval officer reminded the German officials that the ships in Dar-es-Salaam Harbour were all British prizes, and informed them that he had come to inspect these ships, to take such steps as might be necessary to disable them, and to withdraw from the harbour or disable any small craft which might be used against the British forces. Now, one of the ships in the harbour was the s.s. *Tabora*, which had been painted as a hospital ship, and according to the Germans was being used as such, At Lindi we had found the s.s. *Prasident* painted in the same way, and had been told the same yarn—that she was being used as a hospital ship—but we had discovered by inspecting her that the yarn was all a tissue of lies, and that the ship was palpably a collier, which had recently been used for supplying the *Königsberg*.

So we were naturally suspicious about the *Tabora*, and the senior naval officer pointed out to the German officials that she had not complied with the international regulations, necessary to convert her into an accredited hospital ship. He added, however, that he had no wish to cause suffering to any sick persons, who might be aboard her, and that he would send a medical officer to inspect her. He would also send a demolition party to disable her engines, but nothing should be done in this direction if the medical officer was of opinion that it would be injurious to any of the patients on board. He further assured them that no damage should be done to the town or its inhabitants, so long as no opposition was offered to the working parties, whom he was going to send into the harbour, to do what was necessary for the disablement of the engines of the various ships.

The acting governor was obviously very uncomfortable and ill at ease. All he could say was that he would like to confer with the military authorities at Dar-es-Salaam. Military authorities in an undefended port seem to be rather out of place, but the senior naval officer waived the point, and merely told him that he would be given a good half-hour or so after landing, before the British boats entered the harbour. The governor then asked rather a curious question. Would these boats carry on their operations under the white flag? The senior naval officer, somewhat surprised at such a question, naturally answered in the negative, and at that the German officials took their departure and returned to the town.

A good deal more than the half-hour's grace was allowed before a steam-cutter was sent in to sound and buoy the channel into the harbour. It was noticed that two white flags had been hoisted on the flag-staff over against the look-out tower at the entrance, and these floated conspicuously in the breeze, so that they could be seen from all directions. The occupants of the steam-cutter, as soon as they rounded the bend, noticed a lady driving in a carriage drawn by a pair of horses along a road close to the water's edge. Everything looked so peaceful that one would have imagined that our dear German brothers in Dar-es-Salaam had never heard of the war.

When a channel had been buoyed, one of the tugs (the *Helmuth*), accompanied by the *Goliath's* steam-pinnace, was ordered to proceed into the harbour with the demolition party. The other tug (the *Duplex*), owing to some engine-room defects, did not enter the harbour, but lay at anchor about two miles from it. The two ships. *Fox* and *Goliath*, were about five miles from the shore, and those on board them were taking only a languid interest in the proceedings, for the two white flags at the lookout tower were flaunted in their faces, and war seemed to them a very tame affair after all. It is very easy to be wise after any event, and to say that this or that precaution should have been taken, but it must be borne in mind that there were the two white flags, conspicuous to everyone, and the enemy was not a barbarous tribe from the African jungle, but purported to be a civilised European people.

So the *Helmuth* proceeded up the harbour to where two ships, called the *König* and *Feldmarschall*, were lying, and the demolition party boarded the *König*, and proceeded to destroy her engines by placing an explosive charge under the low-pressure cylinder, followed by another one inside it. The crew of the *König* appeared to consist mainly of Lascars, and the only officers on board were the chief engineer and the fourth officer. From these it was learned that all the rest of the officers and men were ashore, and at the time it did not occur to Commander Ritchie, who was in charge of the demolition party, that there could be anything unusual in this circumstance. He ordered all the *König's* crew to go down into the ship's boats, informing them that they were prisoners of war.

Shortly afterwards the *Goliath's* steam-pinnace came up, bringing some more men of the demolition party, with Lieutenant-Commander Paterson in charge. Commander Ritchie instructed this officer to complete the disablement of the engines of the *Feldmarschall* and *König*, while he himself went farther up the creek in the *Helmuth* to another ship, called the *Kaiser Wilhelm II*. The *Helmuth*, however, ran on the mud, and had some difficulty in getting off, so Commander Ritchie took her back to the *König*, and tried the steam-pinnace in place of her. In this he successfully reached the *Kaiser Wilhelm II*, disabled her engines, and destroyed two lighters that were lying near her. But what first gave him a sense of uneasiness was the fact that the *Kaiser Wilhelm II* was absolutely deserted. Her crew were nowhere to be seen, but on her deck were found some Mauser clips—one containing three bullets with the pointed ends sawn off—suggesting that the ship's crew had recently been busy overhauling their rifles. The absence of the officers and white ratings from the other two ships now assumed a new significance.

Lying near the ship were five other lighters, and it occurred at once to Commander Ritchie that it might be useful to have one of these on each side of the steam-pinnace, by way of protection, for there was evidently mischief of some kind or other brewing. The other three lighters he towed astern, and, thus encumbered, the pinnace made the best speed she could down the creek. As she passed the *König* and *Feldmarschall*, Commander Ritchie saw that the *Helmuth* had already started her return voyage, and though he scrutinised the two ships carefully through his glasses, he could see no signs of anyone in either of them. So he proceeded down the creek, but found that the pinnace made such slow progress that he was finally obliged to drop the three lighters astern, only retaining the two which were made fast on either side of the pinnace.

In order to keep to the chronological order of events, we must now return to the *Helmuth* and Lieutenant-Commander Paterson. He was engaged with his demolition party on the engines of the *König* and *Feldmarschall*, and in the meantime some thirty prisoners from the *König* were sitting in the two boats belonging to that ship. Lieutenant Orde had received instructions from Commander Ritchie to proceed down the harbour, towing these two boats, to stop at the s.s. *Tabora* and put Surgeon Holton aboard there to inspect the ship, and then proceed out to sea and deliver his prisoners over to the *Duplex*, afterwards returning to the *Tabora* to pick up Surgeon Holton. This, at any rate, was how Lieutenant Orde understood his instructions, and he not unnaturally concluded that Lieutenant-Commander Paterson and his working party intended to return in the steam pinnace with Commander Ritchie.

It is not very clear why he should have thought that the sole object of his returning to the *Tabora*, after the safe delivery of his prisoners, was to pick up Surgeon Holton, for it had always been intended that a demolition party should board the *Tabora*, and should disable her engines if Surgeon Holton was of opinion tliat this could be done without injury to any of the patients. Possibly, however, Lieutenant Orde was unaware of this arrangement.

It may here be stated that the *Tabora* was genuinely being used as a hospital ship. There were doctors and nurses and some wounded men in her, and she was fitted with cots and other hospital equipment.

And now we must return to H.M.S. *Fox* and the senior naval officer. It was late in the forenoon when he ordered the steam-cutter alongside, and, accompanied by an army staff officer, went in to have a look at the sunken dock at the mouth of the harbour. It was a morning of bright sunshine, and through the clear water he could see the obstruction lying about ten feet below the surface, but, without sounding, it would be difficult to say whether or not it effectually blocked the channel. He then thought he would go round the bend, and see what the harbour looked like, and how the demolition parties were getting on. He gave the order to the coxswain to go ahead, and leaned comfortably back in the sternsheets of the boat, enjoying the pleasant sunshine and possibly wondering why the Germans had hoisted two white flags on the flag-staff, when one would have answered the purpose.

Suddenly the sharp crack of a rifle was heard, and a bullet struck the water on the port side of the steam-cutter. Next moment a blaze of rifle fire came from either bank, and bullets began to rain against the sides of the boat. The hottest fire seemed to come from the vicinity of the flag staff, where the two white flags still floated in the breeze. "Lie down everyone," shouted the senior naval officer, and to the coxswain he gave the order "Hard-a-port." The bullets were whistling over their heads, were pouring into the boat, and were piercing the thin iron plates, which had been rigged for the protection of the boiler and of the coxswain in the sternsheets. The stoker tending the fire was dangerously wounded, but Lieutenant Corson ran forward and took his place. In the after part of the boat a seaman was hit in the head, and the coxswain had a bullet through his leg, but pluckily stuck to his job, although another wound caused the blood to pour from his mouth. "That's nothing, sir," he said. "I'm all right. We shall soon be out of the channel."

No one in the boat was armed, and so there was no way of replying to the fire. To make matters worse, speed had slackened owing to the furnace having been neglected before it was noticed that the stoker was wounded. But the efforts of Lieutenant Corson soon increased the steam pressure, and after a while the boat got beyond the danger zone. The coxswain stuck to his post in spite of his wounds, and eventually brought the boat alongside the *Fox* about half-past one in the afternoon. Stoker Herbert T. Lacey died of his wounds.

Immediately afterwards the firing broke out again, and the senior naval officer saw that the *Helmuth* was coming through the neck of the harbour, towing astern of her two boats full of prisoners. She had put the doctor on board the *Tabora*, and was on her way to the *Duplex* to hand over the prisoners, when field-gun, rifle, and machine-gun fire was opened on her from the north bank. The coxswain was immediately wounded, and his relief had no sooner taken his place than he, too, was wounded. Then Lieutenant Orde, who was in command, received a wound, but the worst piece of bad luck was that a bullet struck the breech-block of the *Helmuth's* only gun—a 3-pounder—and put it out of action, so that she became as defenceless as the *Fox's* steam cutter had been. The bullets came pouring into her, and some of them punctured the steam pipes, with the result that there was a heavy escape of steam, and the speed of the tug slackened considerably. There was a certain amount of grim satisfaction in seeing a stray bullet hit one of the boats astern, and wound a German prisoner, but this was the only consolation to be derived by the *Helmuth's* unfortunate victims.

The senior naval officer in the *Fox* promptly signalled to the *Duplex* to open fire on the shore with her 12-pounder, and both the *Fox* and *Goliath* bombarded the shore whence the enemy's fire seemed to be coming. This had the desired effect of causing some slight abatement, and after a while the *Helmuth* got beyond the danger zone. The *Goliath* was then ordered to put a few shells into the governor's palace, which she proceeded to do with one of her 12-inch guns, and after two or three rounds the palace was reduced to a heap of ruins. Then there came a lull in the proceedings, and one would have supposed that the Germans hiding in the vicinity of the look-out tower would have occupied their leisure in hauling down the white flags from the flag-staff. But the white flags continued to float serenely in the breeze, and the Germans beneath them stood waiting for their next victims.

We must now return to the steam-pinnace and Commander Ritchie. Having satisfied himself that there was no one aboard the *König* or the *Feldmarschall*, he continued his way down the harbour, and, as already related, he dropped the three lighters which were in tow astern, in order to increase speed. When he was approaching the *Tabora* he saw Surgeon Holton put off from her in a boat, and head towards the steam-pinnace. He had just eased down the engines to enable the doctor to come alongside, when a heavy fire was opened on him from both sides of the harbour. The crew of Surgeon Holton's boat took fright, and began to pull back to the *Tabora*. At this the steam-pinnace tried to get up to the boat, but with her two lighters in tow on either side of her, she was difficult to steer, and finally had to abandon the attempt. But the two lighters proved to be her salvation, for some field guns were now firing shells at her, and without the protection of these lighters she must inevitably have been sunk.

As she rounded the bend the shot and shell came at her from all directions, and though the *Fox* and *Goliath* again opened fire to cover her retreat, it did not seem to make much appreciable difference. For the enemy were well hidden among the palm trees, and from the ships, lying five miles out to sea, it was impossible to locate them. Two men in the steam-pinnace were hit almost at the outset; one of them was the coxswain. Petty Officer Clark, whose place was taken by Able Seaman Upton. Then Upton was hit, and Clark, whose wound had been temporarily dressed, tried to resume his place at the wheel, but fainted away from loss of blood. This was the critical moment, for the narrow entrance of the harbour and the sunken dock still lay in front of them, and there was need of a cool head and a steady hand to steer the boat through.

Commander Ritchie had by this time been wounded in several places, and was in considerable pain, but he saw that the only chance of escape lay in skilful steering, and so he took the wheel himself. Amidst the ceaseless shower of bullets whistling over his head and singing past his ears, he piloted the boat through the neck of the harbour, and had just got clear of it when a bullet struck him in the leg. It was his eighth wound; simultaneously the boat ran on a sand-bank, and the commander fainted. Fortunately, however, the worst of the danger was now over; the boat got afloat again without much trouble, the two lighters, having served their purpose, were slipped, and in less than an hour the boat reached the *Fox*. In addition to the commander, one officer and five men were wounded.

Throughout the whole or these proceedings, the two white flags flew majestically from the flag-stall—the emblems of Germany's high ideal of universal peace and the brotherhood of man. But the whole of the tale of treachery is not yet told. It soon became known that Lieutenant-Commander Paterson and his section of the demolition party were missing. The party included Lieutenant (E) V. J. H. Sankey, Chief Artificer Engineer W. E. Turner, one chief petty officer, and seven other ratings. The solution of the mystery of their disappearance was only revealed when these officers and men were released from their captivity nearly three years later. It appears that while the party was at work in the *König*, Lieutenant-Commander Paterson became aware that armed troops were on the river-bank in a position commanding the deck of the ship. When the firing started lower down the harbour, he realised at once that they were in for trouble, and, in fact, he had anticipated it. He therefore kept the whole of his party down below, fully expecting that Commander Ritchie, when he returned with the steampinnace, would come alongside the ship.

Presently he saw on the other side of the estuary two large lighters, with the funnel of a small steamboat just appearing above them. At first he failed to recognise that this was the steam-pinnace of his own ship, but when it had steamed straight past the *König*, and he was able to get a better view of it, he realised the awful truth that there had been some misunderstanding, and that he and his party were left in the lurch. He knew that if he showed himself on the upper deck the Askaris would open fire on him, and he knew that Commander Ritchie would not be able to hear his voice, unaided by a megaphone. There was only one chance that if they all kept very quiet the troops on the bank might think they had left the *König*, and under cover of night they might be able to find a boat and slip out of the harbour. It was a forlorn hope, and unfortunately it was doomed to disappointment. In the early evening the Germans came and took them all prisoners.

On 30th November 1914 the senior naval officer addressed a letter to the governor of Dar-es-Salaam, recapitulating what had taken place, and warning him that the town would be subjected to bombardment, but the *Tabora* would be spared, not as an accredited hospital ship, but because there were reported to be wounded men in her. The governor's reply (which was somewhat belated) was a truly marvellous piece of composition. First of all he said that though he had agreed to the British visiting the ships in the harbour, he had never agreed to allow them to disable the engines; then he stated that the British boats came into the harbour filled with armed men; and finally he excused the presence of the white flags by saying that there was no possibility of hauling them down because the fight was so intensive. Apparently his idea of an intensive fight is hiding behind a palm tree, and potting at defenceless men in open boats. The letter was a poor production, even as a specimen of German mendacity.

At half-past two that afternoon there was another "intensive fight" in Dar-es-Salaam, in which the government buildings, the warehouses, the railway stations, the customs house, and the barracks received special attention. The debris of these buildings was seen flying above the tree-tops, but only two small fires were started, as most of the houses were built of coral slag. But it is a fair surmise that, by the time the entertainment was over, the governor and people of Dar-es-Salaam had had enough of "intensive fighting."

Commander Henry Peel Ritchie, for his heroic conduct in taking the wheel of the steam-pinnace, and bringing the boat out of harbour, after he had received eight wounds, was awarded the Victoria Cross.

CHAPTER 10

Bottling up the "Königsberg"

During the month of September 1914 H.M.S. *Pegasus*—an old light cruiser of about 2,000 tons—put into Zanzibar Harbour to repair her boilers. Now Zanzibar is a British protectorate, but this fact afforded no guarantee at that time that the island was not swarming with German agents, and lying as it does not far from the mainland of German East Africa, it followed as a matter of course that the Germans were kept fully informed as to what was happening at Zanzibar. By means of wireless stations, which were quite plentiful down the coast of German East Africa, they were able to communicate interesting news to any of the German cruisers that were roaming the seas in those days. And so it came about that the German cruiser *Königsberg* received a message to say that a small British cruiser was lying disabled in Zanzibar Harbour—an old third-class cruiser with out-of-date guns, that could not be expected to put up any kind of a fight, and could be easily outranged by the German guns. Here was just the kind of job the *Königsberg* enjoyed, and so on 20th September she pounced down on her prey, and very quickly pummelled the poor old ship to pieces.

Out of the destruction of the *Pegasus* the only compensation to be gained was the knowledge that the elusive *Königsberg* was on the East African coast, and it was a fair assumption that she was receiving her supplies of coal and stores from the shore, by means of German merchant vessels. There were several of these vessels dancing attendance on the raider, and, according to information received, one of them was called the *Präsident*, and another the *Somali*. There were other ships in Dar-esSalaam harbour, which were under suspicion, but the Germans had themselves blocked the mouth of that harbour by sinking an obstruction, and for the present we were content to believe that the ob-

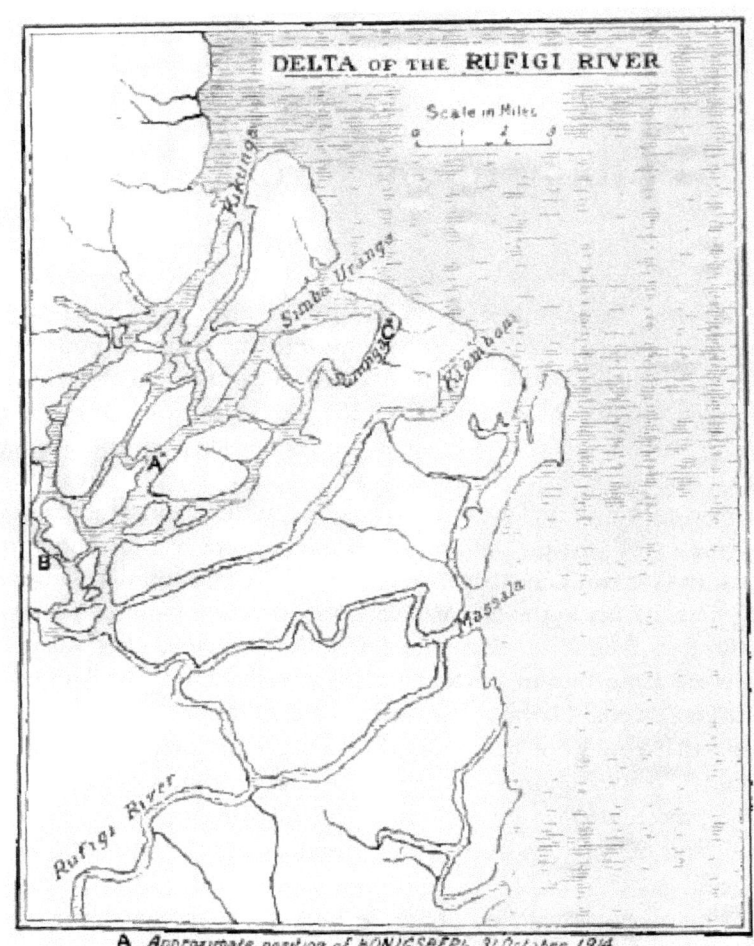

A Approximate position of KÖNIGSBERG 31 October 1914
B   "   "   "   "   4 December 1914
C Position where "NEWBRIDGE" was sunk

struction was effective, and to leave the Dar-es-Salaam ships out of the account. When, therefore, three British cruisers were told off to search for the *Königsberg*, they worked upon the basis that the discovery of the *Präsident*, or the *Somali*, or both, might be of material assistance.

The search was not an easy one, because the coast for the major part is fringed with thick belts of palm trees, behind which the harbours, formed by the estuaries of the rivers, wind away out of sight. Thus at Lindi, near the southern extremity of the colony, the *Weymouth* had a look at the outer harbour, which was empty, but could see nothing of the inner harbour behind the palm trees, nor of the river beyond it, and, owing to shallow water, was unable to approach to such a position as would command a view of these. But a few days later the *Chatham* called at Lindi, and sent in a steamboat, armed with a maxim-gun. Commander Fitzmaurice went in with the steamboat, carrying a letter to the governor of Lindi, which was only to be delivered if it were found that a German ship of any kind was lurking in the inner harbour. The letter contained an order to the governor, to send out to sea any ships that might be in his harbour, and gave him half an hour to carry out this order, before anything unpleasant should happen to him.

Now, as soon as the steamboat turned the corner, the first thing to meet the gaze of Commander Fitzmaurice was the *Präsident* moored about three and a half miles up the river. But he had to rub his eyes to make sure of her, for, instead of a ship looking like a collier, or even like an ordinary merchantman, he saw what looked uncommonly like a hospital ship. At her mast-head the Geneva Cross was floating in the breeze, and on her side was painted a large white cross. And yet she was not by any means perfect in her make-up, for she had not painted her hull white, nor had she the broad band of either green or red running from stem to stern, which is used to denote the hospital ship. For once the Teuton lacked thoroughness in his methods.

Next came a boat from the shore, flying a white flag, and in it sat the governor's secretary, to whom Commander Fitzmaurice delivered the letter. Then came an interval of waiting for an hour or two, while the governor was considering his reply. Presently the secretary came oil again in the boat with the white flag, and the governor's reply in his best official German was duly conveyed to the senior naval officer. In a tone of injured innocence the governor asked plaintively how could he comply with the Senior Naval Officer's order. The *Präsident* was the only ship in the harbour, and how could he be expected to order a hospital ship to go to sea? It was affording shelter to the women and children of Lindi, and to all the sick men of Lindi; to send it to sea would be an act of barbarism. Moreover, its machinery was incomplete, and the wheels would not go round, so the senior naval officer would see at once that it was quite out of the question to send it out of the harbour.

Meanwhile, however, the senior naval officer had been writing another letter to the governor, which proved to be a very suitable reply. He pointed out that the name of the *Präsident* had not been communicated, either to him or to the British Government, as a hospital ship, in accordance with the terms of the Hague Convention, and that her hull had not been painted as the hull of a hospital ship should be painted. He then briefly informed the governor that he was sending an armed party to board her, and, if possible, to bring her out of the harbour, or, if this proved to be impossible, to disable her engines.

That was the end of the negotiations; the governor made no further tax upon his powers of romance, but bowed to inexorable Fate. And so the armed party was sent into the harbour in a steamboat, and went on board the *Präsident*. There are still some strangeminded folk who cling to their faith in the honesty of purpose of the much-abused German; it may come as a shock to them to learn that the hospital ship *Präsident* had no cots, no medical equipment of any kind, no doctors, and no nurses; nor were there any sick men on board, nor any women, nor any children.

There were, however, unmistakable traces of the collier to be seen everywhere about her; and it was evident that she had been recently employed in this capacity. There are other strange-minded folk who will exclaim, "How clever those Germans are!" But when they come to think it out, they will see that there was nothing remarkably clever in painting a white cross on a collier, when she was threatened with capture or disablement. It was a childishly simple trick, as most of the German tricks are.

The *Präsident's* engines were disabled by the boarding party, and they brought away with them a few useful mementoes, such as a chronometer, a set of charts, a set of sailing directions, and some compasses. So ended the career of the *Präsident*, collier and supply ship to the German raider *Königsberg*.

Nearly a fortnight later, on 30th October, the *Chatham* lay at anchor off the Rufigi River delta, and sent in a steamboat to the shore, in quest of information. Three natives were seen wandering about among the palm trees, and were persuaded by cogent arguments that it was their duty to pay an official visit to H.M.S. *Chatham*. In other words, they were brought off to the ship in the steamboat, and through the medium of an interpreter they unfolded their tale. Yes, there were two ships lying up the Rufigi River behind the forest of cocoanut palms, and one of them had big guns, that made a big noise. *Boom!* The other was like a handmaiden to the fellow with the guns—like a good and faithful wife to him, who waited on him and gave him *ghee* and rice and *dhurra* when he was hungry. They described the ships in their own language, and the description was good enough to set all doubts at rest. The *Königsberg* and the *Somali* had been traced to their lair at last. From the *Chatham*'s foretop it was just possible to see the masts of two ships sticking up above the palm trees, but nothing could be seen of their hulls. One useful piece of information derived from the natives was that the *Königsberg* had run short of coal, and that her men had been felling palm trees to obtain fuel. This shortage of coal served to explain why she had been lying idle up the Rufigi River ever since her exploit at Zanzibar a month ago, when the old *Pegasus* met her doom.

It was one thing to discover the *Königsberg*, and quite another thing to get at her. To start with, there was a bar between the open sea and the mouth of the river, which the *Chatham* could only cross at high water; then there was a likelihood of obstructions sunk in the river channel, and of mines; and then there was the certainty of opposition from the shore on either side of the river mouth, for the Germans had been busy digging trenches, rigging up barbed wire, and making gun emplacements, in which they had mounted the guns of the *Königsberg's* secondary armament. All these defences were well concealed behind the palm trees and thick undergrowth.

The first thing the senior naval officer did was to inform by wireless the Dartmouth and the *Weymouth*, who were searching the coast farther south, that their quest was at an end, and that they were to rejoin the *Chatham*. He then set about sounding and buoying a channel towards the river mouth. By the river mouth must be understood that passage through the delta where the two channels, called Simba Uranga and Suninga, make their exit to the sea. According to the information gleaned from the natives the other three channels were impassable by large ships.

Meanwhile the range was taken of the *Somali*, which was lying a little nearer than the *Königsberg*. It was found to be just over 14,000 yards, and so the *Chatham* opened fire on her with 6-inch lyddite shells. The effect of the fire could not be ascertained, for the *Somali's* hull was invisible behind the palm trees, and even her masts could only be seen by the spotters at the mast-head.

One result of the bombardment, however, soon declared itself. The masts of the *Königsberg* were seen to move, slowly at first, but as the ship gathered way, they glided rapidly past the tops of the palm trees. For a moment there was a state of keen anticipation on board the *Chatham*, for they really thought that the German cruiser was coming out to engage them, and, as Alexander Pope says, hope springs eternal in the human breast. But the *Königsberg* had no such intention; all she wanted to do was to make sure of being outside the *Chatham's* range, so she slunk away another six miles farther up the river, and there dropped her anchor again.

Was she now safe from bombardment? It must be remembered that the *Chatham* was five or six miles out to sea, but, supposing she managed to cross the bar and to reach the river's mouth, it was just possible that she might find the *Königsberg* within her range then. At all events it was worth trying, and so the work of buoying a channel continued briskly. One morning, however, a look-out from the mast-head reported that the *Königsberg'*s masts had disappeared, and he could see nothing of her anywhere.

Here was a startling mystery, but the explanation of it was not hard to guess, and the *Chatham* carried on with her work. As soon as the channel had been buoyed and the spring tide came round, she crept in gingerly, passed over the bar, and anchored about a mile and a half from the entrance to the river. And then the look-out in the foretop was able to solve the mystery of the sudden disappearance of the *Königsberg's* masts. The top-masts had been struck, and in their place had been rigged the tops of two cocoanut palms, so that in the distance nothing but these could be seen. It was a better trick than painting a white cross on a collier's hull, and besides having the merit of being a legitimate device of warfare, it was worthy of any of those animals who make a practice of protective mimicry, such as the arctic *fox*, who changes his coat to white when the snow comes, or the mantis, who pretends he is a pink flower.

The *Chatham* opened fire at once, for she had no time to lose if she was to get back across the bar with the ebb of the tide. Her trouble was that the gunlayers could see absolutely nothing of their objective, and her spotters found it almost impossible to spot the fall of the shells amidst the thick vegetation of the delta. It became very obvious that there was very little chance of settling accounts with the German raider until some aircraft arrived to help in the operations. When the *Chatham* recrossed the bar she had less than a foot of water underneath her, and her captain made up his mind that he had had quite enough of that experiment.

Meanwhile the *Dartmouth* and the *Weymouth* had arrived on the scene, and had filled in their time with frequent bombardments of the trenches and barbed-wire entanglements on either side of the river entrance. The result was that the trenches at the extreme ends were evacuated by the Germans, who came to the conclusion that life in them had too many crowded hours to it to be comfortable. The *Chatham* devoted her attentions to the *Somali*, and though her fire was indirect, and the spotting extremely difficult, she succeeded in plumping at least one shell into the ship, and in causing a fire to break out on board.

The next experiment was a scheme to send in armed picket-boats, carrying a couple of torpedoes, to be fired at the *Somali*, but it turned out a failure. The boats were greeted with a heavy fire from rifles and machine-guns, which were so effectually hidden in a mangrove swamp on the south side of the river that it was impossible to locate them. An extraordinary accident occurred to one of the torpedoes, which no one was able to explain. Possibly the releasing gear was struck by a bullet, or possibly a torpedo man lost his nerve amidst the rattle and clatter of the enemy's shot; but, anyhow, the torpedo was released prematurely, and all it did was to sink to the bottom without either a run or an explosion. The other torpedo was out of gear, and so the experiment had to be abandoned, and the boats returned to their respective ships, fortunately with nothing more than very light casualties.

One result of these experiments was the decision that, since the *Königsberg* refused to come out of her retreat, she had better be locked up inside it. With this object in view, a large collier of venerable antiquity was brought from Zanzibar and preparations were made to take her into the river, moor her athwart the fairway, and then sink her, so as to block the channel. Iron plates were fixed round the steering-wheel of her forebridge to protect the helmsman from rifle fire, and her crew were taken out of her and replaced by officers and men of the *Chatham*. A flotilla of steam-cutters and a picket-boat belonging to the three ships, together with a vessel of light draught, called the

Duplex, were to accompany the *Newbridge*, covering her advance, as far as possible, by their fire, and assisting her in various other ways. The picket-boat was to carry a torpedo, which was to be fired at the *Newbridge*, if other methods of sinking her failed. One of the steam-cutters was to stand by to take off her crew when she was abandoned. Another steam-cutter was to land a party on the left bank of the river, to see what they could find there. All the men were to wear life-belts, and to carry their rifles, and the steamboats and the *Duplex* were to be armed with maxims.

Before daybreak on 7th November the flotilla headed for the mouth of the river, the *Newbridge* leading, and arrived there at half-past five in the morning. All seemed quiet at first, and not a soul was to be seen on shore, but as soon as the *Newbridge* turned round the bend, the music of maxims and rifles broke the silence, and the bullets pattered like hailstones against the iron plates which protected her crew. But she kept steadily on her course, entered the Suninga Channel, and just before six o'clock reached her destination.

It is not very obvious from the map of the Rufigi Delta why the Suninga Channel was selected to be blocked. More direct access to the sea is afforded by the Simba Uranga Channel, and it was in this channel that the *Königsberg* was lying when she was first discovered. Since then she had moved up above the point where the two channels met, and one might suppose that either of them could be used by her. This, however, was not the case, according to the opinion of the natives. They were unanimous in the view that only the Suninga Channel had water enough to admit of the passage of a ship of the *Königsberg's* size, and for the present we had to be content to accept this view as correct.

When the *Newbridge* arrived at the position marked C on the map, she shut off her engines, and proceeded to anchor bow and stern. This was carried out to the accompaniment of a ceaseless patter of bullets, occasionally varied by the dull thud of something heavier striking her sides and superstructure. The enemy evidently had some small guns commanding the spot, and they were resolved to make things as unpleasant as they possibly could. To sink a vessel in the exact position required for blocking a channel is not so easy as it sounds. The Turks tried it many times up the Tigris and Euphrates, and invariably made a mess of it; the Germans tried it on a large scale to bar the approaches to Duala, in the Cameroons, and they, too, did the work very badly, using up quite a large number of ships before they succeeded in making a barrage. It is the kind of job which cannot be done in a hurry, and to do it under fire requires a remarkably cool nerve. The Germans knew this, no doubt, and by pouring shot and shell into the *Newbridge* they hoped to spoil the operation.

This hope, however, was doomed to disappointment. As soon as the ship was moored securely across the channel, the main inlet valve was opened, and she began to settle by the stern. Her commanding officer was fearful at first lest the force of the current should carry her stern round, but the anchors held firmly, and in a short time the stern had grounded on the bottom. The crew were ordered to assemble near the port ladder, and in spite of the heavy fire directed at them, they fell in as unconcernedly as though they were in Sheerness Harbour and the quartermaster had piped "Both watches fall in for exercise." The steam-cutter, which was waiting to take them off, also came in for her share of the enemy's fire, but it failed to disconcert her crew.

The last thing to do before abandoning the ship was to place an explosive charge in her, and connect it to an electric circuit, of which the ends were carried into the steamcutter, and, as soon as they were at a sufficient distance, the charge was exploded and the ship, listing to port, sank to the bottom of the river, where she lay very nearly at right angles to the line of the channel. No one could have made a neater job of it.

Then came the exciting business of getting out of the river again. The enemy's 3-pounders, rifles, and machine-guns were busy all the time, but our boats were also armed, and replied as well as they could, though the Germans took good care to keep themselves in hiding. The *Duplex* was there to lend her support, and did useful work in keeping down the enemy's fire. But her commanding officer, Lieutenant Triggs, H.N.R., received a nasty wound in the back of his shoulder from a bursting shell. The coxswain of one of the steamboats and the leading torpedo man in the picket-boat were unfortunately killed, and eight other men were wounded. But considering the nature of the work to be performed, our casualties were remarkably light.

So the Suninga Channel was blocked, and at the time we confidently believed that the *Königsberg* was bottled up. But after a few days the *Kinfauns Castle* arrived, bringing a seaplane with her, and the aerial reconnaissances started. The officers of the R.N.A.S. would seem to take a positive delight in upsetting everybody's preconceived notions, and they found that the Rufigi River gave them endless scope for this pastime. First of all they said that the Simba Uranga was a beautiful channel, such as would delight the heart of the *Königsberg's* navigator; whereat the senior naval officer said, "Then we will block it," and began to make arrangements to bring another old packet from Zanzibar to be sunk as an obstruction. Then the airmen said that the Kikunja Channel, although not so attractive to a navigator as the Simba Uranga, was sufficiently tempting to induce a bold spirit to try his luck there. Finally they said they that did not believe that the Suninga Channel was blocked by the *Newbridge*, as there seemed to be quite a lot of space between the wreck and the north bank.

And then the senior naval officer decided that he would sink no more vessels in the Rufigi River, for he might continue that game until he had sunk the whole of Great Britain's mercantile marine, and even then the R.N.A.S. would not be satisfied. He still had his own private opinion that the *Königsberg* was securely bottled up, but in view of these reports of the airmen there was no alternative but to keep watch outside, until measures could be taken to destroy the *Königsberg* in her lair. He knew that she was short of coal, even if she could negotiate the channel, but in war-time the Navy must take no risks, and so the *Chatham*, the *Fox*, the *Kinfauns Castle*, and the *Weymouth* by turns kept guard over all the exits from the Rufigi Delta.

The *Chatham* spent Christmas Day upon this wearisome job, and it was only natural that her officers should have felt that something should be done to mark the occasion. In those early days of the war, before our stubborn English minds had received an adequate comprehension of the German species, the practice of fraternising was rife everywhere, and the illustrated papers of December 1914 contain many touching little pictures of Tommy and Fritz expressing their brotherly love for each other. It is not easy, however, to fraternise with an enemy some twelve miles away, when he stoutly refuses to come any nearer.

The *Chatham's* officers saw this difficulty, and so they had a raft built, and on the raft they placed the largest lump of coal which could be found in the bunkers, and on this lump of coal they affixed a message of Christmas greetings, and then they let the raft float up the river with the tide. The message ran, "Wishing you a merry Christmas. Get up steam for fifteen knots, and Come Out." But neither the present nor the invitation was even acknowledged.

The occupation of Mafia Island took place early in January 1915. It was a necessary preliminary to the maintenance of a strict blockade on the coast of German East Africa. Several dhows, which had been trading with the enemy, were captured, and these we armed and turned into patrol vessels. Before long the German forces were faced with the fact that they must rely upon internal resources for food and stores, since the great ocean highway was completely closed to them.

CHAPTER 11

Destruction of the "Königsberg"

On 7th November 1914 the *Newbridge* was sunk in the Suninga Channel of the Rufigi River, with a view to bottling up the *Königsberg*, but shortly afterwards our seaplanes reported that in their opinion the German raider could still find a passage out of the river. Consequently a strict guard was kept over all the outlets, until such time as means could be found of giving the raider her quietus.

Six months later two of our monitors, the *Severn* and the *Mersey*, arrived on the scene, and under the directions of Vice-Admiral King-Hall preparations were made for the attack. The Germans were still strongly entrenched on either side of the only channels which were believed to be navigable, and they had taken the guns of the *Königsberg's* secondary armament to support their men in the trenches. Both trenches and guns were well hidden in the mangrove swamps, forests of palm trees, and thick undergrowth, which fringe the banks of the river, so that it was impossible to say what was the strength of the enemy's forces here. To land in a mangrove swamp, and make a frontal attack on hidden trenches and guns, is bound to be a costly operation at all times, and was certainly to be avoided if other means could be found of getting at the *Königsberg*.

The monitor seemed to offer the best solution of the problem, for its light draught would enable it to proceed by channels which were impassable by the ordinary ship, and its long-range guns would be able to compete with the guns of the *Königsberg* with some degree of equality. In fact, the guns of the two monitors were of larger calibre than those of the *Königsberg*, but the latter had the advantage of better facilities for spotting, and the still greater advantage of having the ranges of various points along the river carefully calculated.

The spotting for the monitors could only be carried out by aircraft, for in that dense belt of vegetation it was impossible from their fighting tops to see anything more than the *Königsberg's* masts, and even these were invisible to the gunlayers below. The hull of the ship was never seen throughout the operations by anyone except the observers in the aeroplanes. The enemy on the other hand had no aircraft for spotting purposes, but a very simple device took the place of it. They knew all the possible positions from which we could attack, and so they stationed men in the tree-tops somewhere in the vicinity of these positions, and arranged a simple code of signals. As will be seen later on, it was some time before we discovered this device.

On 6th July 1915, about four o'clock in the morning, the *Severn* and the *Mersey* proceeded to cross the bar, and by half-past five they had entered the Kikunga (Channel of the river. As will be seen from the map, this is the northernmost channel, which, according to seaplane reconnaissances, afforded a possible exit for the *Königsberg*, but according to the opinions of the natives was not navigable by any large craft. The monitors were followed as far as the entrance to the channel by a variety of craft, which came in to support them. The *Tweedmouth*, a light draught steamer, bore the flag of the commander-in-chief; two small whalers, the *Echo* and *Fly*, swept ahead for mines, while the *Childers* sounded to find the channel; and the light cruisers *Weymouth* and *Pyramus* also crossed the bar.

The *Weymouth* then proceeded to bombard a position on the delta known as Pemba, where we were informed that the enemy had a spotting station. It meant long-range firing, without the satisfaction of knowing the result, for there was no aircraft spotting for the *Weymouth*. It seems fairly certain, however, that the German observation station at Pemba, assuming that it existed, was of very little service to them. More important work for the *Weymouth* was that of keeping down the fire of the enemy's anti-aircraft guns, for it was essential that our aeroplanes should be as free as possible from interruption in their work. It is at all times unsatisfactory to fire at an invisible target in the thick of a forest, but there is no doubt that the *Weymouth* succeeded in planting shells near enough to the antiaircraft guns to restrict their activities within reasonable limits.

It must be remembered that the *Königsberg* was defended by a good deal more than her own guns, that military forces and military guns of unknown strength were hidden in the thick vegetation, and that the destruction of a ship, situated as she was behind an impenetrable delta, was no ordinary naval operation. The operation would, in fact, have been almost an impossibility had it not been for the assistance of the aeroplanes. The aerodrome was on Mafia Island, some thirty miles from where the *Königsberg* was lying, and as there were only two aeroplanes available, and they necessarily had to relieve each other from time to time, there were some wearisome pauses in the proceedings.

Flight Lieutenant Watkins started off at half-past five from the aerodrome, carrying six bombs, which he dropped as near as he could to the *Königsberg*, to keep her attention occupied while the *Severn* and the *Mersey* were getting into position. The two monitors on their way up the river had been liberally fired on by pom-poms and 3-pounders, but this had not worried them much, and by half-past six in the morning they were anchored head and stern at their allotted stations. By this time the second aeroplane had arrived, with Flight Commander Cull as pilot, and Flight Sub-Lieutenant Arnold as observer, and the monitors opened fire.

Let no one imagine that spotting from an aeroplane is a simple job. It is hard enough for a stationary observer to declare with any degree of accuracy the number of yards by which a shot falls beyond or short of its objective, but when the observer is moving through the air at a speed of eighty miles an hour or more, the problem is rendered a good deal harder, and when shells from anti-aircraft guns are popping all round him like champagne corks at a banquet, he is apt to be distracted by the thought of such pleasant associations. The aeroplane observers over the Rufigi Delta had other little troubles all their own. The climate was responsible for the worst of these, for the effect of a cool monsoon wind blowing over a surface of land heated by a tropical sun is very startling at times.

A "bump" of 250 feet is not uncommon, and I suppose the scientific explanation is that a *stratum* of warm air rises rapidly through the cold air, and when the aeroplane strikes it the diminished density has much the same effect as releasing the catch on a winch with a heavy weight at the end of the hawser. Another trouble was the thickness of the palm forests surrounding the *Königsberg*. In these the monitors' shells fell to explode unseen, like flowers wasting their sweetness on the desert air.

On 6th July the two aeroplanes between them covered a distance of 950 miles. The first one broke down soon after midday, and the other one followed suit about half-past three in the afternoon, whereat it became useless to continue the operations, and the two monitors had to withdraw from the river.

Their experiences had not been by any means devoid of excitement. The *Severn* had no sooner reached the river entrance in the early morning than she saw two men seated in the boughs of a tree overhanging the water's edge. Beneath them was a log, and alongside the log was a torpedo. Three rounds of lyddite promptly fired from one of her guns left nothing recognisable of either the torpedo or the log, and the two men disappeared completely. When she got into her position up the river, the *Königsberg* opened fired on her with four and sometimes five guns, and the firing was marvellously accurate for range, but slightly out for direction. This was a fairly clear indication that the *Königsberg's* gunnery lieutenant had been carefully calculating the ranges of certain points on the river. Presently the *Mersey* was hit twice, one shell striking the gun-shield of one of her big guns on the port side, and killing four men, while part of the burst shell went through a bulkhead into the sick bay, and wounded the sick berth steward. The other shot struck a motor-boat lying on the port side, and sank it, but did no further damage beyond making a dent in the ship's bottom. It was a piece of luck that the motor-boat was there, or the *Mersey* would undoubtedly have had a big hole below her waterline.

After this she retired, and had only just left her anchorage when another salvo fell upon the exact spot. She anchored 500 yards lower down-stream, where she found the atmosphere rather more healthy. The *Severn* then received the enemy's attention, and later on, after a long pause occasioned by the absence of our aeroplanes. Captain Fullerton came to the conclusion that it would be wise to try a change of billet. As the stern of his ship swung round three lyddite shells fell together on the position he had just vacated, showing beyond doubt that the enemy had both range and direction to a nicety.

It was just about this time that somebody in the *Severn* spied a party of four men up a tree. Here was a complete explanation of the *Königsberg's* accurate firing, and it showed that she had a very shrewd idea as to where the monitors would come to make their attack. A few shots from a 3-pounder gun brought those four down with a run, and after that the *Königsberg's* firing was far from accurate. Captain Fullerton, however, suspected the presence of another observation post at Pemba, and was careful to keep well in to the west bank, so that the hull of his ship could not be seen from that direction. Soon afterwards the second of our aeroplanes broke down, and a withdrawal from the river became necessary.

The result of the day's proceedings was not altogether satisfactory. According to the aeroplane observers, four hits were recorded on the *Königsberg*, but it was quite evident that a further attack would have to be made in order to complete her destruction. It was not by any means a pleasant occupation to take ships up that shallow channel, with every possibility of running aground at any moment, and with unseen field and naval guns firing continually from the recesses of the forest to supplement the shells coming from the *Königsberg*. The *Mersey* already had four men killed and four wounded (of whom two subsequently died of their wounds), and one of her port guns had been put out of action. The *Severn* was more fortunate, having neither casualties nor damage to report. But the day's experiences were enough to show that the task undertaken was far from being a light one.

Five days later, on 11th July, the aeroplanes were again ready for service, and the two monitors crossed from Mafia Island and entered the Kikunga Channel shortly before noon. Their progress up the river was heralded by a chorus of field-guns, machineguns, and rifles, mostly from the east bank, and the *Mersey* had three men wounded by a 9-pounder shell. But our return shot, crashing blindly through the thicket in the direction of the sound of the hostile guns, soon had the effect of quieting them. Shortly afterwards the *Königsberg* opened fire with four guns, concentrating her fire on the *Severn*.

This was inconvenient, because the arrangement was that the *Severn* should get into position first, and the operation of anchoring bow and stern is not an easy one under fire. So the *Mersey* remained in the open to attract the *Königsberg's* gunners, and in a very short time the *Severn* was in position 1,000 yards nearer the enemy than she had been before, and comfortably steady between her anchors. A sharp look-out was kept for spotting parties in the tree-tops, but apparently they had come to the conclusion that it might be too warm up there to be healthy.

None the less the *Königsberg's* fire was uncomfortably accurate. The splash of her shells flooded the quarter-deck more than once, but fortunately no damage was done. About half-past twelve one of the aeroplanes came on the scene with Flight Commander Cull and Flight Sub-Lieutenant Arnold, and the *Severn* opened fire. The first five salvoes were lost in the thick forest of palm trees, and the aeroplane could give no account of them. But the officer in command of the *Severn's* guns took upon himself to make a big reduction in the range, which turned out to be a fortunate guess. The sixth salvo was signalled by the aeroplane to be 100 yards over and to the right. The necessary adjustment was made, and the gun fired again. This time the aeroplane signalled too much to the left. Again the direction was adjusted, and another round fired.

All eyes were impatiently watching the aeroplane to learn the verdict. As it gracefully swooped round in its circle Sub-Lieutenant Arnold signalled the joyful message—a hit! The *Severn's* guns were all adjusted to the ascertained range and direction, and for the next few minutes Arnold was kept busy making the same signal. Occasionally, however, he had to record a short, or an over, or a left, or a right, but the finding of the range had been accomplished, and the hours of the *Konigsberg* were numbered.

In the *Severn* they were all so much engrossed in their task, which had now for the first time promised a successful issue, that they had no time to notice any peculiarity in the movements of their friends in the sky. The aeroplane had been at an approximate height of 3,200 feet, but just as the first of the *Severn's* shells had been spotted, a lucky shot from the anti-aircraft guns burst beneath them, and a piece of it hit their engine. There was no room for doubt about it, for the behaviour of the engine afforded ample evidence, and in ten minutes Flight Commander Cull found that he had descended to 2,000 feet. The situation became decidedly ticklish, for at that height a direct hit by a shell was well within the range of possibilities, and the chances of coming out of the ordeal alive would be remote, to say the least of it. But Commander Cull realised that the crucial moment had come, and that to leave the scene just when the *Severn* was getting on to her target might very well ruin the chances of the whole undertaking. So he set his teeth, and determined to hang on as long as ever he could.

Then Sub-Lieutenant Arnold signalled the first hit, and the excitement grew as the hits became fast and furious. But all the time the anti-aircraft shells were bursting round them, and presently another fragment struck the aeroplane's engine. Nothing remained now but to volplane down as best they could, so they made a signal to the *Severn*, "We are hit; send boat for us," and Commander Cull steered with a view to landing in the river somewhere near the two monitors. During the descent Sub-Lieutenant Arnold continued to send his spotting corrections, until the machine dipped below the tree-tops and the *Königsberg* was lost to view. The observer's last signal to the *Severn* was to bring her salvoes farther aft, and he had the satisfaction of seeing her shells fall into the *Königs*berg amidships before the palm trees obscured his view. By that time nine salvoes had been signalled as having hit the enemy.

The aeroplane fell into the river not far from the *Mersey*, who promptly sent a boat to the rescue. Sub-Lieutenant Arnold was thrown clear of the machine into the water, but Commander Cull was strapped to his seat, and was in an awkward predicament, as the machine turned right over. But Arnold went to his assistance at once, and managed to extricate him; within a few minutes both of them were safely in the *Mersey's* boat. The wreck of the aeroplane was blown up by gun cotton, as a precaution against its falling into the hands of the enemy.

By this time two of the *Königsberg's* guns had ceased fire; a few minutes later only one of the guns was firing, and after another minute or two there was silence. But the silence did not last long, for almost immediately a loud explosion was heard, and dense clouds of smoke rose up above the palm trees, and drifted away in the wind. The *Severn* still continued firing with two of her guns, and soon there were no less than seven distinct explosions heard, and the yellow smoke made a big cloud over the tops of the trees.

The monitors were then ordered to proceed upstream and close to within 7,000 yards of the enemy. The navigation was no easy matter, as there appeared to be a bar right across the river, but they crept up gradually, and when the soundings showed eight feet of water, the *Mersey* put her helm over and dropped anchor. By this time the other aeroplane had arrived with Flight Lieutenant Watkins and Flight Sub-Lieutenant Bishop, and with her third round the *Mersey* scored a hit. The *Königsberg* was now visible from the topmast heads of the monitors, in their new position, and Captain Fullerton himself went aloft to reconnoitre. He saw that the enemy was on fire both fore and aft, that her foremast was leaning over and looked on the verge of collapse, and that streams of smoke enveloped her mainmast. In fact she was a complete wreck, and at half-past two in the afternoon the Admiral, satisfied that the difficult task at last had been accomplished, signalled to the monitors to retire.

Captain Fullerton of the *Severn*, Commander Wilson of the *Mersey*, Squadron Commander Gordon in charge of R.N.A.S. detachment, Wing Commander Cull, and Flight Lieutenant Arnold were all awarded the Distinguished Service Order for their respective shares in this achievement. It was a task which in many of its features was unique in the annals of the navy. Certainly no naval engagement has ever before been fought under circumstances even remotely similar, for it may be described as a naval battle in the midst of a forest. It is equally certain that the new branch of the Navy, the Royal Naval Air Service, had never before been called upon to carry out such important work under such climatic conditions. Perhaps only flying men can appreciate how difficult those conditions were, but the story of those exciting minutes when, with damaged engine, the spotters were guiding the *Severn's* shots nearer and nearer to the target, is dramatic enough to appeal to the imagination even of the most prosaic among laymen.

Chapter 12

An Airman's Adventures

At Chukwani, in the island of Zanzibar, Squadron No. 8 of the Royal Naval Air Service established its headquarters for the purpose of making reconnaissances over enemy territory in East Africa, taking photographs, dropping bombs, and otherwise aiding the military operations. The seaplane carriers, H.M.S. *Himalaya* and *Manica* were lying off the island, and the Flag Commander, the Hon. R. O. B. Bridgeman, D.S.O., had general charge of the operations. Although he was not an airman himself, he was keenly interested in the airman's craft, and moreover he fully appreciated the special difficulties attending aviation in that climate. The R.N.A.S. had every reason to be grateful to him, for he helped them in their work as only an officer with a sympathetic understanding of their troubles could help them.

In January 1917 the *Manica* and *Himalaya* were lying off the island of Nyroro near the Rufigi Delta, and on the 5th of the month the former ship sent Flight Sub-Lieutenant Deans over the delta in a seaplane. On his return journey, when he was just over the wreck of the *Königsberg* and was circling round to get a photograph of a pinnace in her vicinity, he was fired at by rifles, one shot hitting his port wing. He was fired at again lower down the delta, but suffered no further damage, and returned in safety. His machine had refused to ascend with an observer on board, and he had therefore made the flight alone.

Since the *Manica's* seaplane was temporarily incapable of carrying both pilot and observer, it was decided next day to send up the *Himalaya's* machine, piloted by Flight Commander E. R. Moon, and with Commander Bridgeman himself as observer. Soon after seven o'clock in the morning they started off, taking with them a camera and enough petrol to last for three hours, and they flew over the delta with the intention of making a thorough reconnaissance of it. As the hours slipped by, and there was no sign of them, their shipmates began to grow anxious, and, when anxiety had given place to alarm. Flight Sub-Lieutenant Deans was sent off from the *Manica* to discover what had happened to them.

He searched up and down the various channels and creeks, but at first could see no trace of them. On his return, just as he was passing over the Suninga Channel, he noticed something lying on the water at a spot which he estimated to be about six miles from the mouth of the channel, and on descending towards it, he found it to be the wreck of the missing seaplane. He came down close beside it, and saw that it was lying upside down with the bottom of the floats just above water, and that large portions of the wings, tail, and rudder were burnt. For some time he remained alongside, firing a Verey's light to attract attention, but of the pilot and observer he could see no trace. So he returned and made his report.

Several days later the squadron received information from the enemy that Commander Bridgeman had been drowned, and that Flight Commander Moon was a prisoner of war. The full story, however, remained unknown for nearly a year, until the progress of the allied forces brought about the flight of the Germans and the liberation of their prisoners.

I tell the story of Flight Commander Moon in the form of a personal narrative, but it must be understood, of course, that I do not profess to quote the exact words in which he told it to me on his return to England. He has assured me, however, that the following account is correct both in substance and in detail. I need only add that at the time when these events occurred he had been awarded the D.S.O. for many meritorious performances in aircraft work, and that he has since been awarded a bar to the decoration.

> Commander Bridgeman and I started off about a quarter-past seven on the morning of 6th January 1917 from the *Himalaya* at Nyroro Island. It has always been my practice to wait until I return from a flight before taking a meal, because I believe that work of this kind is better done on an empty stomach, and so I had nothing more than a cup of tea before leaving. If I had known what was in store for me, I might have been tempted to stow enough inside me to last me a week, after the manner of the pelican.
>
> We made a very thorough reconnaissance of the delta, flying

over all parts of it, and at the end of an hour or so the commander said he was quite satisfied, and ordered me to return. We were over the south end of the delta when the engine revolutions suddenly began to drop, so that I was obliged to descend. I steered for the inshore end of the Suninga Channel, and landed in a creek which forms a junction between this and Kiomboni Channel to the south of it. I taxied along the creek, while the commander took the pilot's seat to give me an opportunity of attending to the motor.

I found that the after magneto drive had failed, and presently the pressure in the petrol tank gave out, and the engine stopped altogether. I made several attempts to restart it, but without success. The only way to discover what was wrong with it was to take it to pieces, but of course I had no idea whether I should be able to repair the defect when I had found it. The commander decided that under the circumstances there was nothing for it but to destroy the seaplane, and to try to make our escape to the mouth of the river, where we might either be picked up by one of the ship's boats, or find a native boat in which we could pull off to the *Himalaya*.

We happened to have come down close to the spot where a party of Germans had fired at the *Manica's* seaplane on the previous day, and it was therefore probable that the enemy was not far away. Owing to the windings of the creek and the thick vegetation on either side of it, we could not see far in any direction, and we quite expected that a party of Huns might come round the corner of a bend at any moment. We felt certain that they must have seen us coming down, and must have sent men to look for us. As a matter of fact I learnt afterwards that the search party misjudged our position, and wandered along the Kiomboni Creek some miles to the south.

The first thing we had to do was to destroy our seaplane, which we did by soaking it with petrol and setting fire to it with a Verey's light. We watched it burn until it was a useless wreck, and then we started off down the creek, swimming across it after a while with the idea of covering our tracks. The commander had a Perrin belt, which served him in good stead so long as it remained inflated, but unfortunately the air gradually leaked out of it. I happen to be a fairly strong swimmer, and consequently I had no need of anything of the kind. When we reached the Suninga Channel we found the bush on either side so dense that it was impossible to make our way through it, but, as the tide was well down, we were able for some time to walk along the mud bank without entering the mangrove swamp.

It must have been about noon when we saw the *Manica's* seaplane flying over the delta. We had anticipated that it would be sent to look for us, but we knew that we should never be able to attract its attention. Of course we waved our arms and did all we could, but it was quite useless. That the pilot would see our machine we fully expected, but it was clearly impossible for us to remain in its vicinity if we wished to escape capture. I confess that it never occurred to me that, when he saw the burnt wings and tail, he would come to the conclusion that we had caught on fire before we descended and had been burnt to death.

The tide was coming in fast, and it was about high tide when we reached a point just opposite the wreck of the *Somali*. This was the ship which had been a tender to the *Königsberg* in the days of her glory, until a shell from one of our ships set the old packet on fire, and she burned herself out from stem to stern. We thought we saw a green-painted native boat lying alongside the bank close to the wreck, and I decided to swim across to examine it. I thought, too, that I might find a receptacle of some kind or other on the wreck where the rain water had collected, for we were beginning to get thirsty, and of course the water in the channel was as salt as the sea.

I left the commander on the south bank, as his belt had become deflated, and it was a fairly long swim for anyone but a strong swimmer. As it turned out, I found it quite an easy swim, for the current seemed to strike right across the channel towards a creek leading northwards to the Simba Uranga Channel, and I was carried across with it fairly rapidly. But, alas, I found that the boat was no boat at all—only the trunk of a tree overhanging the water's edge. I scrambled on to the wreck to search for water, and here again I was disappointed. There was not a vessel of any kind, and the deck had buckled upwards with the heat of the fire, so that there was no cranny or hollow in which a pool of water could collect. There was just one small spot where a few drains had gathered together, and by lying flat on my face I just managed to wet the tip of my tongue.

My next task was to swim back to the south bank and rejoin the commander, but I found this a more difficult undertaking than I had anticipated. The current which had helped me across to the *Somali* was now against me, and was running at such a pace that I could do little more than keep myself from being carried backwards. I had to give up the attempt, but when I heard the commander shout and fire his revolver to attract my attention, I made another effort to get across. It was equally unsuccessful, and though I shouted at the top of my voice to reassure the commander that I was all right, I failed to make him hear me. Five times during the night I tried to swim to the south bank, but could make no headway against the current, and finally I decided that there was nothing for it but to wait for slack water.

As soon as the sun goes down the mosquitoes in the Rufigi Delta come out in their myriads, and hang over the surface of the water. I must have swallowed some scores of them when I was trying to swim across, and I found them a most unsatisfactory form of diet. While I was waiting for slack water, they swarmed round me, and the only way to keep them off was to stand in the water up to my neck and duck my head from time to time. They had been bad enough even in the daytime, but at night the whole air seemed to be thick with them.

It was just before daybreak when I managed at last to struggle across to the other bank. I found that the commander had gone on downstream, so I swam down with the current (for the tide had turned) until I came in sight of the deserted village of Salali, which lies on the north bank. Opposite to it on the south bank is a solitary hut, and here I saw the commander, but I was carried past him by the current some considerable distance before I could gain the shore, and I had to wade back to him. Standing near the hut was a clump of palm trees, and we were lucky enough to find some cocoanuts on them. In the hut we found two empty bottles, into which we poured some cocoanut milk. We next came across three wooden poles, which we tied together with wisps of sisal, and across them we lashed some old window frames with lattices. It was a poor makeshift of a raft, for the materials were too scanty to bear our weight, but it was the best we could improvise,

The commander sat amidships, while I sat aft, trying to manipulate an old canoe paddle which I had picked up, but it was no easy matter, for the water was always up to my shoulders, and occasionally up to my neck. It must have been some time after midday when we shoved off. We soon found that three submerged poles do not provide the most comfortable of craft, especially in a river where there are plenty of sharp snags to tear one's clothes and scratch one's skin. My stockings were torn beyond the possibility of repair by the most conscientious of darners, and my khaki shorts also became considerably less than respectable. As luck would have it, I was wearing nothing better than a service cap, which is all very well for a flight in the early morning, but is hopelessly inadequate to protect the head from the noontide sun.

As we passed Salali we saw a few broken boats and canoes lying on the bank, but they were too far damaged to be of any use to us. Just before nightfall we reached Mnasi Moja Point, where we saw another smashed canoe, on which we carried out a rapid survey and decided to report that in the absence of docking facilities this vessel could not be recommended even for temporary commissioning. We spent the night near the Point, dodging the attentions of the mosquitoes by keeping as much as possible of their rations beneath the surface of the water. The commander suddenly started laughing, and when I asked him to let me share the joke, he said, 'I cannot help seeing the funny side of our predicament. There really is something very comical about it.'

Undoubtedly there was, and, strange as it may seem, the humour of the situation was always uppermost in our minds, in spite of our physical discomforts. Of course we never had any doubt that we should get back to our ship somehow or other, and we talked as though it were a certainty. I remember the commander reminding me once that we were not yet out of the wood, when I was looking rather too far ahead, and discussing future projects after our return to safety.

Next day (8th January) we started off at dawn, and presently we sighted the wreck of the *Newbridge*—the old packet which had been sunk to block the channel before the *Königsberg* was destroyed. I tried to bring the raft alongside her, but overshot the mark, and finally had to beach the raft some distance to the east of the wreck. We now found that the salt water had penetrated both our bottles of cocoanut milk, making it unfit to drink, but fortunately we still had an untapped cocoanut, with which we were able to quench our thirst. By this time the necessity of finding food and drink completely outweighed all thoughts about the risk of capture, and we decided that we must push away from the river through the mangrove swamp in the hope of coming across some natives who might be able to supply us, and whom we hoped to bribe into giving us a passage in a boat or canoe to our ship.

It was a brave decision, but we had reckoned without the mosquitoes. I had no sooner pushed my way into the thicket than the buzz of a mighty army sang in my ears, and the swarm was upon me. The plague of flies in Egypt may have been a pretty bad business, but the virtue of the common fly is that he feeds on jam and dead meat, like a civilised human being. The female mosquito feeds on live victims, and with a callous selfishness almost unsurpassed in the scheme of creation, she injects a poison which makes her food more digestible for her, but makes her bite ten times worse for her prey. Before five minutes were up I was rushing out of that mangrove swamp as though all the furies of hell had been let loose on me. We had to give up the idea of getting away from the river by a tramp through the bush; for no human being could endure the ordeal of it, unless he was armed like a bee-keeper wrestling with a swarming hive. Our only way was to continue our course downstream until we reached the river mouth.

In the meantime the question of food and drink was becoming urgent. We looked across the river towards the wreck of the *Newbridge*, and the hope, which springs eternal in the human breast, made us dream of the possibility of finding something there which would be of service to us. As soon as it was slack water we pushed off on our raft and managed to make the wreck without much difficulty. I don't know exactly what we really expected to find there, beyond perhaps a small pool of rain water collected in some hollow of the upper structure, which was sticking out above the level of the river, but even in this we were disappointed. There was absolutely nothing on the wreck which could be of the least use to us in our predicament.

The starboard stanchion of the bridge, being painted white,

presented to us the idea of writing a short note to serve as a guide to any of the ship's boats which might happen to come along in search of us, and the commander took a pencil from his pocket and scribbled a few words on the paint. It is a curious illustration of how one loses count of the passage of time when one is deprived of the ordinary routine of regular meals and sleep, that he and I could not agree as to the day of the month. It was really the 8th, but he insisted upon dating his message the 10th. Long afterwards I heard that that message was seen after several days by some of our shipmates, but that they could not make up their minds whether it was genuine or not.

At nightfall we had another drink of cocoanut milk, which very nearly exhausted the supply, and then we settled down to the usual game of hide and seek with the mosquitoes. Once I tried to snatch a little sleep by lying down on the wreck, but I might as well have chosen a bed of red-hot needles; sleep was impossible in the company of that voracious horde. Only the salt water could keep them off, so there was nothing for it but to get back into the river again, and to keep my face and head wet by constant immersion. It was a process which soon grew monotonous, so much so that we did not wait for daybreak before shoving off again upon our raft.

Our plan was to cross to the east bank of the river, run the raft on the mud, and then wade towards the mouth of the channel, where we hoped to come across a native boat or canoe, or, better still, to find one of the ship's boats coming in to look for us. At first we were carried upstream by the tide, but when it turned, we were carried rapidly towards the sea. All the time I was struggling hard with my paddle to bring the raft to the bank, but the tide was too strong for me, and, almost before I realised it, we were being taken right through the entrance of the channel.

At first I failed to appreciate the full extent of our danger. The thought that we had escaped from that horrible delta, with its swarming population of winged torments, was uppermost in my mind. But when we reached the open sea, and found that the wind was blowing up against the tide and causing heavy waves, the full possibilities of the situation dawned upon me.

Our raft was overturned, and, though the poles hung together, they were in a hopeless tangle, and gave us little more support than a single floating spar would have given us. I watched the shore gradually recede into the distance, until I could not see the tops of the trees above the waves, and still the tide seemed to be drawing us farther and farther away from land. Of course I knew that when it turned it would carry us back again, but the question was whether we could remain afloat long enough.

Of those next few hours I cannot speak in detail, for the tragedy of Commander Bridgeman's death blots out all other memories of them. When I saw that his strength was giving out, I tried to encourage him by telling him that the tide had turned and that we should soon be on the beach, but I realise now that he had lost all consciousness of his surroundings, and that, although the instinct of self-preservation made his muscles retain their hold, he was already wrapped in the long last sleep. I could not make myself believe this, and even when his grip relaxed I still clung to the idea that I could save him. I caught hold of him and struggled to keep his head above water. How long I struggled I do not know; it may have been but a few minutes, or it may have been an hour; but to me it seemed like a lifetime. And then my own strength failed, and I was forced to let go of him.

It was fortunate that I was not in a mental condition to appreciate the full force of the tragedy. My mind was dazed through lack of sleep and my actions had become subconscious. So long as my strength had lasted I had clung tenaciously to the idea that my one aim and purpose was to save the commander, and even though I dimly realised that he was dead, I could not relinquish the struggle. When my strength gave out, I had no very clear idea of my own circumstances, but the ordinary animal instinct kept me clinging to the remnants of the raft, until the tide had carried me well inshore. Then I struck out with such strength as I had left in me, and gained the shallow water, where I sat down in the surf to regain my breath. How long I sat there I have no notion, but after a while I must have staggered up the slope of the beach towards the belt of palm trees skirting it.

My next clear recollection is of meeting a native—a young man with only a loin-cloth round his waist, to whom I uttered the magic words 'British man-of-war,' and went through the motions of paddling a canoe. Then I said '*Rupees*,' which was a word he well understood, and I indicated with my fingers that his reward should be considerable. Presently an older man came up, wearing a pair of blue trousers, adorned with many patches. I went through the same pantomime again, and he nodded his head in comprehension. I had four *rupees* in my pocket, which I handed to him as a token of good faith, but he gravely returned the money. I also had a large pocket compass, which I handed to him, fearing lest he might suspect that it was some kind of infernal machine, and that I was going to annihilate him. He kept this at the time, but handed it back to me next day.

The elder man took me by the wrist, and led me towards a grass hut, where I remember sitting down on something or other—probably a wooden bench, though I have no recollection of seeing any furniture in the hut. By this time my mental faculties were almost dormant. I was conscious that I was in need of food, but beyond the need of expressing this elementary desire I had no definite thought. I pointed to my mouth, and the natives nodded their heads. Presently a woman appeared on the scene, and brought me two mangoes, which she cut into slices for me. I think of those mangoes now as the most luscious fruit I have ever tasted. I am afraid that my manner of eating them must have resembled that of a wild beast rather than a human creature, for it was nearly five whole days since I had had any solid food.

I was so much absorbed in satisfying the first primitive desire of a live animal that I had completely forgotten my surroundings. But presently, when I had eaten the fruit, I looked round, and noticed that the two men had put on blue tunics, and were winding khaki *puttees* round their legs. I also saw that each of them had a rifle, but my mental condition was such that I attached no significance to these phenomena. It would have been all the same to me if they had put on surplices and carried a couple of big Bibles. The one idea firmly fixed in my mind was that they were going to take me back to my ship, and when they made signs to me to follow them, I struggled to my feet, and passed out of the hut.

Of that walk through the palm grove by the seashore, I can only remember one or two trivial incidents. I have since calculated that it must have occupied an hour and a half, but I was not conscious of fatigue; I was not conscious of anything but a feeling that the whole situation was quite unreal, and that presently

I should wake up. I remember that the younger of the two natives showed great concern about my stockings, which had slipped down to my feet, and he kept on making signs to me to indicate that the mosquitoes would attack my bare legs.

At last he stooped down himself, and pulled them up for me. Later on he took off his red cap—a very dirty relic of what had once been a Turkish *fez*, but all the stiffness had long since departed from it, so that it looked more like a skullcap. Before I had realised his purpose, he was very tenderly wiping my mouth with it. I suppose that the remains of the mangoes were clinging to my lips and cheeks, and the good-hearted fellow was shocked to see me in such a condition.

The place to which they brought me must have been one of the German outposts. I should observe that, although all the harbours and towns along the coast were by this time in the hands of the Allies, the Rufigi Delta had been left in the undisturbed possession of the enemy. It was not such a desirable spot as to be worth the expenditure of any effort to acquire it. In an open space a large number of natives were congregated round a fire, stoked with cocoanut husks, whose smoke drove away the mosquitoes. Here I sank down on the ground, and was dimly conscious that many pairs of inquisitive eyes were staring at me; but somehow they seemed to belong to another world than my own.

I kept on saying to myself, 'They are going to take me back to my ship,' and this was the only idea that my bemused mind was capable of entertaining. During the march my guides had spoken to a group of women whom we encountered, and I had assured myself that they were telling them of the reward which I had offered, and were impressing on the women the need of holding their tongues about me.

I am not quite sure what happened next. I may have gone off in a faint, or I may have simply fallen asleep. The Germans told me afterwards that I was in a faint, and it is not altogether improbable. The next thing I remember is that a big man with a beard was leaning over me, and as I looked up into his face I saw that he was a European. He said something to a smaller man, who was dressed in the rig of a sailor, and, as my scattered wits returned to me, I recognised the German tongue. Then, and only then, I realised for the first time that I was a prisoner of war.

For some time I was allowed to rest, and then the smaller of the two men, who spoke quite good English, told me that I should have to walk inland with them. I told him that I was quite unfit to walk, but he asked me to make an effort, explaining that it was impossible for me to stay where I was. He turned out to be a very good fellow, and before we started he had a chicken cooked for me. I was sensible enough to appreciate this kindness, for roast chicken is a rare delicacy in the Rufigi Delta, but when the food was put in front of me I found myself quite unable to touch a morsel of it. I could see that this genuinely distressed him, and I told him how sorry I was, but I could not explain to him why a man who has been five days without food loses the power to eat it when it is put in front of him. I only knew that in my exhausted condition I should have turned away from the most tempting delicacy that a Paris *chef* could devise. Later on this little sailor man proved a good friend to me by rigging me out in an old suit of khaki clothes belonging to him—the only clothes I had from the Germans during my captivity.

My experiences as a prisoner of war hardly belong to this story. Suffice it to say that they were not such as to give me any great pleasure in dwelling on them. To start with, I went down with fever, and remained on the sick list more or less continuously for the next six months. The prison camps were in a constant state of being moved from place to place, as the progress of the Allied troops drove the Germans from pillar to post, I estimate that altogether I travelled 600 miles during my imprisonment, walking when I was well enough, and being carried by natives at other times. To make matters worse it was the rainy season of the year, and frequently I had no other bed to lie on than the wet grass.

One piece of news, which the Germans gave me, brought me some comfort. They told me that the body of Commander Bridgeman had been washed ashore, and had been buried with full military honours. In these days of wholesale carnage, when hundreds of men are hurled in a few hours across the gulf between life and death, many of us have grown callous about our fallen comrades. But the thought that one who had been so closely associated with me, and had shared with me the hardships of those four days in the Rufigi Delta, had gone to some unknown resting-place in the wide ocean had preyed on my mind. It was an indescribable comfort to me to know that he had received Christian burial, and the honours due to a brave officer. His memory will long live in the minds of those who knew him, and no man can have a truer inscription on his monument than that which is engraved upon the hearts of his fellow-men.

I have to thank a strong constitution rather than the German doctors for the fact that I survived those months of sickness, and have come back little the worse for them. The medical service of the Germans in East Africa used to remind me of Alice in Wonderland, who had jam yesterday and jam tomorrow, but never jam today. At every camp the doctor told me that, although he was unable to give me proper treatment, I should receive it all right at the next camp. Occasionally I was given a dose of quinine, and occasionally some ointment for my sores, but there was an element of chance as to whether I got even these, and the attitude of the doctors was always perfunctory.

Nevertheless, I had gone far to regain my health when at last the rescue came. I shall never forget those last few days in the prison camp. We heard the guns drawing nearer and nearer as the Allied forces steadily closed in from two directions. Then the commandant gave us the joyful intelligence that the prisoners were to be left behind, together with all the sick Germans, and those who were not likely to be of service in future fighting.

Only about 200 Germans and some 1,800 Askaris made their way across the border into Portuguese East Africa; all the rest were left behind and were made prisoners. The senior German officer in our camp, accompanied by Lieutenant Commander Paterson, and armed with a white flag, went out to meet our troops. And then our fellows started singing 'God Save The King.' I betook myself to a quiet corner, for I knew that, if anyone had spoken to me, I should have broken down and sobbed.

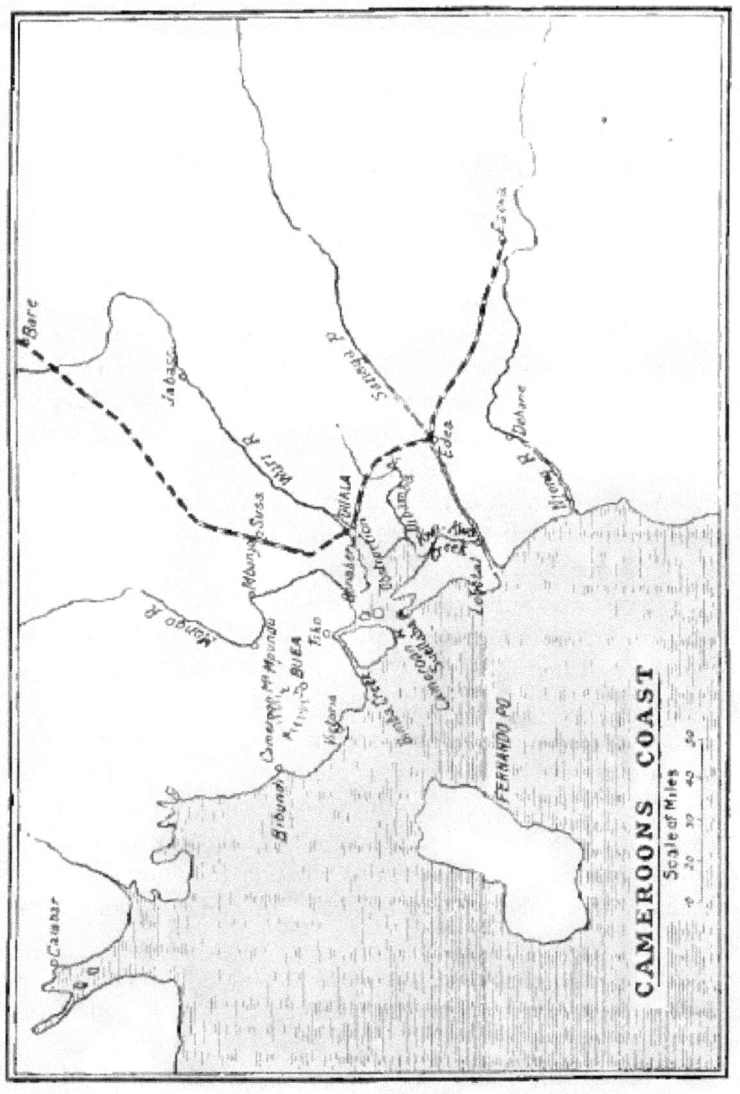

THE NAVY IN THE CAMEROONS

CHAPTER 13

The Story of "King Bell"

When H.M.S. *Cumberland* first cast her anchor off the bar of the Cameroon River in September 1914, this German colony in Darkest Africa was a sealed book to most of us. We had seen it on the map, and were therefore quite ready to believe that it existed, but as to what the country was like, what kind of people inhabited it, what industries were in progress there, our knowledge was meagre in the extreme. We had heard perhaps that German efforts at colonisation had proved to be costly failures for the most part, but few of us had ever worried our heads to find out why they were failures.

On her way down the coast the *Cumberland* had called at Lagos in Nigeria, among other places, and there had picked up a small band of natives who had fled from the Cameroons early in August, and were now eager to lend their aid to the British in driving the Germans out of the country. One of them explained that he was King of Duala, and that the others were his courtiers in attendance on him. This came as rather a shock to the officers of the *Cumberland*, who were not quite prepared for the honour of receiving a reigning monarch into their midst, and were in some doubt as to whether they had committed a grave breach of etiquette in not firing a salute and providing a Marine guard of honour at the gangway.

His Majesty, however, was quite unassuming in his manner, and put them all at their ease by agreeing to accept, as remuneration for his services, the regal sum of one shilling a day. He was even democratic enough to allow his courtiers to be rewarded at precisely the same rate. The only difficulty that arose was in entering their names upon the ship's ledger. The accountant officer's staff grappled in vain with the orthographic problems those names presented, and finally compromised matters by rechristening the entire suite. One gentleman became known as "Jack Friday," while another, who fulfilled the functions of Prime Minister, was named "Lloyd George." The king himself was entered on the books as "King Bell."

Now this was not the original King Bell. In fact the original "King Bell" dates back many generations, for the name has been preserved throughout the ages. Just as there were sixteen kings of France called Louis, so there have been quite as many kings of Duala called Bell, but somehow or other the exact number has been buried behind a veil of antiquity, so that the present monarch can only be designated as King Bell the Umteenth. This story, however, is not so much concerned with him as with his predecessor, who was his uncle.

Before I go any farther, let me explain how it is that the kings of Duala glory in such an English name as Bell. The explanation is that amongst the West African natives for many hundreds of miles up and down the coast the English language is the *lingua franca*, the common vernacular by means of which all the tribes can communicate with each other. It is a kind of pidgin English, which seems to have grown on the coast in some mysterious way, and to have spread itself inland to a considerable distance. It was not deliberately invented as a new language, like Esperanto, but accidentally it has become the Esperanto of Western Africa. By a curious irony of fate the natives of the Cameroons speak better English than any other natives on the coast. This must have been very galling to the Germans, who were obliged to learn pidgin English before they could drill the native troops, or even issue orders to the servants in their own houses.

The story of "King Bell," the uncle of the exile whom the *Cumberland* found at Lagos, is a tragedy. It was first introduced to me by an entry in the diary of Lieutenant Nathnagel, the German military officer, who was found at Duala when the town surrendered. The bulk of the German forces, both European and native, had been withdrawn when the Germans realised that they could not hold the place, and Nathnagel had been left behind to hand it over to the British forces. He happened to have kept a diary, and here is one of the first entries after the commencement of the war:

> *8th August* 1914.—In the afternoon Rudolph Bell and Ngoro Din were hanged in front of the prison for high treason. A great outcry among the populace all night long.

I start thus with the end of the story because that is how it happened to come to my notice. There is nothing in the diary to tell us who were these two malefactors, Rudolph Bell and Ngoro Din, what was the treasonable act committed by them, nor why the populace expressed so much sympathy with them. All the rest of the story I had to collect from other sources, and, although I cannot guarantee its accuracy in every detail, I have no reason to doubt that it is true in its main essentials. Of Ngoro Din it is sufficient to say that he was associated with Rudolph Bell in the charge of treason, but I have not inquired into the particulars which caused him to be implicated.

Rudolph Bell was chief of the Duala tribe, as his father and his grandfather had been before him. His kingdom extended over the town of Duala and its vicinity. The chief industry of his subjects was fishing in the numerous creeks and rivers, and trading in fish. Now the German governor was faced with a problem which sometimes occurs when civilisation sets its great foot upon a country. The traffic of the port of Duala was increasing, and more accommodation was needed for wharfage. The only solution was to clear out a native settlement along the riverbank, and commandeer the space for building new wharves. Where the German governor blundered was in his choice of a new home for the evicted natives. For some incomprehensible reason he ignored the fact that they were fisherfolk, and planted them in a settlement at some considerable distance from any of the rivers. The natural result was that they were profoundly discontented by the change.

"King Bell," as their accredited chief, took up the matter with the German authorities, but the governor, now conscious of his blunder, had not the courage to acknowledge it. He feared that, if he were to show any irresolution in the matter, it would be construed in the native mind as weakness on the part of the German governor, and power on the part of "King Bell." So he told this officially unrecognised monarch that the natives in a colony belonging to the All Highest Emperor of Germany must go and live where they were told, and be thankful that they were allowed to live at all. At this "King Bell" flew into a regal rage, and said, "Your emperor plentee much beeeg man, but Rudolph Bell he know plentee much beeeger man, and he will write letter to English emperor and ask him to come to Duala in a plentee beeg sheep, and take the Cameroons away from you. Then we shall have nice English governor —no more German governor."

Here was a flagrant case of *lèse-majesté*. Apart from the insult to the German emperor contained in the suggestion that any mortal man could be greater than he, there was an invidious comparison of the merits of German and English governors, which could not be overlooked. So "King Bell" was promptly clapped in prison. I am told that he did actually write a letter to King George, and with child-like innocence requested his captors to forward it, but I cannot vouch for the truth of this part of the story. The letter has never been discovered, and, if it was written, it was probably destroyed by the German authorities. This is very regrettable, for it must have been a wonderful piece of composition.

When the curtain next rises upon the drama, the momentous fourth of August has come round, and England and Germany are at war. Up and down the coast of West Africa, and far inland along the banks of the many rivers which water the country, the news is passed from village to village that the great emperor of the English has ordered the emperor of the Germans to release "King Bell" from prison, and if he does not do so at once, then the English emperor will send his big ships and mighty armies to take the Cameroons from the Germans.

Of what transpired at the trial of Rudolph Bell I have no record, but I have no doubt that it was a simple matter to produce sufficient evidence to convict him of high treason. He had many relations and friends eager enough to do his behests, and from the German point of view he was an inconvenient person to have even in prison when the country might at any moment be invaded by hostile forces. Probably the German governor felt that so long as the man was alive he would be a danger in the country, and that neither native jailers nor native troops could be trusted to keep him safely in prison. The simplest solution of the problem was to hang him, and so Rudolph was hanged.

The Germans were in an awkward fix, for they knew that the natives had no love for them, and that their only chance of maintaining their ascendancy was by means of a reign of terror. The diary of Lieutenant Nathnagel contains many indications of the official distrust of the native, and of the strained relations subsisting between governors and governed. Thus on 17th August—nine days after Bell was hanged—we find the following entry:

If the English do not come soon, we shall be going for each other.

Then came the report that an English man-of-war was off the coast of Togoland, shortly followed by the report that Togoland had been surrendered. Both these reports were received at Duala by wireless. On 27th August the diary says:

> From today all telegraphic work is to be carried on by Europeans.

The native telegraph clerks were no longer to be trusted at such a juncture, for they might use the instrument for conveying information to the enemy.

On 31st August H.M.S. *Cumberland* arrived at Fernando Po, the Spanish island off the mouth of the Cameroon River, and three days later preparations were begun for the invasion of the country. It became obvious at once to the Germans that the majority of the natives regarded the advent of the British forces as the dawn of their deliverance. What perhaps they did not realise was that the sequence of events had caused the natives to connect the arrival of the British Navy at the mouth of the Cameroon River with the hanging of Rudolph Bell. Such, however, was, and still is, the idea in the native mind. It is useless to try to persuade the West African people that this war was brought about by trouble in the Balkans, or in any other of those far-off countries which they associate merely with travellers' yarns. The cause of the war was that the Germans hanged "King Bell" and the English came to avenge his death.

The Germans, realising that the people amongst whom they lived were all potential enemies, proceeded to issue stringent orders to prevent them communicating with the English. The diary on 7th September tells us:

> All canoe traffic in the creeks is stopped. No less than 48 Dualas have been captured by the patrols and brought up for judgment. Eight are to be hanged. No Duala native may cross the road after dark.

The order stopping the canoe traffic in the creeks meant starvation for those natives who made their livelihood by fishing. And yet it is only fair to say that from a military point of view it was necessary in order to stop communications with the enemy. As a matter of fact it failed completely in its object, as will be shown later on. The German method of enforcing it was characteristically thorough. Sentries at the outposts along the river-banks were ordered to shoot any natives they saw passing them in canoes. Long after Duala had surrendered, and when the scene of the operations had been shifted far inland, it was quite common to see canoes floating down the streams with no other occupants than the dead bodies of natives.

On the arrival of the *Cumberland* at the mouth of the Cameroon River, "King Bell the Umteenth" and his suite were landed by night, in order to obtain information as to the nature and position of the German defences, and to collect river pilots. The pilots, it may be mentioned, did not prove to be of much assistance, for they failed to grasp the fact that a British man-of-war cannot go exactly where a native canoe goes, but they all meant well. The information collected by the natives was valuable as far as it went, though it usually lacked precision. Thus they reported that the ship channel all the way up to Duala had been extensively mined, but they had no idea where the mine-fields lay. They also stated that ships and lighters had been sunk to obstruct the fairway, but they did not know whether they were all sunk in the same locality, or whether there were several barrages.

As it turned out, the enlistment of the exiles whom the *Cumberland* found at Lagos proved superfluous, because there were plenty of native volunteers all too eager to supply information. For the attempt of the Germans to stop the canoe traffic was a failure, and no sooner had the *Cumberland* anchored at the mouth of the river than canoes came alongside filled with natives, who seemed to regard the ship as an asylum. The reign of terror had begun in grim earnest, and many of these miserable creatures had tasted the cup of bitterness. Of the tales they told, and of the marks on their bodies, which bore testimony to the truth of their statements, I prefer not to speak.

War is a long succession of horrors, and no useful purpose is served by dwelling upon the details of them. Suffice it to say that the ship's doctors were kept busy patching up these wretched victims of German *kultur*, and let us disabuse our minds of the notion that the medieval practice of inflicting torture on human beings has been stamped out by the march of civilisation. For these natives had been literally tortured, until the mere sight of them was enough to turn one sick. A parliamentary committee was afterwards appointed to investigate the matter, and its report, together with some photographs that no one can look at without shuddering, is available to all who care to read it.

In the absence of reliable information from the native spies, the senior naval officer had to proceed with caution in approaching the problems presented to him. Fortunately he had the assistance of the officers of the Nigeria Marine, who were thoroughly familiar with local conditions, and with the creeks and waterways of Central Africa. The initial work consisted mainly of mine-sweeping and reconnoitring, followed by the gradual approach of the *Cumberland* into the mouth of the river, and the establishment of a naval base inside Suellaba Point. The next work to be undertaken was to clear a passage through the obstruction which the Germans had made by sinking ships and lighters. This was rather a lengthy operation, and was necessarily attended by some risk, for it was not very likely that the Germans would leave the working parties to carry on their work unmolested.

On 23rd September six transports arrived, under the escort of H.M.S. *Challenger*, bringing British and native troops from Nigeria and the Gold Coast. Two days later five more transports arrived bringing French troops. The navy, however, was not quite ready for them, for there was nowhere to land them, or establish a base for them. One attempt was made to send a detachment up the Dibamba River, and to land them with a view to cutting the enemy's line of retreat along the Midland Railway. A portion of this force was actually landed, but they found it impossible to make any progress through the mangrove swamp and dense bush bordering the river, and so they had to be re-embarked. Until the navy had prepared the way the army could not even make a start with its work.

The abortive attempt up the Dibamba River was not, however, without its effect. It made the Germans nervous about their line of retreat, and undoubtedly put a period to their hopes of holding the port of Duala. A more cogent influence was, however, brought to bear on them by H.M.S. *Challenger*, who, after lightening ship, managed to scrape through the barrage of sunken ships, and so bring her guns to bear on the town. On 27th September, after one day's heavy bombardment, Lieutenant Nathnagel, who was then in command of what troops were left at Duala, received instructions by telephone to destroy the wireless station and all military stores, and to hoist the white flag.

We captured quite a nice little haul of ships at Duala, including eight large and three small vessels of the Woermann line, one Hamburg-Bremen liner, an armed yacht, a stern-wheel gunboat, tugs, trawlers, launches, and lighters. There was also among the booty a floating dock capable of accommodating ships up to 1,200 tons. Later on the navy proceeded to raise the vessels which had been sunk to obstruct the fairway, to repair them, and commission them for service.

The capture of Duala marks the end of the purely naval operations in the Cameroons. Next day the transports anchored in the harbour, and the troops were disembarked and billeted in the town. From that point onwards the campaign became amphibious for some months, and finally, when the scene of operations had gradually receded inland, it became purely military. There are, however, some rather curious incidents in the early operations, which I will describe in another chapter.

Chapter 14

Some Incidents of the Earlier Operations

It is not my purpose to give a detailed account of the earlier operations in the Cameroons, preceding the capture of Duala. There are, however, a few incidents deserving special mention, not because they had any important bearing upon the operations, but because they are sufficiently extraordinary to have some historical interest.

The first two of these incidents take one back a hundred odd years to the good old days when cutting-out expeditions were of common occurrence, and when naval warfare was largely made up of a succession of duels between ships at pistol-shot range. Cutting-out means capturing an enemy ship from beneath the protection of shore batteries. It was accomplished by manning the boats on a dark night, quietly stealing up to the prize, and boarding her before the enemy had realised what was happening. The cable was then cut, the sails set, and the prize taken out of the harbour.

The ship had to run the gauntlet of the shore guns, but this was not a very serious matter, because the gunners were naturally reluctant to fire on a ship manned by their own friends, even though those friends were safe prisoners under hatches. The real risk in the undertaking was that the boats might be detected before they reached the prize, and so come under the fire both of the ship's guns and the shore guns. This sometimes happened with disastrous consequences, but on the other hand many successful cutting-out expeditions are recorded in the annals of the navy extending from the seventeenth until the early part of the nineteenth century.

The twentieth century example of a cutting-out expedition took place on 6th September 1914, and the prize consisted of six large lighters, which were moored off the pier at Victoria, a small port in Ambas Bay, on the north side of the Cameroon River estuary. It was a fairly dark night, and our men took the precaution of leaving their white-covered caps behind, and of wearing shoes with india-rubber soles, so that they could board the lighters without making a noise. So far as was known there were no shore batteries to take into account, but the German trenches about twenty-five yards from the lighters were manned, and at that range it was reasonable to suppose that a heavy rifle-fire might do considerable damage.

Our men were armed with nothing but revolvers, as it was desirable that they should be encumbered as little as possible. The ships of the navy and the Nigeria Marine flotilla were lying about fourteen miles from Victoria. Two vessels of the latter—the steam-launch *Vampire* and the tug *Walrus*—provided with tow-ropes, etc., took the men inshore, while the gunboat H.M.S. *Dwarf* accompanied them. Commander Strong taking charge of the expedition. Of course all lights were extinguished, and as they approached the lighters the men were strictly enjoined to keep silence. In spite of all precautions, however, it seemed almost inconceivable that the Germans in their trenches could be unaware of the approach of the three vessels.

Still, there was no indication that they had been detected, so the men silently boarded the lighters, slipped the mooring chains, and attached the tow-ropes from the *Vampire* and the *Walrus*. They expected every moment to hear the sharp crack of a dozen rifles, followed by a shower of bullets, but it never came. They got back into the two boats, and in a few minutes the party was well under way with the prizes in tow. In triumph they brought them back to the anchorage—a very useful addition to the flotilla.

The silence of the German rifles remained a mystery until the officer commanding the detachment became one of our prisoners of war, and told us his version of the story. From his trench he saw three vessels off the pier, and several large boats beside them, which seemed to be filled with troops. The large boats were of course the German lighters, which had been there for several days, but, being a soldier and not a sailor, he had forgotten about the lighters, and it never occurred to him that they could be anything else than British boats with British troops in them. "They are going to land," he said to himself, "and will try to rush the trenches." He ordered his men to reserve their fire until they saw the first man leave the boats, and then they were to shoot them down like ninepins.

When he saw the three vessels and the large boats retire into the darkness, he said, "They have thought better of it; they will not try again tonight." In the morning one of his men pointed out the absence of the lighters. "The lighters?" he said. "What! the lighters! *Himmel!* they have stolen the lighters,"

The second incident reminds one of the old sea duels when two ships lay alongside each other, and hammered away at a range so close that the gunners had their hair singed by the flames of the enemy's guns. In these days of modern gunnery such an engagement as this cannot last more than a few minutes, but, while it does last, enough excitement is crowded into those few minutes to satisfy most men for a lifetime.

H.M.S. *Dwarf* was exploring Bimbia Creek, to find out whether the enemy had any defences along its banks, and generally to gain information about the possibilities of the creek as an alternative entrance to the Cameroon River. On either side were thick mangrove swamps, through which the creek pursued a tortuous course with many sharp bends. It was not a particularly pleasant creek, for a mangrove swamp has little to recommend it from the aesthetic or any other point of view. The peculiarity of the mangrove tree is that it is not content with the roots beneath its stem, but keeps on dropping from its boughs long tentacles, which strike the soil and so become subsidiary roots. A cluster of these trees presents a thicket as impenetrable as any that Nature has devised.

Another peculiarity of the tree is that it will grow nearer to the seashore than most other forms of vegetation; in fact the roots seem to be perched on top of the sand, and to find sustenance in such refuse as the sea washes up to them. At low tide they look like a mighty cluster of snakes burying their noses in the slime, which the receding tide cannot suck away from them, because of the network they form to retain it. Beneath these roots the crabs and shell-fish cluster, while the branches of the trees afford a home for swarms of voracious mosquitoes.

Through such a swamp as this the Bimbia Creek winds its way, and on 16th September the *Dwarf* anchored for the night about six miles up the creek. On a large-scale map it can be seen that at this point the creek bifurcates, a northern channel coming down from the village of Tiko, and another channel winding towards the Cameroon River. Near this junction the *Dwarf* lay at anchor, and, as the mangrove trees made it impossible to see round the next bend, and as there were known to be enemy craft prowling about the creeks, she darkened ship and her men went to action stations.

It was a dark night, and in that thick jungle it was impossible to see more than a few yards ahead. The officers had finished dinner, and were smoking vigorously to keep off the mosquitoes, when it was reported to the Captain that a light was coming round the bend a little more than a hundred yards away. Behind the light there loomed the shape of a fairly large ship, which seemed to be coming from the direction of Tiko at a good speed. Commander Strong at once gave the orders to slip the cable, get under way, and open fire. It was almost point-blank range, when the for'ard 4-inch gun and two of the 12-pounders let fly.

Of what happened during the next two or three minutes it is difficult to convey any adequate idea through the medium of cold print. The general impression left on the mind was of a sudden stream of light, as the *Dwarf's* searchlight was switched on, of the ping of a new army of mosquitoes attracted by the light, of the crash of many guns, of a big black ship coming full tilt at the *Dwarf* down the stream of light, of a mighty crash when the collision came, and of a mighty blaze from stem to stern of the big black ship. The *Dwarf* had been lying athwart the creek, and though she got under way at once, she had no time to avoid the blow. The *Nachtigal* struck her abreast of her funnel, and in so doing got dragged round, so that the two ships lay alongside each other. And all the time the 4-inch and 12-pounder guns of the *Dwarf* were blazing away for dear life.

The *Nachtigal* had a gun in her bows, but before she reached the *Dwarf* both the gun and its crew had been blown over the side into the water by a salvo from the *Dwarf*. I do not know what other guns the German ship had, but at all events they had no chance of coming into action, for within a moment after the collision the ship burst into flames along her whole length. The *Dwarf* hastened to extricate herself from the unwelcome embrace, steaming towards the south bank, crossing the bows of the *Nachtigal*, and turning right round to port until she ran aground on the north bank. The burning ship drifted to the south bank, where she soon blew up. Of her crew the captain and thirteen ratings (three Europeans) were rescued and taken prisoners. All of them were wounded. The rest of the ship's company, consisting of eight Germans and twenty-five natives, had been killed.

The *Dwarf* came off with no casualties at all, but she had a large hole in her side, and one of her compartments was filled with water. She was able, however, to return to the base, and within a week the engine-room staff of the *Cumberland* had patched her up so satisfactorily that she could resume her duties.

The shape of the hole made by the *Nachtigal's* stem suggested that a ram with a round head had been fitted to her, and that the whole episode had been premeditated. It seems more probable, however, that the ship was on her way from Tiko into the Cameroon River, and so to Duala, and was unaware of the presence of the *Dwarf* in Bimbia Creek, until she got round the bend, and the *Dwarf* opened fire. Escape was impossible, and the foremost gun having been blown over the side, ramming was the only method of offence left. The captain must have realised that his vessel was doomed to destruction in any case, and pluckily resolved to take a course which gave him a chance of doing some damage to the enemy. This view is borne out by an entry in the diary of Lieutenant Nathnagel, the officer left at Duala to surrender the town after the German troops had evacuated it. The diarist is a soldier, who is often rather vague about naval matters, but his diary is interesting as a sidelight on the early operations in the Cameroons. Here are the entries relating to the *Nachtigal*.

> In the evening just after 9 p.m. there is distant gunfire, and news comes from Victoria that the *Dwarf* is engaged with the *Nachtigal* two kilometres from Tiko. At 10 p.m. a message comes from the *Dwarf*—'Have been rammed by a steamer and have put my ship aground.' Unfortunately he completed the news later as follows—'Only one compartment full; ship in order; hope to come off at daylight.' The *Nachtigal* seems to be lost, and the ramming adopted as a last resource. The *Dwarf* is again afloat.

The above messages from the *Dwarf* were made *en clair* and intercepted by the wireless station at Duala. After the first one some German wag sent a sarcastic message to the senior naval officer offering the loan of a carpenter, but before an appropriate reply could be sent the second message came through, and obviated the necessity of making any rejoinder.

Two days later, on 18th September, the diary records:

> The *Nachtigal* is lost. Deck hands are reported prisoners; engine-room staff killed by boiler exploding.

While these two incidents—the cutting-out of the lighters and the engagement in the creek—bring back to us the naval warfare of a hundred years ago, there was a third incident which savours of the old days when torpedoes were in their infancy, and the outrigger torpedo was seriously regarded as a weapon of war. The inventor of a new design in outrigger torpedoes was a German missionary at Duala, and though his contrivance has the demerit of being a good deal more complicated than the old scheme of a bomb stuck on the end of a pole which was balanced on a swivel, it was at all events ingenious. He rigged two upright poles, one on either side of a motor-boat, and secured them in position by means of struts athwart the boat.

To each pole he attached a hydrogen gas-cylinder (such as is used for making soda-water) which was filled with dynamite. The ends of these cylinders projected beyond the boat, and, though the cylinders were above water when the boat was under way, they were lowered to the requisite depth below the surface by sliding brackets on the upright poles. In the old outrigger torpedo the bomb was lowered beneath the water by simply raising the near end of the pole to which it was attached, just as the blade of an oar is dipped in the water by raising the handle. Possibly the missionary had never beard of the old outrigger torpedo, for it is difficult to see why he should have considered his elaborate contrivance an improvement on it.

Two boats were fitted up, each with a pair of torpedoes. The story of their fortunes is told in Lieutenant Nathnagel's diary, but not with absolute accuracy, so I must take the liberty of correcting him when he goes wrong. Let me first explain that the Germans had sunk a whole row of ships across the fairway of the Cameroon River to obstruct the passage, that the navy was busily engaged in making a channel through this obstruction with the aid of explosives, and that the *Dwarf* was anchored close by at night to prevent the enemy from sinking any more ships there, or interfering with the work in hand. The Germans decided that the *Dwarf* should be the first victim of the missionary's great invention. An abortive attempt was made on 11th September, and here is what the diary says about it:

> *11th September.*—Tonight a launch with a mine built in under her keel is to be let loose upon the *Dwarf*. The engineer who will have to remain on board almost until the last will be as good as lost, but none the less three brave men have volunteered for the fatal journey.
>
> *12th September.*—The night was bright moonlight, and the torpedoes could not get near enough. At 8 o'clock the *Dwarf* steamed away.

As a matter of fact, the *Ivy*, a vessel belonging to the Nigeria Marine, was then doing duty as guardship at the obstruction, and for some reason or other the Germans did not consider her worthy of receiving the attentions of their torpedo-boat. On 13th September the *Dwarf* relieved the *Ivy*, and another attempt was made that night to torpedo her. On 14th September the diary says, "*Dwarf* working at the barrier. The torpedo-boats cannot get near enough; they are always observed too soon and fired upon."

But on 16th September Lieutenant Nathnagel records that an attack has actually been made at last.

> The first torpedo attack on the *Dwarf* has unfortunately failed. The man in charge lost his head, and jumped out with the rudder wrongly lashed. In consequence the boat ran round in circles with the torpedo set, and endangered the other boat, which had to retreat, and in the meantime the torpedo-man was drowned. The torpedo exploded uselessly in the mangroves.

As to the result of the attempt, and as to the cause of the failure, the diarist is correct, but his details are lamentably inaccurate. First of all, the rudder was not lashed, but the tiller was fixed by means of an iron pin, and the man in the boat became so much rattled when the *Dwarf* opened fire that, instead of fixing it amidships, he fixed it hard a-port, so that the boat swung to starboard and ran on the mud. The other boat did not retreat because of the vagaries of its companion, but because of the *Dwarf*'s fire. It is not clear whether this other boat was the second torpedo boat, or merely a boat to pick up the man who ran the first boat. Its intention may possibly have been to divert the *Dwarf*'s attention from the first boat, for it had come downstream below the *Dwarf*, and then turned to approach her from the seaward side, at the same time signalling with a lantern.

This boat escaped in the darkness. The man was not drowned, as reported by the diarist, nor did the torpedoes explode. The man was found next morning seated on a spar of one of the sunken ships, and clad in nothing but a pair of trousers. He was a lanky, miserable fellow, and very much frightened when he was taken prisoner; but a cup of hot cocoa soon restored him. The torpedoes were recovered intact, and brought aboard the *Dwarf*, where they were duly admired; but Commander Strong did not care for them as ship's pets, so they were eventually buried.

Of the other torpedo-boat the diary says:

20th September.—The second torpedo-boat has been out since yesterday evening. We hope it has not been blown up by its own torpedo. Anyhow, the *Dwarf* has not been blown up.

21st September.—Till now no news of the torpedo.

22nd September.—Some of the native crew of the torpedo-boat have returned, and report that the boat was attacked from in front and behind by launches; the benzine tank caught fire, and the crew then surrendered. A thousand pities, but still better than if it had been uselessly blown in the air.

Lieutenant Nathnagel is evidently a born optimist, for he finds consolation in the fact that the boat has fallen intact into the enemy's hands, so that it may be of some use after all. He omits to mention that the great inventor was captured at the same time, and was retained as a prisoner in spite of the plea that his missionary work in the Cameroons was likely to suffer by his absence. The launches he refers to were ship's boats belonging to H.M.S. *Cumberland*.

There are two other incidents in the early operations which are worthy of mention; but both of them are essentially modern in their character, and both of them offer an insight into the peculiar psychology of the German. The first occurred on 25th September, when a channel through the obstruction had been completed, and H.M.S. *Challenger*, having reduced her draught by the removal of heavy stores, passed up the river to within range of the town of Duala. Transports had arrived bringing British and French troops, and preparations were being made to supplement a frontal attack on the town by sending a detachment of troops up the Dibamba River, to cut off the enemy's line of retreat to the eastward.

The *Challenger* anchored at Bwape Sand just short of a mine-field, and a party was sent ashore under the white flag to convey to the governor of Duala a demand for the surrender of the town. An interval of two hours was allowed to enable the governor to frame his reply, and in the meantime the *Challenger* and all the vessels in company with her flew the white flag. The party reached Duala and handed the message to the governor, and then followed the interval of waiting. But it was by no means a dull, uneventful interval. While the governor was drawing up one of those models of evasiveness for which Germans seem to have a special aptitude, the commandant and his officers were getting very busy. It would seem to be one of the axioms of German military tactics that, when the enemy hoists the white flag, an exceptionally favourable opportunity is offered for attacking him.

In this case, however, the methods of attack were severely limited, for it is obviously futile to send a body of infantry or cavalry to attack an armoured cruiser, and an artillery attack, to be effective, needed guns of larger calibre than any the Germans had available. There was, however, one method of attack, which had a very fair chance of success at a time of truce, when it might be supposed that the enemy's vigilance would be relaxed— the floating mine. On the swift current the Germans released a large number of floating mines, and waited expectantly.

Fortunately for the *Challenger* the vigilance of her look-out had not been relaxed. The mines were seen approaching the ship, fire was opened on them with rifles and maxims, and all of them were exploded before they came near enough to do any damage. The chagrin of the Germans at the failure of their tactics was expressed in the version of the story which they sent by wireless to Germany.

> The British, having hoisted the flag of truce, opened fire with rifles and machine-guns

A perfectly accurate statement, only they forgot to mention the floating mines.

Two days later, when they saw that the forces confronting them were too formidable for them, and that their line of retreat was in danger, they surrendered the town of Duala and the suburb of Bonaberi across the river. The final entry in Lieutenant Nathnagel's diary reads:

> *26th September.*—The commandant goes to Edea. A slow bombardment; various buildings destroyed, but no loss of life. At noon news comes that large bodies of troops are landing, and advancing from Gori, Pitti, and Japoma.[1] I am now Commandant of Duala.
>
> *27th September.*—Out at 5 a.m. under full protection as the bombardment may be expected at once. At 7.30 instructions from Captain Haedicke that the companies are to retire. I am still keeping up telephonic communication with the commander, and receive the definite order to give up the useless opposition, march off the coloured troops with arms, make all war material useless, and hoist the white flag.

---

1. Pronounce Yapooma.

After the capture of Duala and the neighbouring country, one of the problems confronting the Allies was the administration of the cocoa plantations. The German overseers, who controlled the native labourers, pointed out that the workers would not continue their work without supervision, and, as the Allied forces had no one available at the time to take the place of these overseers, it was decided to place them under parole and let them carry on. If there were any misgivings as to the value of a German's parole, it was not long before they found ample justification. These overseers promptly enlisted in the German secret service, and sent all the useful information they could to the German forces upcountry. Very soon it became apparent that these men were an infernal nuisance, and would continue to be so until they were interned.

With a view to putting a check upon their activities, surprise visits were paid to the cocoa farms, and occasionally the European staff were brought off to the Senior Naval Officer's ship to be examined. The farm buildings were searched for firearms, etc. but the Germans contrived somehow or other to keep some of their rifles securely hidden. To convey information to one's friends in spite of a solemn promise not to do so is one thing; to engage in active operations of hostility in contravention of a pledge to which one owes one's liberty, is another thing. Both are not only permissible, but even praiseworthy, according to the German code of morals. It would seem, however, as if Nemesis, with righteous indignation, was lying in wait for these German traders.

A landing party had been sent ashore to one of the cocoa farms, where they found a small German staff, some papers which, on translation, might prove incriminating, and some money. They brought the party aboard with the papers and the money, and they also brought off from the shore a boat belonging to the German traders. The money and the papers were retained, and a formal receipt was handed to the farm manager. The Germans were then sent back in their own boat, unaccompanied. By this time night had fallen, and it was quite dark. From the ship they could hear the splash of the oars as the boat approached the river-bank, when suddenly the sound of rifle-shots rang out through the darkness, and quite a heavy fusillade was opened upon the unfortunate Germans in the boat.

The explanation was that some of their compatriots, having succeeded in retaining their rifles, thought that a splendid opportunity had come to strike a blow for the Fatherland. They saw a boat pull away from a British man-of-war, and naturally assumed that it was manned by British sailors. Without a thought for their parole they hid behind some bushes, and, as soon as the boat reached the bank, they let drive. The result was that the number of Germans in the world was reduced by two, and Nemesis was satisfied.

CHAPTER 15

Amphibious Operations

I have said that at the opening of the Cameroons campaign the operations were entirely naval, the military forces not appearing on the scene until just before the surrender of Duala. I am referring, of course, to the western side of the colony, which is bordered by the sea. In the north-east there were military operations as early as August 1914, culminating in the unfortunate disaster at Garua, when Colonel Maclear, and four other officers were killed, and about 40 *per cent,* of our native troops were lost. After this catastrophe the operations from the Nigerian border of the Cameroons were suspended for over nine months, and it was not until June 1915 that a second attack was made on Garua. This was completely successful, and the town was surrendered, together with a considerable number of prisoners and a big haul of guns and ammunition.

It is noteworthy that, in achieving this result, our military forces had the assistance of a naval gun, transported by Lieutenant Louis H. Hamilton and five seamen over narrow, rough roads through hundreds of miles of bushland. This gun and a small French howitzer had an instantaneous effect upon the German native troops, who were unaccustomed to guns of that calibre, and soon got out of hand and became mutinous. Their officers then realised that the game was up, and Garua was surrendered without a struggle.

For many months preceding the capture of Garua the main part of the campaign had been going on in the west, along the sea-coast, and in those districts made accessible to floating craft by numerous rivers and creeks. The nature of the country near the coast and for many miles inland is such that ordinary military operations are impossible. Mangrove swamps and thick jungle are the natural features of the land, and though the efforts of man have succeeded in clearing spaces here and there for cocoa plantations, in making rough roads, and building railways, the sum-total of these efforts has made about as much impression upon the general appearance of the country as the seven maids with their seven mops upon the sands of the seashore. One cannot move an army with its guns and transport waggons through a mangrove swamp, and, though native carriers can be employed for the conveyance of food along the bush-roads, it is arduous work to convey heavy guns and ammunition by such primitive means.

The only redeeming feature of the country as a terrain for the operations of war is the network of rivers and creeks. To the purely military mind, of course, these waterways only serve to damn it the more, for the soldier must necessarily regard a river as an inconvenient obstacle which has to be crossed. But, to the amphibious mind, the waterways afford the only solution of the transport problem, and to the nation which enjoys the supremacy of the sea they offer an incalculable advantage in the ordeal of war. Granted that plenty of craft, small enough to navigate these narrow channels, can be brought to the scene of operations, the rivers and creeks become, instead of obstacles, magnificent highways for the conveyance of troops, guns, and stores, while the gunboats of the navy provide the artillery, which is moreover of a larger calibre than anything which the enemy can hope to bring against it, faced as he is with the problem of carrying his guns overland.

A typical example of amphibious operations was that which was undertaken ten days after the capture of Duala. The objective was the village of Jabassi, about fifty miles up the Wuri River, which runs into the Cameroon River from the north-east. The flotilla consisted of seventeen steam and motor vessels and eighteen lighters, of which seven vessels and one lighter carried guns. The *Mole* and the armed lighter each carried a 6-inch gun, while the others carried guns of smaller calibre, and there was also a naval 12-pounder field-gun manned by a detachment of seamen. The military force consisted of eight companies of native troops, half a company of Pioneers, 600 native carriers, a medical detachment, etc. This force was embarked in the various river craft, and proceeded up the Wuri River.

Unfortunately, it was the rainy season of the year, when the country is not only unpleasantly moist, but also unpleasantly hot—a sticky, damp heat, which causes the perspiration to exude in a constant stream, drenching one's clothes almost as soon as one puts them on. Moreover, the rain came down in torrents, so that there was moisture both from within and without, and, as the troops were all huddled together in the small river craft, without any protection from the downpour, they had a very uncomfortable time of it. To add to their troubles, there were the mosquitoes, which thrive exceedingly well in the Cameroons during the rainy season, and have a disagreeable habit of carrying the malaria microbe about with them.

This first expedition to Jabassi was a failure, chiefly on account of the climatic conditions; but it is interesting as an illustration of the difficulties which our forces had to overcome in achieving the conquest of the Cameroons, and as evidence of the absolute necessity of naval co-operation in a campaign of this kind. The flotilla actually carried the troops within three miles of Jabassi, and then landed them without any mishaps. They marched two out of the three miles towards the village before they encountered any opposition, so that they were within a mile of their objective when the enemy first showed that he was there, and very much awake. He opened a hot fire on our troops, who were advancing along a road parallel with the river, and upon the armed vessels, which had kept abreast of the advance, and had steadily bombarded the high ground where Jabassi stands. The enemy were hidden in the dense bush, so that it was impossible to ascertain their strength, or form any reliable opinion as to the nature of their defences.

For the greater part of the day a kind of haphazard fight went on, our troops firing at the sound of the enemy's rifles, and gradually crawling towards them through the jungle. The 12-pounder field-gun found a hill from which to pepper the enemy's positions, so far as they could be ascertained, and the armed river craft went on cheerfully firing in the direction of where they thought the enemy ought to be. The result of their efforts was that the German rifles and machine-guns were gradually silenced, and there seemed to be no further obstacle to an advance upon Jabassi. By this time, however, the troops had become hopelessly scattered in the bush, and moreover were quite exhausted. The rain and the heat had told upon them, so that the medical staff found that they had to deal with many more sick cases than wounded men. In fact, the casualties had been remarkably light, for the German marksmanship was poor.

A retirement was obviously necessary, for night was coming on, and to remain in that jungle with the chance of being surrounded by the enemy was not to be contemplated. If the troops had been obliged to retire on foot it would have gone badly with them, for they were thoroughly worn out, and doubtless the Germans would have kept abreast of them in the jungle through which the road runs, and would have sniped at them all the time. But fortunately the flotilla of river transports was there waiting for them, and the naval guns in the armed launches were there to cover their retreat and embarkation. In a very short time they were beyond the range of the enemy's fire, and anchored about three miles downstream from Jabassi.

Probably they would have been able to take Jabassi next day if they had attempted it, but the condition of the troops was such that it was deemed prudent to bring them back to Duala, where the sick men could receive proper attention. In the meantime another detachment of troops was sent up the Wuri River, and on 14th October they entered Jabassi almost without opposition. The officer commanding them paid a very warm tribute to the naval officers and ratings in the armed launches, who encountered the brunt of such opposition as the enemy offered, and were largely instrumental in persuading him that the game was up.

A week later another amphibious expedition was undertaken, with the object of capturing Edea, on the Midland Railway, about forty miles south-east of Duala. A glance at the map will show that it is also on the Sanaga River, and consequently accessible from the sea. The scheme of operations comprised three attacks from separate directions—(1) by the Sanaga River, (2) by the Njong River as far as Dehane and thence overland, and (3) by the Midland Railway. The first two of these required naval co-operation; the third was an entirely military affair, and was undertaken by a small force, mainly with the object of affording a distraction to the enemy. The chief military force was detailed for the Njong River, while the naval forces were divided between the Njong and the Sanaga Rivers.

It will be convenient to deal first with the Sanaga River force. This was divided into two sections—the larger craft, which went round by sea to the river entrance, and the smaller craft, which reached the river by means of the Kwa-Kwa Creek, joining the Sanaga to the Cameroon River. The Kwa-Kwa Creek flotilla encountered some opposition, which caused a delay; but they eventually overcame it, and reached the Sanaga River on 23rd October in the evening, anchoring off Lobetal Beach to await the arrival of the larger craft. These had arrived safely at the river entrance, but had had some difficulty in crossing the bar, and further difficulties awaited them in the lower reaches of the river, owing to the native pilots being unfamiliar with them.

It may be said that the chief virtue of the native pilot is his unfailing cheerfulness. When he has run the ship aground with a big bump, he turns smilingly to the commanding officer, and says "Small water lib 'ere, sah," and he says it too with the air of one imparting useful information. These pilots had all been in the habit of using the Kwa-Kwa Creek to get from Duala to Edea, and consequently they knew the river fairly well above the junction at Lobetal, but had practically no knowledge of it below that point.

They managed, however, to reach Lobetal eventually—on the day following the arrival of the Kwa-Kwa Creek flotilla, and the combined flotilla, under the command of Commander L. W. Braithwaite in the *Remus*, proceeded up towards Edea. The troops were landed on both banks to march in front of the flotilla, but they found it such heavy going that they had to be re-embarked. At nightfall when the flotilla anchored, some troops were again landed, and camped in the vicinity of the anchorage to protect it from a night attack. On 26th October they drew near to Edea, and as they steamed past the riverside village, the natives all came out of their huts, and cheered lustily. To them the British flag was the emblem of their deliverance from rulers whom they had learned to hate, with that undying hatred which is born of a sense of tyranny and injustice.

That they should so regard their German rulers must have been a source of pathetic perplexity to the Teuton mind. For the German Government had sunk large sums of money in the development of the Cameroons; it had reclaimed big tracts of jungle, and cultivated them with cocoa and plantains; it had constructed roads and railways to bring these plantations within easy access of a seaport; it had built huts for the native workers on the plantations, and provided them with well-equipped hospitals. And yet it had failed entirely to win the goodwill of the natives. The explanation is not far to seek. Germany's whole idea had been to exploit the colony and its inhabitants for the benefit of the German trader.

The land was taken away from the native, who was compelled to work on it at a nominal wage of a few shillings a month, which just sufficed to avoid the charge of imposing a system of slavery. To all intents and purposes, however, it was a system of slavery, for the worker was not allowed to leave his work and seek other occupation when he felt inclined, and was always subjected to the practically unlimited powers of the German overseers, who sometimes exercised those powers with unbridled brutality. The German system of colonisation has consistently resulted in economic failure; in the Cameroons it also resulted in completely alienating the sympathy and goodwill of the natives. The Sanaga River flotilla had some fairly heavy guns with them, including a 6-inch gun in the *Mole*, and there is no doubt that the approach of these guns had a very salutary effect on the Germans at Edea, and influenced their decision to evacuate the town. But, to keep to the chronological order of events, it is necessary to relate the experiences of the Njong River section.

Early in the morning of 21st October the *Cumberland*, the *Dwarf*, the French *Surprise*, and six transports conveying about 2,000 troops, mostly native, anchored off the entrance to the river. The smaller craft came up later, and proceeded at once to cross the bar. Unfortunately the weather was bad, and it soon became apparent that there would be considerable difficulty in getting the larger vessels over the bar, no ship as large as any of the transports having been known to enter the Njong River. The officers of the Nigeria Marine had made a reconnaissance of the river mouth, and it was largely due to them that the enterprise was carried out successfully.

Two transports got over the bar without much trouble, but the third one ran aground, and had to wait for the flood-tide before she could be refloated. An armed launch also got stuck, so badly that she had to be abandoned after her guns and stores had been salved. A heavy sea was running the whole time, and consequently there was a good deal of danger attending the operations. Perhaps no one fully appreciated how great that danger was until a sad catastrophe occurred. The senior naval officer (Captain Fuller) embarked in a whaler with a native crew to row across the bar and superintend the operations on the other side. He was accompanied by Lieutenant Child (director of the Nigeria Marine), Commander Gray, R.N.R. (transport officer to the expeditionary force), and Captain Franqueville (a French staff officer). Just as they were crossing the bar a big wave caught the boat and capsized it, throwing all its occupants into the water. Boats were immediately sent to the rescue by the ships lying at anchor, but, owing to the high seas, it was some time before they could reach the spot. Out of the whole party only Captain Fuller and two of the native crew were saved.

That evening the flotilla of small craft proceeded up the Njong River under Commander Cheetham, R.N.R., taking with them a detachment of French troops. Next morning they occupied Dehane and the following day the French column commenced its march towards

Edea, leaving a small guard of British troops at Dehane. On 26th October they reached their objective, and found that the Germans had evacuated the place. The news was passed to the flotilla in the Sanaga River, whose guns had been largely instrumental in persuading the enemy that resistance was useless, and they proceeded upstream and anchored off the town. German prisoners reported that their officers had declared it impossible to bring up heavy guns to Edea; but, when they saw that the impossible had been accomplished, they hastened to effect a retreat.

So far our conquest of the country had extended north-east of Duala as far as Jabassi, and south-east as far as Edea. The next objective was Buea, northwest of Duala, and about twenty-five miles from the coast. Buea was the German seat of government, and was also a health resort, for it lies on the slopes of the Cameroon Mountain—a volcanic formation, which looks as though it had been dropped by accident in the midst of that vast area of swamps and low-lying ground. Further inland there are high mountain-ranges stretching across the Cameroons, but all the country within a hundred miles of the sea is a level plain, thickly covered with forests, and intersected by innumerable rivers and creeks. On the Cameroon Mountain in the vicinity of Buea the rank growth of tropical vegetation has been made to give place to the cultivation of European plants.

English vegetables and fruits are grown there with ease, and the Germans had instituted a dairy farm with real live cows, good pasture, cowsheds, milk separators, and everything complete—except that there were no dairymaids. From all points of view Buea was a desirable place to acquire.

The plan of operations comprised four distinct undertakings: (1) to make a demonstration at Bibundi in order to persuade the enemy that we intended to land a force there; (2) to occupy Victoria, so that they might anticipate an advance towards Buea from that direction also; (3) to capture Tiko, and advance with the main force from there to Buea; and (4) to send a flotilla up the Mungo River to Mpundi, and a detachment of troops up the Northern Railway to Susa, and so make a flank attack from the east. The fortunes of these undertakings, which were all amphibious in their nature, will be described in turn.

The Bibundi expedition was entrusted to Commander Strong in the *Dwarf*, accompanied by a small transport. Upon arrival at the spot, some *krooboys* were sent ashore in surf-boats to make a feint of landing. Apparently the manoeuvre succeeded admirably, for word was sent to the German commandant that a considerable British force was being landed at Bibundi, and the enemy promptly made preparations to meet it. Having achieved his object, Commander Strong re-embarked the *krooboys*, and in due course returned to Duala.

The taking of Victoria was entrusted to a party of Marines under Captain Hall, the transport being escorted by the *Ivy* and two armed tugs, while the French cruiser *Bruix* remained in the offing, to cover the landing with her guns. On 13th November they arrived at Victoria, and Commander Hughes, R.N.R., in the *Ivy*, summoned the German commander to surrender the place, giving him one hour's grace to consider his reply. He refused to surrender, and so a bombardment was opened upon Victoria and the neighbouring village of Bota.

Then the Marines were landed at Bota, and they proceeded to march on Victoria. The enemy, bombarded from the sea and threatened from the land, came to the conclusion that the game was not worth the candle. Within a few hours he had been driven out of Victoria, and he did not even stop to destroy the light railway running inland from Bota, for the Marines found it intact with all its rolling-stock in good condition. Having taken possession of the place and sent all the non-combatant Germans to Duala for internment, they left a guard of native troops and returned to the base.

Meanwhile the main force had proceeded to Tiko. Captain Beatty-Pownall in the *Remus* had charge of a flotilla of six river transports, each towing a lighter laden with troops and equipment, and an armed tug towed a heavy lighter mounting a 6-inch gun. Lieutenant Hamilton was in command of a detachment of seamen with field-guns supplied by the *Cumberland* and *Challenger*. There were 70 European troops, and over 2,000 native troops and carriers. Two despatch vessels were employed as mine-sweepers, and proceeded ahead of the flotilla, which approached Tiko at daylight on 13th November. The Tiko Haben pier, which is at some distance from the village, was reached in safety, and here the troops disembarked, while the tug with the lighter carrying the 6-inch gun pushed up a creek to the west of Tiko to cover the advance.

It had not gone far before it came under rifle and machine-gun fire from trenches well hidden in the bush. But a 6-inch gun has a little way of its own in dealing with rifles and machine-guns, and it needs a brave man to stick to his trench when heavy shells at short range are tearing the trees down all round him, and bursting on every side of him. The enemy's fire was silenced, the enemy melted away, and Tiko was occupied without any further opposition.

Next day the troops commenced their advance on Buea, and, after overcoming some slight resistance, they reached a village called Bole Famba, where they halted for the night, and where we may leave them for the moment.

The Mungo River party, who were to assist the troops sent up the railway to Susa in making a flank attack, had the longest distance to travel, and therefore started earlier than all the rest. It was fortunate they did so, for the Mungo River eclipses most of the other rivers of the country as a test in navigating skill. It is very narrow in parts, it twists about with hair-pin bends, it is full of shoals, and it has a strong current. It was not supposed to be navigable at all after the end of October, and even during the rainy season only vessels with a very light draught ever attempted it.

The flotilla, which was commanded by Lieutenant-Commander Sneyd, consisted of two boats from the *Cumberland*, armed with light guns, a stern-wheel gunboat, called the *Sokoto*, which had been captured from the Germans when they surrendered Duala, and three armed launches. The *Sokoto* had never risked herself in the Mungo River before, and she soon began to wonder whether her new masters had mistaken her for a steam-roller or a hay-making machine. However, she made up her mind to do her best, and struggled manfully round the twists and over the shoals.

Mbonjo was reached on 12th November, and next day the flotilla pushed on to Mpundu, where they found the enemy holding a strong position on the right bank. But the guns of all the armed craft soon induced him to clear out of it, and Mpundu was occupied without much trouble. Here the troops from Susa joined up, and the march towards Buea was commenced. It is difficult to say which of these undertakings was mainly instrumental in persuading the enemy that he could not hold Buea— the feint of landing at Bibundi, the occupation of Victoria, the main advance from Tiko, or the flank attack from Mpundu. All of them were successfully carried out according to plan, and the cumulative effect must have been considerable upon the much-harassed Germans. The main force from Tiko, which we left at the village of Bole Famba on the night of the 14th November, was the first to reach the German capital, and occupied it without opposition during the afternoon of 15th November.

The rest of the work of the navy in the Cameroons presents no startling features, which would justify a description in detail. The conquered area steadily expanded, and, as it did so, the scene of operations gradually passed farther inland, until it became inaccessible to floating craft. This however, did not reduce the navy to a state of idleness, but it tended to make its work more humdrum and devoid of incident. A constant patrolling of the rivers and creeks had to be maintained, to drive off enemy detachments and protect the unfortunate natives from the revengeful habits of their former masters, to stop food supplies and contraband from being smuggled up the rivers, to obtain information as to enemy movements, and, generally, to fulfil the functions of a police force.

These duties brought them into conflict frequently with small bodies of enemy troops, which took every possible opportunity of sniping at them from the jungle. But the most troublesome part of the day's work was in connection with the German monasteries and religious establishments. At first the inmates of these establishments had been placed on parole and allowed to continue their vocation without interference; but soon there was an accumulation of evidence that these holy brethren and their holy sisters were taking advantage of their liberty to forward information to the enemy. Finally, it was decided that they must be interned, and, when Commander Braithwaite was clearing the Dehane-Kribi district of the enemy, he made all the monks and nuns prisoners and sent them off to be interned. The news of this proceeding filtered through to Germany, and, needless to say, it was at once turned to account for propaganda purposes; the neutral Roman Catholic countries were flooded with a heart-rending version of the story of how the brutal British officers had laid sacrilegious hands upon the servants of the Church.

In addition to the patrol of the inland waterways, the Navy had also to undertake the blockade of the sea-coast, which commenced on 23rd April, 1915. This necessitated a constant vigilance night and day, each ship engaged on the patrol covering a certain distance along the coast-line, and plying up and down its beat with a wearisome monotony, which is all too familiar to the officers and men of the navy. A few of the naval force had the good fortune to escape from this patrol work by being detached for service ashore with the military. The expedition of Lieutenant Hamilton and a gun's crew to Garua has already been mentioned. A similar expedition was commanded by Lieutenant-Commander Davies, R.N.R., who took a 12-pounder gun and two maxims to accompany the military expedition up the

Northern Railway to Bare, and did some excellent work with the gun.

When we can quietly devote our minds to the chronicle of this mighty struggle through which we have passed, we shall turn with some feelings of pride to those pages which record the successes of the Cameroons campaign, and possibly we shall wonder how it was that such achievements were received so unconcernedly at the time of their occurrence. Such has always been the fate of all side-shows when the drama of a European war is before the world's public, but the side-showmen may find consolation in the knowledge that the historian always accords them their due place of honour among the makers of history.

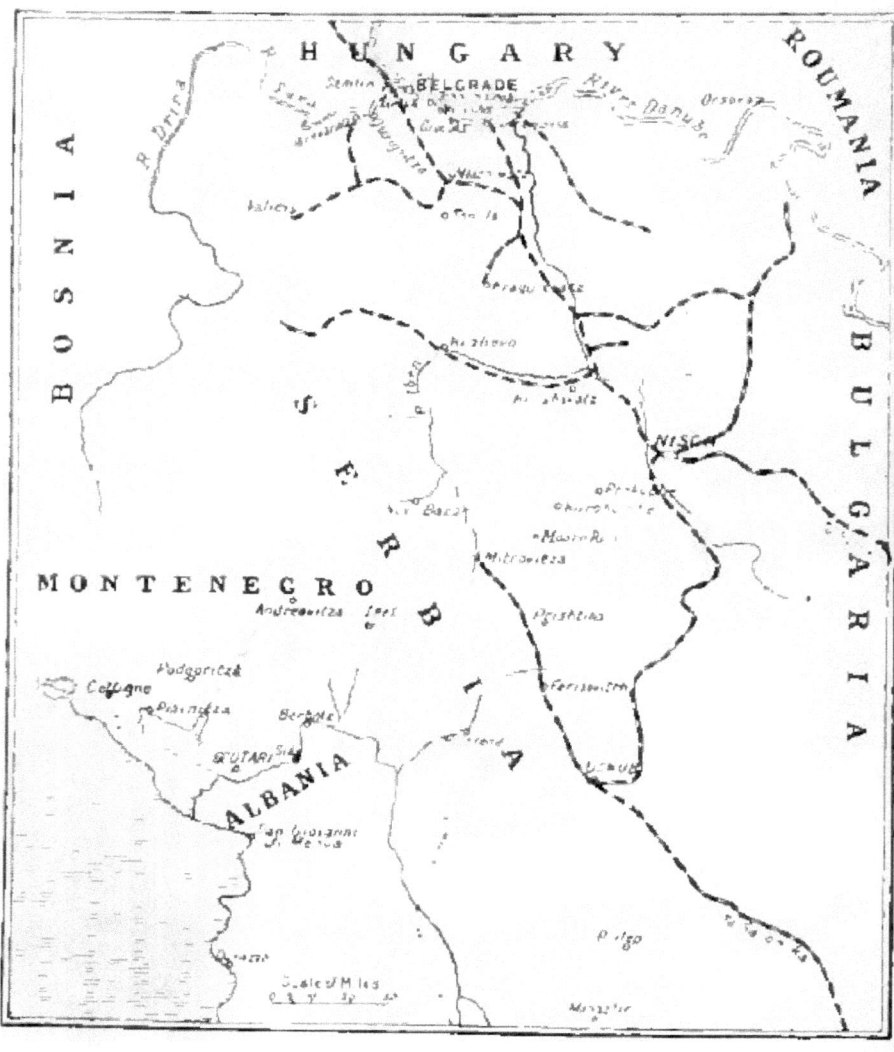

THE NAVY IN SERBIA

CHAPTER 16

The "Terror of the Danube"

When our naval mission, under the command of Rear-Admiral (later Vice-Admiral) Troubridge, went to Serbia early in 1915, no public announcement of its departure there, nor of its doings when it got there, was made. It was sent to co-operate with the French and Russian naval missions in preventing the Austrian monitors and other enemy vessels from having a free run of the Danube. In this it succeeded completely, for the Austrian monitors and munition boats were forced to lie behind a boom defence, and never ventured down the river until the great attack on Belgrade drove the defenders from the city. The story of how this result was accomplished has never been published in detail, but a despatch from the *Times* correspondent at Belgrade, which appeared in that paper on 7th July, 1915, gave the public a glimpse behind the scenes. Here is an extract from it:

> You can ascend to the roof of a favourably situated house, or walk to the higher ground outside the town, and look through glasses up the Danube to where, beyond the Austrian town of Semlin and the island of Grosser Krieg, the Austrian river monitors are lying, black and ugly, in the stream. At one time there were seven monitors, but there are only six now. . . . What you cannot see is that they are lying inside a boom; for, since their number was reduced from seven to six by a pretty piece of torpedo work on the part of the solitary little picket boat, commonly known as the 'Terror of the Danube,' the enemy's monitors have been singularly unenterprising. . . . The young gentlemen who have charge of the 'Terror of the Danube' have great larks with it. They poke their way on dark nights into creeks and passages, where they are not in the least expected,

and annoy the Austrians dreadfully. The Austrians have three picket gunboats, which look like toy Dreadnoughts, with machine-guns mounted in their turrets. Any one of these could eat up the 'Terror' in a few minutes, if it could get at it. But the 'Terror' comes up when it is nice and dark and makes rude remarks with its single machine-gun to one of the Dreadnoughts, and then runs like a hare.

The *Times* correspondent goes on to describe how the "Terror" enticed one of the Austrian "Dreadnoughts" over a minefield, with the result that the "Dreadnought's" remains were floating about in midstream and drifting ashore on Kojara Island. But this happened towards the end of June 1915. The incident I am going to describe—the pretty piece of torpedo work which reduced the Austrian monitors from seven to six—happened in April 1915. These monitors had been in the habit of plying up and down the river at their own sweet will, bombarding with their small guns the Serbian trenches by the riverside, and with their big guns throwing shells upon the positions farther inland. But the "Terror of the Danube" changed all that, reducing the enemy's monitors to a state of impotence and compelling them to lie snugly secure behind a boom defence. Only a very brief account of this pretty piece of torpedo work was published at the time when the decorations were awarded to those concerned in it, but the story has enough dramatic interest to be worth relating in some detail.

The picket-boat was brought from Malta to Salonika and thence forwarded overland by rail to Belgrade some time in March 1915. There it was launched in the Danube, and, as it was the only craft the navy had at Belgrade, they naturally regarded it with tender affection. The Austrians had six monitors and seven patrol-boats lying somewhere above the fortifications of Semlin, higher up the river, and it may possibly have occurred to the more superstitious among them that a fleet of thirteen vessels is bound to meet with a disaster sooner or later. Anyhow, they seemed quite annoyed with our little picket-boat the moment it arrived, and they greeted it by pitching shells upon the dockyard where it was lying. Consequently the admiral decided that it would be wiser to give the Austrians time to forget about it, before sending it out upon any kind of escapade.

It was only a picket-boat, but the navy at Belgrade was quite proud of it, for, when the Navy is condemned by circumstances to play at soldiering, it always has a secret yearning for something that floats, and, just as a doll is supposed to satisfy the maternal instinct of incipient womanhood, so a picket-boat had to satisfy the cravings of our naval men ashore in Serbia. They petted it, and fondled it, and put a maxim-gun in its bows, and rigged up two torpedoes in it, and loaded it up with hand-grenades. And then they waited eagerly for a chance to take it out on a little voyage of exploration, for that Austrian fleet of thirteen vessels was such an obvious challenge against the laws of chance and probability.

The River Sava meets the Danube at Belgrade, flowing into it from the west. The Danube itself flows from the north down to Belgrade, and then turns eastward, so that there is quite a broad expanse of water opposite the town, with rivers running into it from north and east, and running out to the west, By comparing this expanse of water with Parliament Square, we find that the River Sava takes the place of Victoria Street, and that the Danube, having come down Whitehall, turns to the left over Westminster Bridge. Belgrade occupies the position of the Houses of Parliament, Semlin occupies the position of the Local Government Board, and the Austrian monitors were lying up Whitehall somewhere near the Horse Guards. The small islands opposite Belgrade may be marked by the statues in Parliament Square in order to complete the map.

The first attempt was made on 21st April soon after ten o'clock at night, when the picket-boat, commanded by Lieutenant Commander Kerr, glided quietly up the river. His orders were to reconnoitre the position of the monitors, and, if a favourable opportunity occurred, to attack them with torpedoes. If, however, he found that the enemy's defences at Semlin were too formidable, or that the monitors themselves were prepared for an attack, so that the chances of success became hopeless, he was to return at once to Belgrade. "For Heaven's sake don't lose the boat," said the admiral, "for it is all we have." There was another danger to be taken into account. Although the Serbian patrols on the bank of the river had all been warned that the attempt was to be made, it was quite possible that some of them, in a fit of enthusiasm, might open fire on our picket-boat with their rifles, and so awake the Austrian batteries and monitors to the fact that something was going on down below them. Some of the Serbian river patrols were remarkably enthusiastic upon occasions, sometimes inconvenient occasions. Fortunately, however, they managed to restrain themselves during the two nights of the picket-boat's adventures.

On the first night, it was found that a strong easterly wind had caused the monitors to shift berth from the right (or western) bank to the left bank of the river, "where they were better sheltered from the wind. The picket-boat slipped past the Semlin defences without being seen, and continued for about two miles up the river, keeping in to the right bank, but was unable to locate precisely the position of the monitors. The river here is full of shoals and small low-lying islands, which are difficult to avoid by night, and, after running aground once and experiencing some difficulty in getting off, Lieutenant-Commander Kerr decided to return to Belgrade.

As his movements had apparently escaped the notice of the enemy completely, it was decided that he should make another attempt on the following night. The wind had abated, and during the day four monitors and a steamer had been seen to cross the river, and return to their usual anchorage near the right bank. So, just before midnight, the picket-boat again started off for another adventure. As before, the defences of Semlin were passed without attracting attention, and the boat steamed steadily up the river against the fast current.

About half-past one in the morning a monitor was sighted about 300 yards away on the starboard bow (the picket-boat was therefore between the monitor and the right bank of the river). Just ahead of her was another monitor; then came a white-painted steamer; then a third monitor; while the fourth monitor lay about 100 yards to eastward of the first two, approximately on their starboard beam. Lieutenant Commander Kerr's plan was to attack the first monitor with a torpedo, pass under her stern across the river, and attack the fourth monitor with his other torpedo.

The picket-boat crept up to within 100 yards of the first monitor, and was then challenged by the look-out. The reply was the firing of the torpedo, and at the same moment rifle and machine-gun fire was opened on the picket-boat from all directions. The torpedo ran true; there followed a heavy muffled explosion and much shouting, and the picket-boat swung round across stream towards her second objective. But by this time all the monitors and the whole riverside were alive with rifles and machine-guns, and Lieutenant-Commander Kerr remembered the wise saying of Macbeth: "*If it were done when 'tis done, then 'twere well it were done quickly.*" A bullet striking the releasing gear of his remaining torpedo might jamb it fatally, so he stood not upon the order of his firing, but fired at once. Unfortunately he was too close, so that the initial dive of the torpedo carried it right under the monitor and it exploded on the river bank 400 yards away.

The only thing to do now was to get out of it as quickly as possible, and in this the rapid current was of material assistance. Searchlights blazed forth from everywhere, and the bullets kept up a merry patter on the boat. Fortunately, however, nothing larger than bullets assailed her, for the simple reason that the enemy knew that shell-fire across a river in the dark is apt to do more damage to friend than foe.

So the officers and men kept well under cover, and listened contentedly to the music of the bullets on the boat's side. In a few minutes they were clear of danger from that part of the river, but they had still to pass the Semlin defences. Suddenly, just ten minutes after the attack, they heard a tremendous explosion from the direction of the monitors, and for a moment the whole sky was lit up by the glare. Evidently a fire had been started by the first torpedo, and it had just reached the magazine. Next minute the boat was passing Semlin, and all the searchlights there were making frantic efforts to pick her up. But, by good luck, they failed, and she got back safely to her creek in Belgrade after an exciting run of two hours and a half.

Next morning at daylight only three monitors lay at anchor where yesterday there had been four. Three days later the Austrian Press reported that the monitor *Keresh* on 22nd April struck an Austrian mine above Semlin and sank. Apparently they preferred to express it in this way, though it must have made some of the Austrian folk wonder why there should be Austrian mines above Semlin, at the precise spot where their monitors were always anchored.

Anyhow, Lieutenant-Commander Kerr was awarded the D.S.O. in consequence of this untoward accident to an Austrian monitor, and the picket-boat's crew were all awarded the D.S.M.

CHAPTER 17

The Fall of Belgrade

There were many tragedies—national tragedies—during the Great War, but none came with such dramatic suddenness as that which overwhelmed Serbia. Right up to the eve of the disaster Belgrade maintained its reputation as a gay city; the fashionable restaurants were crowded with military officers, and ladies in the shortest of short skirts—a cosmopolitan miscellany of Serbians, British, French, and Russians, with a few Danish and American doctors and nurses thrown in. There they were, going hither and thither in motor-cars, lounging outside *cafés*, arranging social functions of every kind regardless of the enemy just across the river—until the crash came. Possibly the facts that the Austrians had once crossed the Sava, that Belgrade in December 1914 had been evacuated, and that the enemy had soon been driven back again from Serbian territory inspired them with a false sense of security. However that may be, it is certain that the disaster, when it came, fell upon them like a thunderbolt.

With the politics of that time it is not my purpose to deal, save in so far as they explain the military situation. For the Serbians it was a time of bitter anguish, and it is not altogether surprising that they cherished a belief that they had been betrayed by their allies. The tortuous course of diplomatic devices, by which Germany induced Bulgaria to join hands with her, is altogether beyond my scope. It is sufficient to know that Bulgaria demanded, as the price of maintaining her neutrality, such concessions in Macedonia as Serbia could not contemplate without wounding her national honour, and the result was that Serbia concentrated the bulk of her forces on the Bulgarian frontier, in order to resist the threatened invasion.

During September 1915 guns, ammunition, aeroplanes, and general equipment were withdrawn from Belgrade, while the Serbian

Army there of some 37,000 men was reduced to 3,000 men. That the Serbian General Staff expected such a small force to be adequate for the defence of the town is of course an impossible supposition. The probable intention of the staff was to evacuate Belgrade at once if the Austrians crossed the river, just as it was evacuated in December 1914 as soon as the Austrians had crossed the Sava. It must be explained that the Serbians are very proud of Belgrade, for it is the only city in the whole country, and consequently means a great deal to them. Rather than have it destroyed by bombardment, they were prepared to hand it over to the enemy without hesitation.

From the point of view of the foreign naval missions this withdrawal of the Serbian forces from Belgrade could not be contemplated without some alarm. The naval batteries were either in the town, or in its vicinity, and, in addition to these batteries, there were mine-fields, with observation mines, in the Danube and the Sava, as well as some floating torpedo batteries. All the equipment of these undertakings was likely to be lost in the event of a sudden evacuation, just as the French guns had been lost in December 1914 when the city was abandoned.

The intention to evacuate the town was never declared by the general staff, but there can be little doubt that it existed, and would have been acted upon, if events had not taken such a dramatically sudden turn. Admiral Troubridge was frequently assured that he would have three clear days' notice of any contemplated advance on the part of the enemy, and that he would have ample time in which to remove his guns, mines, torpedoes, and all equipment; and this opinion was expressed by the Serbian staff officers with so much confidence that it became useless to mention the possibility of other eventualities.

It must be clearly understood that the naval forces of the allies were never intended to form any part of the defences of Belgrade. They were concerned solely with the Austrian monitors and munition ships on the Danube, and when they first arrived on the scene they found the enemy in full possession of the river, going up and down it at will, and bombarding the Serbian riverside trenches with absolute impunity. But they soon put a stop to that state of affairs. The naval batteries and minefields made the Danube and the Sava undesirable rivers for these pleasure cruises, and the feat of our picket-boat, known as the "Terror of the Danube," in torpedoing an Austrian monitor, caused all the rest of those craft to take refuge behind a boom defence, and to remain there.

It may be said that the naval missions had fulfilled their purpose when they had put an end to the enemy's activities on the river, but they were bound to remain at, and near, Belgrade, in order to prevent the possibility of those activities being resumed. Moreover, Admiral Troubridge saw further possible spheres of usefulness. It was clear that, before the enemy could advance into Serbia, he must cross either the Danube or the Sava, and to do so he must either build a pontoon bridge, or effect a crossing in boats. With batteries commanding the river, and mine-fields in the river, there seemed every prospect that the naval forces might do some useful work, if the enemy attempted an advance.

Such was the situation throughout the summer of 1915, but when, in September, the Serbians removed their guns and nearly all their infantry from Belgrade to the Bulgarian frontier it became clear that, whatever might be the usefulness of the naval forces, they could not by themselves save Belgrade in the event of an attack. The Admiral saw, with some dismay, that the Austrians were quietly occupying some of the islands in the river below Belgrade, more especially the island of Semendria, that they were emplacing guns on this island, and that they had accumulated a flotilla of small boats behind it. He drew the attention of General Jivkovitch to these preparations, but the General assured him that the island was so much under the fire of the Serbian artillery (which had not all been withdrawn at that time) that no enemy gun could exist on it for a moment.

It was quite unnecessary, in the general's view, for the Serbians to occupy the island, but if it was found that the enemy there proved himself troublesome to the Serbian operations, then of course he would be driven out at once. As to the boats lying behind the island, the general said, "I venture to think that you will agree that there is no urgent necessity to destroy these boats with artillery fire, especially as the commandant of this section probably intends to make use of them for bridge-building purposes over the Danube, in case of an advance from our side, for we have a lack of such material." Here was supreme confidence in the might of Serbia. The enemy's boats were not to be destroyed, because, should the Serbian Staff decide upon an advance into Austrian territory, they could be used by the Serbians for a pontoon bridge.

What actually happened was that twenty Austrian guns on the island of Semendria swept the Serbian shore with their fire, while Austrian infantry crossed the river in the boats, which had been hidden behind the island, and landed in Serbia almost without opposition.

This expression of opinion by General Jivkovitch is quoted, not in order to lay stress on the miscalculations of the Serbian Staff, but to explain the position of the foreign naval missions when the great crisis came. At the beginning of October 1915 the only Serbian artillery left for the defence of Belgrade were two 12-centimetre howitzers on a hill to the south of the city, called Topchider Hill. On the same hill the French had two 14-centimetre guns, while the Russians had two old guns of the same calibre in the fortress of Belgrade, and one 65-millimetre Q.F. gun. Of the four British batteries only one, consisting of two 4.7 guns, was in the immediate vicinity of Belgrade, being on a hill to the south-east of the city, called Velike Vrachar. This completes the list of the artillery which could possibly be regarded as belonging to Belgrade's defences when the great crash came.

Of the other three British batteries, each consisting of two 4.7 guns, one was at Ostrujnitza on the Sava, twelve miles from Belgrade, one at Tcholin Grob on the Danube ten miles from Belgrade, and one at Grotska, also on the Danube, twenty miles from Belgrade. The last of these was, however, transferred on 7th October—four days after the great bombardment commenced—to a hill south-west of Belgrade, called Banovo Hill, but was too late to play any appreciable part in the defence of the city.

Of the mining and torpedo sections of the naval forces not much can be said, beyond recording that they were confronted with a hopeless task after the enemy attack had begun, and that they showed wonderful resource in extricating themselves from their unenviable positions. During those three terrible days of bombardment they stuck to their posts on the banks of the Danube and the Sava, until the connecting wires of their observation mines had all been shot away, and only the torpedoes remained. In the case of the torpedo battery opposite Semendria Island the torpedoes had their internal mechanism so badly damaged by the bombardment that it was found at first impossible to fire them. But after the enemy had actually crossed the river, Lieutenant Bullock, R.M., fearing that his torpedoes might be made use of by the Austrians, ran down to the river bank by himself (having withdrawn his men to safety), and succeeded in firing one of the torpedoes, but, before he could make the other one work, the Austrian infantry were within a few hundred yards of him, and he had to run back amidst a torrent of shrapnel and rifle-bullets. He then marched his men away to the south.

The section at the railway bridge over the Sava succeeded in firing their two torpedoes, as soon as they realised that they could remain no longer at their post. They had undergone a terrible bombardment for three days and two nights, but had hung on desperately until they saw the enemy cross the river and land troops in all directions. To illustrate the fearsomeness of that bombardment there is no better testimony than that of Surgeon Merewether, who went down to our post at the railway bridge on receiving a report that one of our men had been wounded. The man unfortunately was dead before the surgeon arrived, so he took the opportunity of visiting the Serbian outposts in the neighbourhood, knowing that his assistance would probably be needed. Upon his return he reported to the admiral that the Serbian soldiers were so much dazed by the bombardment that he had the greatest difficulty in distinguishing the living from the dead. One can well imagine what must have been the condition of those men after three days and two nights of that hellish fire.

A plan of Belgrade, found in the possession of an Austrian officer who was taken prisoner, showed clearly the positions of the batteries, and of the posts of the mining and torpedo sections. It is not surprising, therefore, that these came in for the lion's share of the Austrian shells, which rained upon them unceasingly. The bombardment commenced on 3rd October, and with a steady crescendo of intensity reached its height on the morning of 6th October. There were long-range guns firing from beyond Semlin; there were 12-inch and 9-inch howitzers at shorter range; and there were smaller guns all along the north bank of the Danube and on the islands in the river.

The chief of staff estimated that within the first twenty-four hours of the bombardment 48,000 shells fell upon the area of the Belgrade defences. Houses were swept down like corn before the scythe; telegraph and telephone poles were strewn across the ruins; electric-light standards came crashing down, so that the city was plunged in darkness. And all this while the enemy's aeroplanes, like mighty birds of prey, hovered overhead, directing the Austrian gunners. At first the anti-aircraft batteries tried to hamper the movements of these spotters, but within the first hour or so every battery had been destroyed, and the aeroplanes had free license to go where they listed.

Soon the city was one big blaze, and terrified citizens were fleeing helter-skelter to get away from the deafening roar of bursting shells and falling houses. But all the roads of escape were under fire of the Austrian guns, and these miserable outcasts—old men trundling their worldly possessions in handcarts, women with children in their arms and children clinging to their skirts— had to make their way through bursting shells. The roadside became strewn with dead and wounded, as the fugitives crowded together in their panic, so that the winding road looked like a huge writhing serpent, composed of motor-cars, oxen-carts, horses, and terrified humanity.

We in England, secure behind a deeper and wider trench than ever the hand of man has dug, have never yet realised what war is. When a few German aeroplanes passed over our heads and dropped bombs in our midst, our newspapers, with flaring headlines, used to devote many columns to the incident, and all our tongues were busy wagging about it, until we really believed we had seen war. If only some of us had been at Belgrade during those three awful days, we might know what war really is.

No one had better cause to appreciate the magnitude of Belgrade's bombardment than the occupants of No. 1 Battery on Velike Vrachar hill. The battery was commanded by a Serbian artillery officer, with another Serbian officer, as second in command, and was composed of Sergeant Pearce with a corporal and four gunners of the Royal Marines, and a small crew of Serbian soldiers to assist with the heavy work. During the first two days of the bombardment the battery remained quiet, for they knew that the Austrian gunners were looking for them, and that they would be wise to reserve their fire until the approach of the crisis. On the third day it would seem that the aeroplanes had located them, for shells from fifteen centimetre and many smaller guns fell on them from eleven o'clock in the forenoon until sunset. On the next day the shelling started at eight o'clock in the morning, and again lasted until sunset. But all this time the battery remained quiet, waiting for the first sign of an attempt by the enemy to cross the river.

On Thursday, 7th October, they could wait no longer, but opened fire on the batteries along the river front, and for the rest of that day they carried on an artillery engagement with no less than twenty-four Austrian guns. But the result was a foregone conclusion. So long as they had kept quiet they had smiled contentedly at the Austrian shells shrieking over their heads, and exploding at some distance behind them. But, the moment they fired the first shot, the aeroplanes began to signal to the Austrian gunners, who immediately reduced the range, until their shells were falling in torrents all round the battery.

Fortunately the emplacement was well constructed, with good solid battlements, or the crews of No. 1 Battery would have been wiped out in a few minutes. As it was, they managed to keep up the unequal contest all day long, and most of the next day, until those two guns were all that was left of Belgrade's defences, and nearly the whole of the Austrian artillery was concentrated upon them, though they never realised it.

About eleven o'clock in the morning of 7th October two heavy shells fell on the shell-room of No. 2 gun, causing it to collapse, and killing one of the Serbian interpreters and another Serb. Almost at the same time two of the Marine gunners, Carter and Davies, were wounded, and the other interpreter was severely wounded. Both shrapnel and high explosive shell were pouring on the battery, and the noise inside was deafening. About noon the dug-out between the two guns was blown in, so that it became almost impossible to pass along the connecting trench, or to go from one gun to the other without being exposed to the enemy's fire. But there was another trench in front of the battery, and, though this also was exposed, it seemed to offer a better chance of communication, because the enemy had, so far, ignored it.

When the rain of shells became unendurable, it was decided to abandon the battery for a short time, until the enemy had been led to believe that they had silenced it. So the crews of the two guns crawled forward into the trench in front of the battery, and began to crawl stealthily along this trench towards some haven of peace and quiet. But the accursed aeroplanes had eyes like hawks, and immediately signalled to the Austrian gunners to shorten their range. Then the shells began to pitch into the trench along which our men were crawling, and the Serbian officer, the second in command, received a nasty wound. The rest, however, managed to crawl away in time.

They waited half an hour or so in their retreat, and, as they expected, the enemy's fire eased after a while on the battery, and sought other objectives. So they started to crawl back along the trench, flattering themselves that they had outwitted the Austrians for once. But the aeroplanes hovered over them like inexorable harpies, and immediately passed the word to the Austrian gunners. Again the shells came pouring into the trench, and. though by good fortune they came through unscathed, those few minutes were among the most crowded in those crowded hours of life.

At last the welcome darkness came, and beneath the protection of its cloak they set about repairing the ravages of the enemy. The two poor fellows who had been killed were extricated from a mass of fallen masonry and earth, and the debris was cleared away from the communication trench and from around the guns. The first instinct of a British sailor or a British Marine is to clear up an untidy mess, and make things look ship-shape. If they had had a hose and a squeegee they would doubtless have cleaned the battery deck, and their fingers must have been itching to run over the guns with a polishing rag.

Soon, however, they found more serious work to hand. Some boats were seen off Kozara Island preparing to take infantry across the river, so they loaded up and sent a few shells into the thick of them. Imagine the fury of the Austrian gunners, who thought they had silenced our battery for ever. With one accord they directed their fire upon it, and in a few moments a mighty shell came crashing into the casemate of one of the guns, breaking the sights, the bar, and the bracket. When the sights of a gun are broken it is still possible to use it with the aid of a clinometer, and one of these imperturbable Marines was on the point of getting to work on this suggestion when it was discovered that ammunition was running short. In that case it was better to reserve what was left for the use of the sound gun than to expend any of it with a lame gun. So, with the one gun, they kept up a steady fire, until all the ammunition was expended.

Then they waited until a fresh supply could be passed up the trench by the Serbian soldiers—a risky business, for it meant exposure to the enemy's fire. With the ammunition came an old fellow bringing some hot soup, made of beans, which the men drank with avidity, and poured blessings on the head of the old patriarch, who had risked his life to bring it to them. Later on Captain Kartitch, the commanding officer of the battery, sent for some food, and, when it came, shared it round amongst the men. It was little enough, when divided among so many, but the fact that officer and men stood shoulder to shoulder in this hour of trial was more sustaining than the most luscious masterpiece of a Paris chef.

So night passed into morning, and the undefeated battery still kept on plugging away with its single gun. Presently the Austrian monitors issued forth from their retreat, and came down the river towards Belgrade. "Give 'em a drop of lyddite," said Sergeant Pearce, and the gun was loaded with a lyddite shell. A few seconds later that shell burst amidships on an Austrian monitor, and the little band of defenders watched the vessel struggling to get back upstream with large volumes of smoke pouring out of her. All the other monitors fled for their lives, while the lame duck managed to crawl into the creek opposite Semlin, and remained there to lick her wounds. "I reckon she's *horse dee combat*" said one of the gunners, mopping his face with his handkerchief.

But it was not long before the monitors plucked up courage for another sortie, and at the same moment all the guns for miles round concentrated on the last of Belgrade's batteries. The battery managed to get off one round at the monitors, and then a shell came plunging into the casemate, wounding three men. It was quite evident that the time had come to make themselves scarce again, and they hurried along the communication trench towards their shelter. The last man had only just left the casemate when a whole shower of shells fell on top of it, and the structure fell in. The sights and breech-lever of the one remaining gun were smashed, so that it too was out of action. But Sergeant Pearce was not the man to leave anything to chance. The guns as they stood were possibly capable of repair, and, though the torrent of shrapnel made their vicinity far from comfortable, he and his men went back to strip down the breech and carrier. "The enemy won't make much of that lot," they said, with a grin of satisfaction, as they made their way out of the inferno.

The sergeant, in his official report, says:

"Both guns being thus out of action, we awaited further instructions."

And, while they waited, the city at the bottom of the hill was all ablaze, shells shrieked over their heads, and shrapnel burst within a few yards of them. At nightfall a verbal order to retire came to them, so they tramped through the rain and darkness to a village a few miles to the south, where some hospitable peasant gave them shelter, while they rested for a few hours. In addition to the loss of two men killed, the battery had fourteen men wounded. But the sergeant regarded this casualty list as remarkably small under the circumstances, and ascribed their good fortune to the excellence of the battery's construction and the depth of the trenches. All their personal belongings, which were in a house near the town, had to be abandoned, but what most distressed them was the loss of the Serbian medals which had been awarded them.

And now it was a case of *sauve qui peut* for all in Belgrade. The mining section, under Major Elliot, left the city on Friday morning, 8th October, and marched by a circuitous route to Torlak, whence they were ordered to proceed to Tchupria. There the whole force, except the British guns' crews, was assembled on 10th October. The French and Russian naval missions, who had had all their guns destroyed, also assembled at Tchupria, and for over a fortnight the whole party waited upon developments. Then they made their way by divers routes—partly by rail and partly on foot—to Monastir, whence they took train to Salonika, a day or two before Monastir fell to the Bulgarians.

The three batteries belonging to the British Navy, whose guns were still intact, were attached to the Serbian army at the request of the general staff. On 15th October the admiral received a note from the Serbian general to say that the whole of his heavy artillery had been lost, and all that remained to him were the six British naval guns to resist the invasion of Bulgaria's armies.

CHAPTER 18

The Great Retreat

Of the four British naval batteries sent to Serbia, one was destroyed during the great bombardment of Belgrade, and its crew, after having put up a magnificent fight against impossible odds, abandoned all that was left of their two broken guns, and retreated to Tchupria. But the other three batteries, each having two 4-7 guns, remained intact (except that one of them had two men badly wounded) and on 9th October, 1915, when Belgrade had fallen, one was on the left wing of the Serbian army, one on the right wing, and one in the centre. Lieutenant-Commander Kerr was then attached to the staff of General Jivkovitch for command of the three batteries.

The Serbian army was gradually retreating, and the naval guns had the task of delaying the enemy's advance, so that the Serbians could carry out an orderly retirement. It was during this period that General Jivkovitch wrote to Admiral Troubridge that the only heavy artillery left to his army was that of the three naval batteries, and that they were doing splendidly. It was, however, mighty hard work with very little encouragement, for, no sooner had they taken up positions for the guns, than they were ordered to abandon them and continue the retreat.

On 22nd October they were at Mladnovatz; from there they moved southwards to Topola; and from there on 25th October they moved to a position south-east of Kraguievatz. There the retreat became more hurried, and they had to retire by forced marches in execrable weather, arriving at Krushavatz on 31st October.

These twenty-two days of retreat were not without their excitements but the general impression left on the minds of those who went through the ordeal was one of unceasing rain and endless trudging along muddy roads crowded with soldiers, refugees, ambulance waggons, transport carts, and all the paraphernalia of an army. The transport and the hospital equipment were inadequate; wounded men were plodding along on foot, because that was their only chance of escape, until they grew faint from loss of blood, and fell by the way-side; others perished from want of food, because the facilities for conveying food to them were lacking. It would need the pen of another Zola to describe the harrowing scenes which met the eye at every few paces along the road of retreat, but perhaps it is more decent to draw the veil over the details of Serbia's great tragedy, and let those fill in the picture who can. Let us pass on to the story of the naval batteries.

At the end of October the three batteries had all reached Krushavatz, and early in the morning of 2nd November a request was made to Admiral Troubridge that they should proceed to Nisch to join up with the Second Serbian Army under Marshal Stepanovitch. They had then been either in action or on the march for twenty-two consecutive days, and had had just one day's rest, so it would be useless to pretend that they were in ecstasies of delight when they received the order to trudge ten miles to a railway station and thence take the train to Nisch. They arrived there at half-past three next morning, to find the town very full, but everybody making preparations to evacuate it.

No. 2 Battery took up a position at Alexandrovatz, to the west of Nisch across the Morava River, where it was well placed to cover the road by which the inhabitants of the town must retreat. No. 3 and No. 4 Batteries were placed at intervals of about three miles along the river, but they were at some distance from any road, and Lieutenant-Commander Kerr saw at once that, when the inevitable order came to retreat, there would be considerable difficulty in getting the guns away. No. 3 Battery especially was very inaccessible, for it was on the top of a small hill, and between it and the main road lay a large expanse of soft, marshy ground, lie decided that he must lose no time in pointing out to the chief of staff the precarious positions of the British guns, so he at once rode to Prokuplie— a distance of some thirty miles— where the marshal's staff had assembled.

On arriving there he had some difficulty in getting hold of a responsible officer, to whom he could profitably explain the situation; but finally he succeeded in buttonholing the marshal himself. The result of the interview, however, was far from satisfactory, for, as might be expected, the marshal had many preoccupations, and the troubles of the British naval batteries could not under the circumstances arouse very much sympathy in his mind. Later on Lieutenant-Commander

Kerr returned to the front, and saw Colonel Mattich, commanding the division to which the batteries were attached.

"Don't worry," said the colonel. "You will have plenty of warning before a retreat is ordered, and the ground between your batteries and the main road is not so bad as you think." At this the matter had to be left.

King Peter paid a visit in his car to No. 2 Battery and asked the men whether they were comfortable, and whether they would like to send letters home to England. It was a thoughtful enquiry, but His Majesty did not realise at the time that the postal service had completely broken down, and there was no way of getting the letters out of the country. During the next few days the guns were in action fairly constantly, and, whenever the enemy attempted to mass troops, the batteries succeeded in dispersing them. But, unfortunately, the ammunition was running low, and it was feared that the reserve supply had fallen into the hands of the enemy, as the Serbian officers in charge of the transport arrangements could give no account of it. The time was obviously drawing near when the guns would become useless through lack of ammunition.

This was the period when the daily bulletin issued by the Serbian Staff read, "Situation very serious."

The Austro-German forces were threatening to close the road of retreat into Montenegro, while the Bulgarians were threatening the road into Albania. A Bulgarian detachment was near Prilep threatening the line of communications to Monastir—the railhead of the only railway which was not in the hands of the enemy. In fact, Marshal Stepanovitch's army was in imminent danger of being completely surrounded and cut off.

When, on 12th November, the order to retreat was given, only one small segment of the enveloping circle remained open—to the south-west of Nisch, towards Prishtina—and the whole effort of the Serbians was now directed to keeping open this line of retreat. The batteries were ordered to proceed to Prishtina with a view to joining up eventually with the Anglo-French force, which was supposed to be coming up from the south to the rescue of Serbia. The only question was, could they ever get to Prishtina? The Third Army was sent to cover the defence of the only road of escape, but that they could resist the enemy's advance seemed very doubtful. The Second Army was in full flight along this road, and the British naval batteries were actually in the extreme rear of it and nearest to the enemy.

No. 3 Battery met with disaster at the very commencement of the retreat. As Lieutenant-Commander Kerr had foreseen, that swampy ground proved too much for them. The gun-carriages ran into deep mud, which covered the axles, and all the combined efforts of their crews and their oxen could not move them. So they had to be stripped and abandoned, only the transport and the remainder of the ammunition being saved. So only four of the original eight guns were now left. The other two batteries safely reached Prokuplie, and hurried on towards Kurshumlie, knowing that the flying moments were precious. No. 2 Battery had four men wounded just before the retreat commenced, which did not help to cheer them on their road.

They were the first to get under way, and trudged all through the night beside the weary oxen and the two guns, taking just twenty-seven hours to cover the thirty-three miles from the Morava River to Kurshumlie. The men of No. 3 Battery, minus their guns, were the next to pass through Prokuplie, and finally came No. 4 Battery, so far behind that Lieutenant-Commander Kerr had become more than anxious about them. They, too, had had their troubles, but they came up smiling, in spite of rain and slush and weary limbs.

But there was no time to pause at Kurshumlie, for the Austro-Germans were getting nearer every moment. Just a few hours for rest and food, and then the whole army had to push on towards Prishtina. The oxen attached to the guns were almost worn out, but even the dictates of humanity must give way before dire necessity, and the unfortunate brutes had to be goaded on. All through the night of 15th November the retreat continued along a road which led them over the mountains. It was bitterly cold, and the rain was incessant. A few of the Serbian soldiers, seeking to make better speed than was possible on the congested road, turned aside from it, and in the darkness walked over the edge of a precipice, horses, waggons, and men.

Next morning the batteries reached the Mdare Pass, whence they could see the snow-covered mountains of Montenegro away to the west. But their road lay to the south, and along it this great struggling crowd of soldiers, refugees, transport-waggons, oxen, horses, and guns made the best speed they could. At night they bivouacked in the open to snatch a few hours of sleep, but by half-past three in the morning they were on the road again—struggling on, footsore and weary, men, women, and children. The road grew easier after they were through the Mdare Pass, but the rain continued to pour down in torrents, occasionally varied by a blinding snow blizzard.

Napoleon's retreat from Moscow could have been no worse than this, for at every few yards along the roadside there were cattle, horses, and men dying of hunger and exhaustion. No one knows what was the toll in human life of that retreat through Serbia. We can only thank Heaven that the women and children were comparatively few, for most of them were left behind. Whatever fate awaited them, it could not be worse than that which overtook the refugees. Report has it that the Serbian women were well treated by the invaders; but, on the other hand, there were many ugly stories going round, and the minds of those soldiers who had left behind their mothers, wives, and sisters were filled with persistent forebodings.

So the bedraggled, rain-soaked crowd found its way to Prishtina, and the town soon became filled with a confused mass of dazed humanity, which knew not what to do to get food, or where to go to dry their soaking clothes. Fortunately, the batteries had food of their own, and could look out for themselves. But the question arose, what was to be done with the four remaining guns? The idea of taking them to Mitrovitza, to join the new Anglo-French Army coming up from Salonika, had become impossible, for the enemy had advanced too rapidly, and the new army showed no signs of making its appearance on the scene. One suggestion was to bury them somewhere accessible to the railway, but eventually it was decided that the batteries should be transferred to the Third Army under General Sturm, and that they should retreat with that army in the direction of Ipek, across the Montenegrin border.

On 22nd November they got under way. The congestion on the road was appalling, and an Austrian aeroplane took advantage of the situation to drop a few bombs, but fortunately they fell wide. The men of the navy, grateful for their rest at Prishtina, and taking, as usual, a cheery view of life and things in general, trudged on beside their four remaining guns. They were not sorry to be quit of Prishtina, for typhus had broken out there, and there were some stories going around of weapons being hidden in the Mohammedan mosques for use on the Christian population as soon as the army was out of the town. In fact, Prishtina was developing symptoms of unhealthiness.

At four o'clock in the afternoon they arrived at a swamp on the main road, and one of the guns of No. 2 Battery promptly got stuck, holding up all the traffic behind it for a long time. Men and oxen hauled away at it for dear life without producing the least impression; then more men and more oxen were requisitioned; then a motorcar was harnessed to the gun-carriage, and men, oxen, and motor-car did their damnedest for five solid hours, but that gun refused to budge. The men of the gun's crew and their Serbian soldiers were working up to their knees in water all this time, and it was freezing fairly hard. The rest of the cavalcade had managed to squeeze past the obstruction, so it was finally decided to destroy the breech-block, recoil-springs, and sights, and leave the old gun to its fate. The other gun belonging to No. 2 Battery had still to cross the swamp, and, though it was past nine o'clock at night, there was nothing for it but to make the attempt. The oxen from the first gun were transferred to the second, and an alternative route was tried.

All went swimmingly at the start, and the gun was hauled safely over the river, but the bank on the other side proved too much for it. It slid back gracefully into the mud, until the axles of the gun-carriage were lost to view, and the combined efforts of 80 oxen and 250 men failed to budge it. They laboured until after midnight, but the climax of misfortune came when the driver of the first pair of oxen slipped in the mud, and was trampled under the feet of the struggling beasts. Before he could be extricated the gun-limber passed over his legs and broke both of them. Fortunately two sick berth attendants were on the spot to render first aid.

So the second gun had also to be demolished, and now only two guns were left out of the original eight. The men lit a fire and sat round it until two o'clock waiting for No. 4 Battery to come up. When they arrived they were able to benefit by the experience of their unfortunate shipmates, and, by dint of a combined effort of the oxen and crews of the two batteries, they succeeded in getting the last two guns across the swamp. And so they continued their trek towards the mountains of Montenegro. Here are one or two extracts from the diary of one of the *trekkers*:

> Struck camp at 1 p.m. and started off through wooded hills—no people, no roads, no nothing, except wonderful scenery. A very cold wind struck up about sundown. Progress was very slow. Halted at 5.30 p.m., and got a bit of sleep in an ox-waggon.
>
> *Thursday, 25th November.*—Moved on at 2.30 a.m. Progress a little better. . . . Not a sign of cultivation, and very few inhabitants—only a few Albanian hovels. Passing through forests during the day; quantities of rifle ammunition on all sides, as well as Q.F. and field-gun stuff, all thrown aside to lighten the carts. For the moment we seem to have passed the region of dead

and dying beasts. Marched on until 8 p.m., when we made our bivouac, pitched tents, and settled down for the night.

Friday, 26th November.—Up at 8.30 a.m. Snowing hard, but no wind, and therefore not so cold. Mud, slush, and small rivulets to be encountered all the way, and a great deal of traffic. Mud sometimes 18 to 24 inches deep. Stopped at 8 p.m. in a snowy plain, where we pitched our tents. Two of our men adrift. Whistling them up until midnight, when they turned up, having lost their way in the dark. The men get one biscuit a day from the Serbian authorities, but luckily we still have some of our provisions left. Water is very difficult to get. What we find is chocolate-coloured and muddy, so we prefer eating snow.

It was on this day (26th November) that No, 4 Battery had its first disaster. One of its guns, while crossing a small stream, fell right through the bridge, which had not been built for a weight of that kind. For four hours they tried to extricate it, but found the task hopeless, so they stripped the gun and left it. Only one gun remained, and finally that also had to be destroyed, for the difficulties of transport went on increasing, until it became practically impossible to take the gun any farther.

The diary carries on the story of the travellers, toiling over the mountains all through the days, camping at night by the roadside.

Very hard frost during the night. My towel and valise frozen stiff.

On 29th November they drew near to Ipek, and here they found a recurrence of the old familiar sight—dead and dying oxen on all sides. Ipek was crammed with refugees, and everything was in a state of sublime confusion.

Dead horses and oxen all over the place, and the cold continues.

But the cold unfortunately did not continue.

A thaw has set in, and mud and slush, mingled with decomposing horses and oxen, compel us to pick our way carefully. Yesterday, going into Ipek, we found some nice firm stepping-stones across a brook; but today the thaw has melted the 'stones,' and we discovered them to be the half-submerged corpses of horses.

On 3rd December the journey began from Ipek to Scutari. The track lay over the mountains of Montenegro, where nothing larger than two-wheeled carts could hope to pass. So all the waggons were destroyed, and there was a general holocaust of vehicles, rangefinders, telescopes, and even clothing. The scene of destruction spread for miles round, for a whole army, as well as bands of civilian refugees, were about to take to the mountains. The men of the batteries started at two o'clock in the morning A petty officer and a leading seaman were too ill to walk, and had to ride in the two-wheeled carts, whose wheels were soon buried in mud nearly to their axles. Soon it came on to rain in torrents, and in the thick of the downpour they had to halt in order to stow their provisions and stores in the carts, as the things kept on falling off into the mud.

At two o'clock in the afternoon they decided to camp, because the congestion on the road had become so great that progress was almost impossible. In the twelve hours they had covered little more than six miles. All next day and the day after they remained in their camp, watching the procession of refugees and of all that was left of the Serbian army stream past them—a sorry spectacle of half-starved men in soaking rags, which fluttered in the wind, as though they clothed some decaying scarecrows rather than live human beings.

On 5th December, in the evening, the order came to destroy the two-wheeled carts and their contents, for these carts were the main cause of the congestion, and there was grave danger that the rations of the fugitive army—such as they were—might come to a full stop at any moment. In fact, every Serbian soldier on leaving Ipek had been given five biscuits to last him throughout the journey, and already they had been three days *en route*. Moreover, there were rumours that parties of Albanians, instigated by Austrian leaders, were contemplating an attack on this miserable remnant of an army.

The men of the batteries were not yet reduced to such straits as the Serbian soldiers in the matter of food, because they had brought with them the remainder of a store which had been originally provided by the Admiralty. By means of careful management it was hoped to eke out this scanty store until the men reached Scutari. If, perchance, any of the Serbian soldiers, with their miserable biscuits, saw our men sharing out their few ounces of bully beef, they very probably made some kind of exclamation of which the nearest English equivalent would be "food hogs," but it was manifestly impossible to share out such meagre provisions with the whole Serbian Army, so the charge had to be tacitly ignored. Just beyond Ipek, however, a fresh complication arose.

A Serbian officer, who had been closely associated with Lieutenant-Commander Kerr and the batteries, introduced a party of five women and two children into the family circle. Generous hospitality is one of the oldest traditions of the navy, but it is a tradition which occasionally has its inconvenient side. Fortunately Lieutenant-Commander Kerr had supplemented the official stores by the private purchase of some "ward-room stores," including cakes and some bottles of *rakia* (a drink made from the juice of plums). So he made a gallant effort to maintain the navy's reputation for hospitality, but the diary records that:

> The Serbian womenfolk are not backward in asking for what they want, and expect us to provide them with jam, cakes, and *rakia ad lib.*

The food problem was increased when the order came to destroy all the carts, for the two horses were required to carry the two sick men, and so there was nothing for it but for each man to carry his food on his back, in addition to his kit. Under these circumstances the sacred rites of hospitality are apt to become a trifle irksome. Moreover, the new recruits to the party required other privileges. The diary tells us:

> The women and children bought up all the room round the camp-fire, so I made another one and slept by it, but was somewhat disturbed during the night by a colt, which kept on breaking away and walking over me.

They had, of course, been obliged to leave all tents behind them, as there were no means of transport.

At last they came to the pass through the mountain summits, and here they found a vast concourse of fugitives blocking the trail.

> We fought our way through a scene of panic and disorder, occasioned by a few mountain tribesmen firing on the congested multitude from behind rocks. Horses and oxen were dropping from fatigue on all sides, and many people were crushed to death. Eventually we slipped through the entrance of the pass with all our horses and men, and continued marching through a rocky defile until seven o'clock. It had been snowing for some time past, and the snow lay so thick that progress became difficult. We rested from seven till eight, and then we trudged on

over the Zleb Pass until midnight, when we made a bit of fire in the snow and took another hour's rest. After that we tramped on through the rocks and snow until, at seven in the morning, we arrived at Rosarj, the worst part of the journey over.

They arrived at Andreovitza on 10th December, but by that time their provisions were running very low, and the rations had to be very strictly limited. The diet was tinned mutton and ship's biscuit. The mountain tribes had shown themselves extremely unfriendly all the way, and very little in the nature of food could be bought from them. Occasionally a few rotten potatoes, and occasionally some *rakia*, and for these they extorted such prices as would have made Shylock blush for shame. The diarist has some pathetic little touches on the subject of food. Here is a note of his reflections, as he sat by the camp-fire near Andreovitza.

Most glorious scenery from our bivouac—a wide, swift-running river flowing between the high mountains on each side of us. It is a regular fairyland at night, with all the camp fires on the hills burning, but few of us are in the mood to appreciate feasts of the eye, being more inclined for feasts of another description.

The biscuit had come to an end, and bread was unobtainable locally, but a supply was sent from Podgoritza by motor-lorry to the Serbian Army, and the batteries managed to secure two maize loaves for the whole party—the first taste of bread since leaving Prishtina. Then the tinned meat began to run low, and we come to this pathetic entry:

A beastly evening and night, raining hard, and the men a bit down on their luck. We issued the last ration of tinned mutton.

On 13th December they had a breakfast consisting of some tea and the biscuit crumbs scraped from their pockets, but later in the day they had the good fortune to secure two more maize loaves, bought at a village for twenty-four francs in hard cash, for no one would look at notes. At Podgoritza they found the usual scene of dire confusion, and rain coming down in sheets. After a hard struggle they managed to get a soup ration and a little maize bread. The rain continued all through the night, which they spent in a field without any cover. The next day was one long chase to find something to eat, and eventually they succeeded in getting a little bread from the headquarters of the Third Army; but no one parted readily with food of any kind, for all were in the same extreme of necessity. The next quest was for a roof to cover their heads and a fire to dry their clothes, and they eventually succeeded in finding a *café*, where they were allowed to spend the night.

At last, after many disappointments, they secured a passage in two motor-lorries to Plavnitza, on the borders of the lake of Scutari. Here, after another long wait, they went aboard a schooner driven by a petrol engine, which landed them at the town of Scutari about six o'clock in the evening of 15th December. Here were Admiral Troubridge and the officers of the Adriatic Mission—a British mission sent to co-operate with the Italian Government in providing the necessaries of life to the soldiers and refugees from Serbia—and, needless to say, the admiral was much relieved in his mind when he saw the men of the batteries safely arrived. Here, too, were tidings at last from the outside world—news of the war, news from dear old England. But the best news of all was that the admiral's coxswain had a good square meal ready for them, and when they heard that, everything else paled into insignificance.

The admiral, with his party, had crossed the Serbian border by another route, *via* Prizrend, Berbetz, and Sika to Scutari. It was a six days' march through the mountains; the cold was intense, and snow fell at frequent intervals. A party of French aviators who followed immediately behind the admiral's party had twenty men incapacitated by frost-bite, and lost many of their horses, which walked over the precipices in the blinding snow. Behind them came the members of the Serbian Headquarters Staff, who lost most of their baggage in the same way. But the tail end of the procession had the worst time of all, for they were continually harassed by Albanian tribesmen, who sniped at them from behind the rocks, and, moreover, they had the advancing Bulgarians hard on their heels.

It was noticeable that the only fugitives to meet with friendly treatment from the warlike tribes in the Albanian mountains were the admiral and his party. The explanation of this distinction was afforded when the admiral reached Scutari, and it is certainly a striking tribute to British prestige. The Mufti of Scutari called on Rear-Admiral Troubridge as soon as he arrived and offered him the hospitality of the town.

"I knew the precise moment of your departure from Prisrend, and I knew that you and those with you were unarmed, and that no Serbian soldiers were guarding you. I am proud—all Albania is proud—to think that your great country showed this confidence in us, and I want you to know that throughout your journey a thousand unseen eyes watched you as you walked, a thousand unseen eyes watched you as you slept, and no harm could possibly have come to you."

The sequel to the story of the great retreat concerns the activities of Admiral Troubridge and the officers of the Adriatic Mission at the little port of Medua di Giovanni, where a stupendous effort was made to import sufficient food for the refugees, and to organise its distribution. The food ships, after unloading, took on board as many as possible of the refugees, and in the meantime the Serbian army made good their retreat to Durazzo, whence they embarked for Salonika to continue the great struggle against the invaders. But of what went on at Medua an excellent account has already been written by Lieutenant E. Hilton Young, R.N.V.R., M.P.,[2] and it is sufficient for me to add that, when the Austrians poured into Albania and Medua had to be evacuated, the last persons to leave for Brindisi were Admiral Troubridge and his staff.

---

2. In the *Cornhill Review* for June 1916.

THE FIRST KITE BALLOON SHIP

CHAPTER 19

1. H.M.S. "Manica" at Gallipoli

Early in October 1914 the Royal Naval Division at Antwerp sent in a demand for observation balloons to direct our artillery. For the moment the Admiralty was completely nonplussed, until someone thought of the captive balloons which were used in the South African War. They had been turned over to the Royal Naval Air Service—a few old spherical balloons, two hand-power winches, another winch with a petrol engine, and some cable. These were got together, a Naval Balloon Section was mobilised, and they were standing by, ready to cross the Channel, when news came through that Antwerp had fallen.

About a week later the British monitors, bombarding the Belgian coast, began to complain that the sand-dunes, which lay between themselves and the enemy, made accurate firing very difficult, and the late Rear-Admiral Hood asked that captive balloons should be sent over. So on 14th October, 1914, the Naval Balloon Section arrived at Dunkirk, and next day one of the balloons was in readiness to make an ascent. The section found plenty of problems confronting it as time went on. The visibility was bad as a rule, and worse still was the roundabout method of communicating with the fleet of monitors—by telephone to the Belgian Headquarters, thence by messenger to a field wireless station, and thence by wireless to the fleet. Later on an improvement was made, and by means of a wireless set in a motorcar more direct communication was established, both with the fleet and with the French artillery.

But the main trouble was the balloon itself. A spherical balloon does not take kindly to captivity; it plunges, and pirouettes, and turns and twists, and longs to break away from its thraldom and to chase the drifting clouds into realms unknown. Even in a light wind it never seems really happy, and in a heavy wind it gets beyond the pale of parliamentary language.

One day, our observers noticed a queer-looking object in the air in the direction of the village of Slype, and wondered what it was. What they saw was a Drachen—not at all like the dragon which Siegfried slays in the opera at Covent Garden, but most unromantically like a big sausage. They made enquiries about it, and were told by some French officers that something of the kind had been tried by the French Army at their peace-time manoeuvres, but it happened to be a breathless day in summer, and the advantage of the Drachen over the spherical balloon was not very palpable.

The Belgians also knew about the Drachen; in fact, they had a baby Drachen of their own, which had been presented to them by the Germans, when, in a thoughtless moment, Germany had forgotten that the treaty undertaking to safeguard Belgium's neutrality might turn out some day to be merely a scrap of paper. When a Belgian balloon section appeared on the scene with their baby Drachen, our naval airmen became keenly interested in the creature. They had been daily watching the performances of its father at Slype; they had noticed how much higher he could ascend on his cable than a spherical balloon, how steadily he behaved in a still breeze, and, above all, how accurate were the observations he made and transmitted to the German artillery. So they crowded round the baby Drachen like a lot of matrons invited to a tea-fight where the firstborn is on show.

They examined its nose, and declared that it was the image of its father; they examined its tail, and said that it took after its mother; they examined its stabilisers and came to the conclusion that it really favoured both its parents. They photographed it, took drawings of it, talked about it from morning till night, and then wrote home about it, and said that they would never be happy until they had a Drachen all their very own.

So a firm of balloon manufacturers was instructed to make a baby Drachen by way of experiment; but, as the work was quite new to them, they had to proceed very cautiously. Unfortunately, the tide of war could not wait for them. The naval bombardment of the Dardanelles forts in February 1915 had disclosed the fact that the Turks had concealed their batteries on the peninsula very cleverly, and that aeroplanes and seaplanes had their limitations as directors of gunfire. Apart from troubles with their engines, there was always the self-evident axiom that an observer moving rapidly through the air cannot spot as accurately as an observer sitting in the basket of a stationary balloon. The Dardanelles followed the examples of Antwerp and Dunkirk, and sent out S.O.S. signals for observation balloons, urging that they should be despatched from England at once, so as to arrive in time for the landing on the Gallipoli peninsula.

When this message came through on 8th March 1915, the R.N.A.S. had got as far as the establishment of a kite-balloon division with a training centre at Roehampton, where the owner of Upper Grove House had generously placed his house and grounds at the disposal of the Admiralty. A nucleus of officers and men trained in airship work had been collected, and were busily imparting their knowledge to the new recruits. But there were no kite-balloons, no winches, no cables, no telephones, when the order was received to proceed at once to Lemnos with a kite-balloon section fully equipped.

Now it was quite useless for them to say, "We are not ready," because that is one of the things that no one in the navy is ever allowed to say, and because the answer is obvious—"Then you have jolly well got to be ready." The only thing that could possibly be said in the circumstances was, "Aye, aye, sir; we'll carry on at once, and push off at the earliest possible moment," and when that is said in a cheerful tone of voice by a much-harassed commanding officer, it goes far to persuade the Admiralty that almost anything, short of a miracle, will be accomplished by him.

The first thing to do was to get hold of a kite balloon. Luckily the French had been making some, so an officer was packed off to Paris, who could talk French, and had a winning smile. He came back in a very short time and announced that he had borrowed not only a kite-balloon, but also a winch for its cable, and spoke as eloquently as circumstances would permit about French generosity and French hospitality. The next problem required some careful thought. According to all established precedents, it required a large open space like Salisbury Plain or Richmond Park to negotiate a balloon ascent, and how were they to find such a space on the Gallipoli Peninsula, seeing that the whole of it was in the hands of the enemy? Only one possible solution presented itself—the balloon must be flown from a ship.

They found the ship—it was an old tramp unloading manure from Australia, and was called the *Manica*—and they proceeded to convert it to their needs, by lifting up a long sloping deck from forecastle to waist, fixing a dynamo to drive a hydrogen compressor, installing their winch and connecting it with the main engines, building a wireless telegraphy house, building quarters for officers and men, and generally adapting the fittings and appointments to what they conceived to be the requirements of a kite-balloon ship. Then they collected the necessary personnel and stores, and in an incredibly short space of time—within seventeen days of receiving the order from Gallipoli—they sailed from England.

The *Manica* arrived at Lemnos on 16th April 1915, and a few days later she was in the thick of it. During the next three weeks her observers spotted for various ships of the squadron, including the *Triumph*, *Lord Nelson*, and *Prince George*, but latterly they devoted most of their time to the *Queen Elizabeth*. On 19th April a Turkish camp was shelled under their direction, and thrown into confusion; on 24th April the Gaba Tepe position was shelled and the Turkish barracks destroyed.

On 27th April they had a red-letter day. The observers sitting up aloft in their basket saw something of more than usual interest on the other side of the peninsula, so one of them put his mouth to the telephone and told the fellows in the *Manica* about it. "There's a nice fat Turkish transport in the Straits," he said; "she is lying in Square 215 W. Quite a nice plump bird. Seven thousand tons at least."

The fellow at the other end of the wire told the joke to a signalman, who repeated it by visual signalling to the *Queen Elizabeth*. Now, of course, they could not see the transport from the *Queen Elizabeth*, because there was a peninsula in between, but they looked at their map and found the square marked 215 W, and then, just to make sure of things, they asked for a bearing by the compass. The observers in the basket gave them the bearing, and the *Queen Elizabeth* trained one of her guns accordingly and fired. The thing she fired weighed about as much as twelve fat men put together, and she sent it clean over the peninsula to a distance of about eleven miles. It was a comparatively short range for her; if the distance had been twenty miles, she would not have been disconcerted.

The back-chat comedian in the basket watched the fall of the shell, and remarked tritely down the telephone, "A hundred up; deflection five right." This, being interpreted, means, "Increase your range by a hundred yards, and turn your gun five points to the right." The comment was repeated by the back-chat comedian in the *K.B.* Ship to the signalman, who repeated it to the Q.E., who received it just thirty seconds after they had fired the shot. They made the corrections and fired again.

"Fifty down," said the back-chat comedian in the basket, and the joke was duly passed along the line. Then the Q.E. tried a third time, and waited expectantly to know the result. There was a short pause before the voice of the comedian in the basket came down the telephone wire.

"Got her," he said laconically. "She's sinking by the head."

The joke was so good that, as the signalman repeated it to the Q.E., the whole fleet took it up and began to roll from side to side with laughter.

Here are a few extracts from the official record of the *Manica's* achievements during the next fortnight.

28th April.—Two field batteries silenced; several guns destroyed.

30th April.—*Chanak* shelled; burned for two hours.

2nd May.—Battery of 8-inch guns shelled; three direct hits.

8th May.—Four batteries silenced.

12th May.—House, reported to be Turkish Headquarters, destroyed.

And so the story goes on, each day showing some record of damage to the enemy's defences. It must be borne in mind that two months previously there was not a single kite-balloon in England, that no one had ever attempted before to fly a kite-balloon from a ship, that kite-balloon, ship, stores, equipment, officers, and men had all been scraped together in England within the space of seventeen days, that the whole of the Kite-balloon Division was in an embryonic state, and above all, that they were always face to face with a preconceived notion that aeroplanes and seaplanes had rendered obsolete all lighter-than-aircraft. This prejudice was not altogether unreasonable in view of the comparative failure of the Zeppelin as a weapon of war, but what it did not recognise was that there are certain functions which can only be discharged satisfactorily by means of some craft that can remain stationary in the air. The experiences of the *Manica* at Gallipoli removed the prejudice for ever.

After a while the Turks began to take a violent dislike to our kite-balloon. They tried attacking it and the *Manica* with bomb-dropping aeroplanes, but our anti-aircraft guns kept up a merry tattoo, and "Percy" got frightened. Then they decided to signify their disapproval in a dignified but passive kind of way. As soon as the balloon went up, all the Turkish ships near *Chanak* got under way, quietly and unostentatiously, and disappeared up the Dardanelles, doubtless remembering the fate of the fat transport which had dallied too long in the danger zone. At the same time the Turkish batteries suddenly relapsed into silence, realising that a well-concealed battery can only be detected by the flashes of the guns. So the ascent of the kite-balloon transformed a noisy pandemonium into a peaceful calm.

After the evacuation of Gallipoli the *Manica* went to East Africa to do some more useful work. The *Canning* took a kite-balloon section to Salonika, whence they proceeded to the Doiran front to cooperate with the army. Another section was sent to Mesopotamia, and others to various points along the Western front. The *Arctic*, a specially fitted shallow barge, operated amongst the shoals off the Belgian coast, rendering valuable aid to the work of the monitors. In fact, the prestige of the kite balloon was firmly established for the purpose of directing gun-fire; enthusiastic converts were proclaiming its virtues, and the ranks of the sceptics were being diminished daily.

Among the enthusiasts was Vice-Admiral De Robeck, who had witnessed the exploits of the *Manica* at Gallipoli. In an official report, which had come to his notice, he had come across these words:

> I have observed that fish can be very clearly seen under water from the balloon; if opportunity arises, I intend to apply for a submarine to be detailed for trial of visibility.

Herein began the first chapter in the genesis of the naval kite-balloon, as distinct from the land kite-balloon. The story of its evolution, of the long series of experiments by means of which a balloon has been designed capable of withstanding so great a force of wind that it can be towed by a fast-steaming vessel against a moderate gale, cannot yet be told in detail. Suffice it to say that the naval kite-balloon is now an accomplished fact, and that the work which it is performing with our fleet has brought about its recognition as an essential adjunct to naval patrol vessels.

Not many weeks after the naval kite-balloon came into being a British destroyer found itself in a thick fog, and was very doubtful as to its bearings. Fortunately it had a kite-balloon attached to it, and the observers in the balloon telephoned down to the bridge the compass bearings of various headlands, which they could see quite plainly over the top of the fog. Here was a new function discovered for the kite-balloon. Others may crop up in course of time. With a range of vision extending in ordinary weather to a distance of sixty-three miles, it is surprising what a vast superiority one holds over the ordinary mortal, who crawls about on the face of the earth or waters. All one needs is a good pair of eyes, and a course of training in the science of observation, to make oneself into a very valuable aid to the work of the navy. The telephone will do the rest.

CHAPTER 20

2. H.M.S. "Manica" in East Africa

After her exploits at Gallipoli the *Manica* went home to refit, and it was not until the 10th March 1916 that she left Birkenhead in search of fresh laurels. A month later she was off the island of Zanzibar, where an air station had been established to assist the operations in East Africa. Here the *Manica* spent the first two or three weeks in carrying out balloon evolutions, and rectifying minor defects in the balloon's envelope and telephone equipment. Next came a period of that wearisome routine, all too well known to the Navy in war-time, which has been inadequately designated by the words "patrol duty."

The expression may be apt enough, from the official point of view, as indicating that the ship turns herself into a peregrinating policeman, but it fails altogether to convey any idea of the boring monotony of the job. In home waters there is always the interesting possibility of bumping a mine, or being hit by a torpedo, to lend variety and charm to the routine, but off the coast of East Africa there are none of these attractions; the only possible variation to a dreary prospect is the sight of an Arab dhow trying to smuggle supplies across from Arabia for the use of the enemy. There is also the certainty that the time must come when the ship must put into harbour to coal, and, though coaling ship in the humid tropics is not Elysium, the anticipation of such a break even as this helps to make life tolerable.

In May the *Manica* added to her usefulness by shipping a seaplane as a kind of auxiliary to the kite-balloon. The first machine, however, proved to be a failure, and had to be exchanged for a second one, which in turn developed symptoms of an unhealthy constitution, such as a tendency to burst its petrol-pipe, and to suffer other parts of its complicated organism to refuse duty at inopportune moments. A board of aeroplane doctors would probably have relegated it to C.3, but, as there are no aeroplanes growing on the palm-trees in Zanzibar, it had to be passed as A.1 and told to carry on.

On 7th July, while flying over Tanga, it was hit by gunfire, had its pilot wounded, and its floats badly damaged. The damage to the floats worried the pilot more than his wound, because it left him in a state of disagreeable uncertainty as to whether he could come down on the water without foundering. At a height of some 3,000 feet the observer volunteered to climb down the rigging and examine the floats, and performed this little job as cheerfully as though he had been a steeplejack all his life. The floats were badly punctured; but, nevertheless, when the machine came down, the *Manica* managed to hoist it in before it capsized altogether.

On this same day (7th June 1916) our military forces, which had landed at Manza Bay under cover of the guns of the *Talbot* and *Severn*, occupied Tanga, after encountering but slight opposition from enemy patrols. The place had been the scene of a bad disaster in the early stages of the campaign, and consequently its occupation was not without dramatic interest. The enemy made no real attempt to defend the town, but cleared out of it before our troops had time to reach it. The *Vengeance* (flagship) sent her band ashore to play the National Anthem when the Union Jack was hoisted over the governor's house, and, except for the embarrassing attentions of a few persistent snipers, all was as merry as a marriage bell. So the first of the seaport towns of German East Africa fell into our hands.

The next on the list was Pangani, a few miles farther south. Here it was a race between navy and army to see who could get into the town first. As soon as the navy arrived on the scene the Germans hoisted a white flag, whereat a landing party was sent in to take possession, and they made a dead heat of it with the advance guard of the army, which had marched overland. That was on 23rd July. Nine days later the two services again combined in an attack on Sadani, the third town on the list, which also was secured after overcoming a very feeble opposition.

I pass over these events rapidly because they involved no serious fighting, and consequently the work of the observers in the *Manica's* balloon was little more than that of spectators in the gallery watching the smooth progress of the drama. It may, however, be in place here to explain briefly the position of the campaign at this stage, prefacing my explanation with a warning that no conscientious study of maps will give any true idea of what was happening.

When we were following the progress of the war in France and Flanders we used to look at the maps, which our newspapers obligingly published, and we saw a thick black line that approximately marked the position of the front. But in East Africa there was no clearly defined line of front. Scattered detachments of the enemy's forces were here, there, and everywhere, and were continually being shifted to fresh positions as the allied forces closed in on them. On the map the positions occupied by the enemy would appear to be quite haphazard, because the map does not reveal one of the most important factors in determining the conduct of the campaign—the African bush. Those who know only the sylvan glades of England, or the forests of France, can form no adequate idea of what this bush is like.

An almost impenetrable mass of vegetation extending for hundreds of square miles; an undergrowth with thorns three inches long and curved like scimitars; overhead a foliage so thick that the glare of the tropical sun is reduced to a dim religious light; a hot, reeking atmosphere filled with the droning of countless myriads of insects, which give no peace to the rash intruder who tries to force his way through this rampart of Nature's contriving. On such ground as this the soldier finds that all he has learnt about the theory of warfare, about lines of communication, salients, and *points d'appui*, must be relegated to the scrap-heap.

To get at the enemy he can approach only along those paths where the hand of man has made some progress in the struggle with Nature, and, instead of exercising his mind upon such refinements of modern warfare as Lewis guns, trench mortars, and hand grenades, he must devote his attention to the primitive needs of an army—how to keep them supplied with food and water, and how to mitigate the ravages of malaria and the tsetse-fly.

By June 1916 the German forces had been completely cleared out of British East Africa, had been driven out of Aruscha by a detachment under the command of the South African General, Van Deventer, and thence had been hustled southwards as far as Kondoa Irangi. Another German force had been chased from the range of hills on the east side of the Ruvu Valley down as far as the Pangani River. But all the coast towns—Tanga, Pangani, Sadani, Bagamoyo, and Dar-es-Salaam—remained in the enemy's hands, and, though the blockade of the coast carried out by the Navy prevented these seaport towns from receiving any supplies of food or munitions, there was still a danger that German troops in them might strike westwards, and make flank attacks upon the allied forces working southwards. In these circumstances, it was decided that the towns on the coast must be wrested from the enemy, and the navy was called upon to assist in the task.

In the capture of the first three of these seaport towns—Tanga, Pangani, and Sadani—I have already shown that we had virtually a walkover, in which the navy and the army joined hands. It is not until we come to the story of the capture of Bagamoyo, which followed a fortnight after that of Sadani, that we find the navy acting alone, and the Germans putting up some kind of a fight. On 13th August, Lieut.-Colonel Price, who was in command of the troops at Sadani, made the following wireless signal to Rear-Admiral Charlton:

> Latest intelligence points to Bagamoyo being evacuated. If it is still held, only a small force can be there—about ten whites and forty Askaris. The general officer commanding asks if navy will take and occupy the town, as its occupation is essential at the earliest possible moment. All my available forces are engaged in Mandera operations, but when these are completed they could relieve the navy (at Bagamoyo). Please inform me if you are willing.

The admiral's reply was brief and to the point:

> Inform general officer commanding that this will be arranged.

He added that he would like to have the assistance of the Marines of H.M.S. *Talbot*, who had been left ashore at Sadani to supplement the military forces, and of a detachment of Zanzibar Rifles, if any could be spared. The intelligence officers were somewhat out in their estimate of the strength of the Bagamoyo garrison, for, as it turned out, the enemy was numerically stronger than our landing party, having a total force of sixty whites, and between 350 and 400 Askaris (including a small detachment at Mtoni Ferry, a short distance inland from the town). The number of white German troops sounds small, as indeed it was, but it must not be imagined that the Askaris were a negligible factor.

There is often a tendency to assume that in a composite force of this character it is only the white men who really count; such an assumption would be very dangerous where Askaris are concerned, for, in spite of certain limitations, they are among the finest soldiers to be found anywhere outside the continent of Europe. To give an idea of their fighting qualities I cannot do better than to quote the tribute paid to them by Lieutenant-Commander Whittall, R.N. in his book, *With Botha and Smuts in Africa*.[1]

In common with all who know him I have a great respect and admiration for the native soldier; whether he be King's African Rifleman, or German Askari, he is as good a fighting man as you would ask to have beside you in a tight corner, or as worthy an enemy as the veriest fire-eater could desire as an opponent. He is first and last a soldier. He comes of a stock whose business has been fighting for many generations, and he is thus rich in warlike traditions. Full of courage, he is as faithful as a dog to his officers, if these know how to handle him and humour his prejudices. Watch him on the march, and you will see him, when he halts for even a short interval, employing his leisure in cleaning his rifle, until it is speckless without and within—no matter when and where, you will never find the native soldier with a dirty rifle.

He has got it deep down in his child-like mind that his rifle is his only friend, to be cherished and tended against the time that it win be all that stands between him and sudden death. He cannot shoot as a rule, and when you are opposed to him the safest place is usually in the firing-line. With infinite trouble you may make a third-class shot of him in about a year, but that is the best you can expect. But, if he is not much of a shot, he is a magnificent bayonet fighter, as might be expected when it is remembered that he is almost born with a spear in his hand. Let him once get to close quarters with the ' white arm,' and he will give the best European troops as merry a scrimmage as they could want—and it will not be more than even money on the result. . . . Like all native troops he requires understanding, and thinking for, all the time, but once you have got his confidence he is yours to lead to the nethermost pit if need be.

It may be regarded as a piece of good fortune for us that in East Africa the Germans did not know how to handle the Askari, and consequently did not inculcate in him that spirit of fidelity, which would have made him face the horrors of the nethermost pit rather than abandon his masters. The wholesale desertions, by which the German forces were being constantly reduced, afford evidence enough of the inability of the German officer to gain the unquestioning confidence

---

1. *With Botha and Smuts in Africa* by W. Whittall is also published by Leonaur.

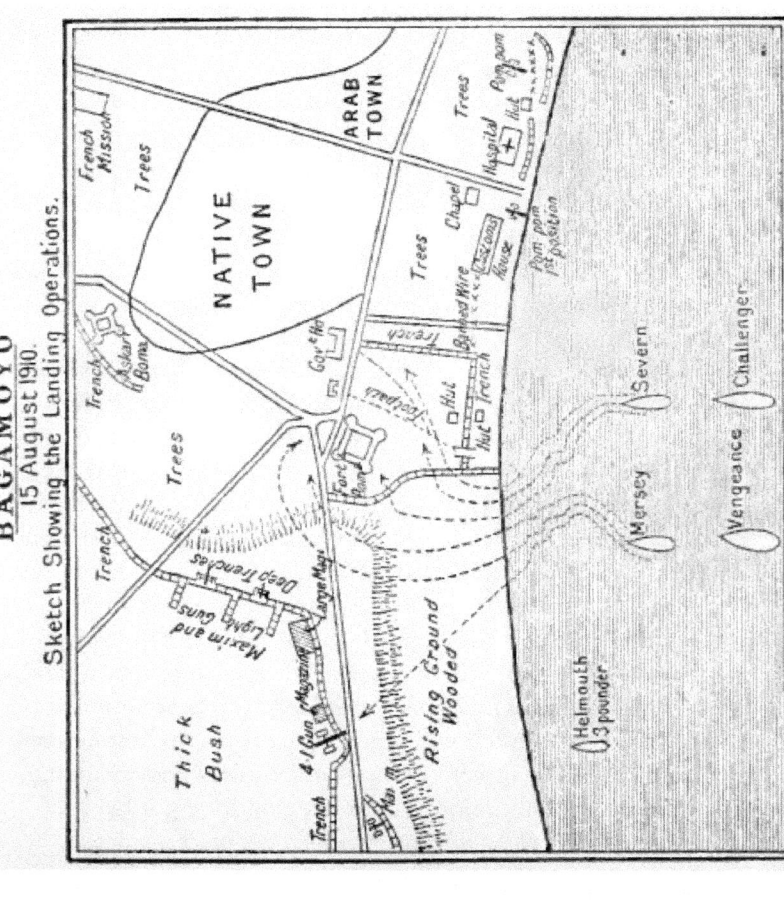

of the native soldier, and in this there is nothing surprising to those who know the German officer. For there are two kinds of military discipline— that born of the fear of punishment, and that born of a personal respect, amounting almost to affection. The German knows only the former kind, which is good enough in times of normal prosperity, but fails lamentably when adversity comes upon him who seeks to rule with a rod of iron.

It was half-past three on the morning of 15th August 1916 when the *Vengeance, Challenger, Mersey, Severn, Manica,* and the armed tug *Helmuth,* dropped anchor off Bagamoyo, and an hour later he landing party was making towards the shore. Owing to the bright moonlight it was useless to expect that the attack would be a complete surprise to the enemy, but we managed by a simple device to deceive him as to the exact spot where we intended to land. The boats, having proceeded on a straight course towards the trenches in front of the governor's house, suddenly turned six points to port, and then steered a zigzag course, partly to keep up the deception, and partly to baffle the enemy's range-finders. The result of this manoeuvre was that the Germans had the greater part of their force in the wrong place, and our landing was effected with very little difficulty.

At the spot where the boats ran on to the beach a thick belt of trees clothes the sloping ground almost to the water's edge. Immediately above it the Germans had emplaced a 4.1 inch gun, which had been taken out of the *Königsberg*, and had been dragged by *coolies* first to Tanga and then to Bagamoyo; but it stood about ten yards back from the top of the slope, and consequently could not be depressed sufficiently to bear on our landing-party. It was, however, engaging the *Mersey* and *Severn*, while machine-guns, rifles, and a pom-pom on the starboard side of the boats were keeping up a steady fire. But the crew of the 4.1 soon found that the flashes of their gun made them unduly conspicuous. The *Helmuth*, one of the steam barges, and a picket-boat, had each a three-pounder mounted in the bows, with which they let drive at the 4.1 at a range of about 500 yards, until the German gunners could stand it no longer.

As soon as our men had landed. Sub.-Lieutenant Manning was sent in charge of a machine-gun section to rush the hill and capture the 4.1. This he did very skilfully, taking cover as soon as he reached the top of the rise, and peppering the Germans relentlessly, until they abandoned their gun and took to their heels. In addition to the gun, over 80 rounds of ammunition were found in the magazine near by, and a few days later both gun and ammunition were shipped to Zanzibar, where they were on view to admiring crowds of natives.[2]

At the commencement of the bombardment the kite-balloon and the seaplane had been sent up by the *Manica* to spot for the guns of the bombarding ships. Unfortunately, the seaplane started engine trouble almost immediately, and was forced to come down, but the kite-balloon continued to do useful work at a time when accurate spotting was much needed, for the thick vegetation on shore made it impossible for the gunners to see their objectives. About six o'clock there arrived a seaplane belonging to the *Himalaya*. This ship was then just leaving Zanzibar to join in the bombardment of Bagamoyo, but her seaplane did not wait to be carried across the twenty odd miles between the island and the mainland. Immediately on receiving the admiral's signal it flew over to Bagamoyo, piloted by Flight-Lieutenant E. R. Moon, whose subsequent adventures in the Rufigi Delta have been recorded in another chapter. On his arrival he immediately started to drop bombs on the enemy's trenches, and, when all his bombs had been discharged, he supplemented the efforts of the kite-balloon in controlling the fire from the ships.

At 6-30 a.m. the observers in the kite-balloon reported that the enemy was abandoning his trenches, and falling back towards the French Mission behind the native town. The same report was made by the seaplane's wireless set, and by a portable wireless set which the landing party had taken ashore with them. Now the whole of the mission buildings were hidden from the view of our gunners by the dense foliage of the trees behind the native town, and consequently there was considerable risk that, if we continued to fire on the retreating enemy, we might hit some of these buildings. They are fairly extensive (Bagamoyo being the headquarters of the mission) and include a cathedral, solidly built of stone, dwelling-houses, and workshops where the natives receive a technical education, for the French Mission is essentially practical, and provides courses of instruction in carpentry, smithy work, shoe-making, and other industries. From all points of view it was very desirable to avoid doing serious damage to an establishment of this kind, but at the same time it was out of the question that the enemy should be allowed to get away scot free.

It afterwards transpired that the German commandant had foreseen the dilemma which would confront our gunners if his troops moved

---

2. In the autumn of 1918 this gun was exhibited in the Mall near the north door of the Admiralty.

back towards the mission, and had deliberately planned his retreat accordingly. The circumstances are related in some detail by the Vicar Apostolic François Xavier Vögt, who is a Frenchman by birth, but had been a naturalised German for the past ten years. As soon as he saw the troops approaching along the road which skirts the Mission, he went up to Captain von Bock and pointed out to him that the cathedral and other mission buildings were likely to become endangered. One can picture the scene—the priest, as calm and dignified as his natural nervousness at the sound of roaring guns and shrieking shells would allow him to be, and the young Prussian officer, immaculately clad in white ducks, but with a hot and dusty face beneath his white *topee*, and showing very plainly that he was not in the best of tempers. His reply to Father Vögt was typical of the breed. "I do not need to ask the bishop where to place my men."

Father Vögt complains that the captain said this in a loud voice before a throng of people, as though to show that he was not afraid to snub a priest, nor anyone else who should dare to interfere with him! Apparently, however, the priest was not the man to be snubbed so easily, for he persisted in pressing his point, observing that he had never heard that Prussian officers were in the habit of taking shelter beneath the walls of sacred buildings during an action. Whereat Captain von Bock condescended to argue the case in a lower key, quoting the Geneva Convention, which, he said, allowed combatants to approach within a hundred metres of the mission walls. Father Vögt was not sufficiently familiar with the terms of the Convention to dispute the matter any further, and so withdrew to his own precincts.

The kite-balloon and the seaplane did their best to keep the shells off the mission, but there were four or five ships firing simultaneously, and it was quite impossible to maintain an accurate check upon every gun. It speaks well for the efficiency of the spotting that only one direct hit was made on a mission building—unfortunately by a 12-inch shell on the cathedral—while the splinters, although they played havoc with the stained-glass windows, and caused some damage to the baptistery, did practically no harm to the main structure. More important is the fortunate fact that, although the cathedral was packed with people, not one of them was injured. The vicar, however, ascribes this deliverance to another agency than that of the kite-balloon and seaplane. "When one thinks," he says, "of the vast number of people who were assembled here, their immunity can only be explained by a special protection of the good God." Without any derogation of the work of the observers, we may heartily subscribe to these sentiments.

We are fortunate in having a description by Father Vögt's own pen of that scene in the cathedral during the early hours of the morning of 15th August 1916. With the first streak of dawn the thunder of the guns began, and gradually the shells, following the line of the Germans' retreat, began to fall nearer and nearer to the mission. Father Vögt had hurriedly thrown on his robes and taken his stand at the confessional. "The church trembled," he says, "and I trembled too; and I think that every one confessed well." Such delightfully human touches, all too rare in these sinister days, serve to remind us that even war is a very human affair when you come to close quarters with it.

By six o'clock the sun was well up, and the vicar gave orders that the *Angelus* should be rung. What a strange congregation was that which thronged into the cathedral! Swahilis, Indians, Arabs; men, women, and children; clad in every description of garb, from the white duck suit of the *babu* clerk to the simple loin-cloth of the humble peasant. Some came barefooted, others wore sandals, and others wooden clogs; some of the women wore frilled cotton trousers, others encased their legs, body, and shoulders in the multiple folds of the cotton *sari*; some were clad in white, others sported the most startling colours, and made a lavish display of cheap necklaces and bangles.

The Arab women for the most part wore either veils or black masks over their faces, but the Swahili women openly flaunted the beauties of their features, adorned with pendants as large as table-napkin rings, hanging from their ears and noses. Some were bare-headed, their back hair well greased with cocoanut oil, others wore white or coloured turbans, and others made the all-sufficing sari provide a headgear as well as a skirt and blouse. Such was the motley crowd that trooped into the cathedral as the thunder of the guns grew louder and louder.

Facing this strange assembly were Father Vögt, who had mounted to the altar, and Father Gallery, who stood beside him and read Mass. In the distance the guns roared unceasingly, but more terrifying than this deep rumble were the shrieking and explosions of the shells, which were falling all round them. Father Vögt says:

> My feet and hands were cold. But I was quite calm, and confident in the protection of Heaven. Our Christians prayed with fervour. At the moment of the elevation of the Host the building received a mighty shock from the burst of a shell, of which several fragments fell on the church. During communion the

whole church shook violently—we heard the noise of a great fall—a small side-tower had been struck. I expected a precipitous rush from the church. But no! not only was there no panic, but they moved closer to the altar rails and to me.

Picture that assembly of strangely diverse creeds—a few Christians, many Mohammedans, many fetish-worshippers, with a faith made up of child-like beliefs in fairies, hobgoblins, unsightly deities, and awesome devils—all brought face to face with the prospect of being suddenly hurled into eternity. Before them stood two honest, God-fearing men, who, with blanched faces, but showing no other sign of fear, calmly performed their religious offices. More than half the congregation knew nothing of the faith which upheld these Christian priests, and understood not a word of what they were saying; but one and all felt instinctively a sense of protection in their proximity, and, with that mysterious accordance that so often characterises a crowd, one and all moved nearer to the altar-rails as the sound of the devastating shells grew louder in their ears.

Possibly their primitive minds attached strange significations to those deafening sounds, and refused to believe that mortal hands had produced such diabolical torments. Were they not the devils of Hell let loose on earth— raging, tearing, screaming devils, sent by the Prince of Devils in a paroxysm of fury to destroy the whole world? And were not these two white-robed priests striving with prayers and incantations to exorcise the devils, and drive them back whence they came? They were the white man's priests, and surely they must have power to combat the Evil One, else the white man would not have entrusted them with such a task. So this flock of frightened children, young and old, were urged by fear towards an unquestioning faith, which we sophisticated folk can only envy, and, when the tower came tumbling down with a mighty crash, their one idea was to creep closer to the altar-rails—to the visible emblem of a power beyond their comprehension.

At last Father Vögt decided that it would be safer to take them out of the cathedral by way of the choir and sacristy to the big Mission House, which stands farther from the sea. They had only just left when the baptistery chapel collapsed, so that the nave was filled with a cloud of choking dust; but no one was injured, and soon the whole congregation found sanctuary inside the dwelling-house. Shortly afterwards the bombardment ceased, for the Germans and their Askaris had fled at the approach of our men, and found their way into the neighbouring country. Captain von Bock was killed by one of our shells not far from the mission. Another officer, Captain von Boedecke, was standing near the pompom to the right of the Customs House when a well-placed shell from the *Severn* scored a direct hit on the gun, and he, too, was killed outright.

In the meantime the Marines, led by Captain Thomas, R.M.L.I, had taken possession of the governor's house, where they were joined by a small detachment of Zanzibar Rifles, with whose aid they proceeded to clear the country in a westerly direction. They found enemy parties concealed in the long grass, and were subjected to a heavy rifle-lire by which Captain Thomas unfortunately was killed, and about half a dozen others were wounded. Simultaneously the seamen had pressed forward past the Boma, that flanks the governor's house, and had captured many of the enemy in their dugouts. Other parties of seamen worked round behind the governor's house, cutting off the enemy's line of retreat, and causing him to abandon his maxims and light guns. Thus the attack was driven home from several points at once, overwhelming the enemy with its rapidity and vigour, so that they lied in confusion, disheartened by the loss of their two officers, and quite incapable of initiating an orderly retreat.

Having routed the enemy, it now remained for us to secure possession of the town, and to prepare for the possibility that the Germans might draw reinforcements from neighbouring posts and make a counter-attack. Headquarters were established at Government House, dead and wounded were collected, pickets were stationed over a prearranged area, defences were strengthened, and scouts despatched to report on the movements of the enemy. When the navy goes a-soldiering it has its own methods of doing business, and they are usually both simple and effective. It knows no such luxury as an Army Service Corps, but it just tells one of its officers that so many men will be landed, and that they will want to be fed. Gunner Moore, ably assisted by Leading Seaman Doney, and supervised by Commander Wilson of the *Mersey*, cheerfully undertook to keep the 350 men of the landing-party supplied with food, and carried the arrangements through without a hitch. The medical department had a rather larger personnel, but fortunately it was not called upon to make use of all its resources, and it did what it had to do with ease and efficiency.

It must always be remembered that the navy owes much to the fact that its units are self-contained, so that the organisation of an expedition virtually resolves itself into a joining up of forces which are already organised. Every man-of-war has its service corps, its medical corps, its machine-gun corps, its artillery, and its infantry; you have only to add together the complements of enough men-of-war and you can form an army—complete except for the absence of cavalry. And, with regard to the cavalry, it is a peculiar characteristic of the sailor that he usually fancies that he would make an excellent cavalryman. I have no doubt that he would try his hand at it if he were given half a chance, and, if he found that horses were unavailable, he would accommodate himself quite as happily on a camel, a donkey, or a pig.

Commander Watson, who was in charge of the landing-party, had a busy time during the next three days after the capture of Bagamoyo in dealing with the Arabs, Indians, and natives, as well as with the Askaris who deserted in ever-increasing numbers from the German forces. The taking of the town was an important event in the native mind, for it had been the capital of a large district in the days of the slave trade, and the terminus of the great caravan routes from the interior. The result of its falling into our hands was immediately apparent in the demoralisation of the enemy's troops. A strongly fortified point at Mtoni Ferry, six miles up the Kingani River, was promptly evacuated, and Askari deserters began to flock in from all sides.

Commander Watson's diplomacy was largely instrumental in securing the latter result, for, with the aid of Captain Dickson as interpreter, he handled the situation with admirable adroitness. First he assembled Swahilis, Arabs, and Indians on the beach, and told them that the British would respect their property, and allow them to return peaceably to their houses in the town, but that they in turn would be expected to give any information they could about the enemy's movements. He explained that by doing so they would be serving their own interests because, if the enemy counter-attacked and were allowed to approach the town, there would be such a bombardment from the ships as would make that of 15th August pale into insignificance. Then he told each tribe to select two or three men to report to the commander every morning, and to be generally responsible for the good behaviour of their people.

The Bagamoyans received this speech with applause, and with many expressions of gratification that the British forces had assumed control of the country, and, as an earnest of their goodwill, they proceeded to bring in all the German cattle they could find, and present them to our headquarters. The information they gave us about the enemy's movements proved to be both valuable and accurate. Soon the Askari deserters began to filter in, and Commander Watson made a point of interviewing them all. He told them that the British had no quarrel with them, but only with their German masters, that the British did not compel the natives to fight for them, and that all who gave themselves up and handed in their rifles could go free.

Soon the number of deserters increased by leaps and bounds, so that Bagamoyo was filled to overflowing. The congestion was increased by bands of fugitives from neighbouring villages, who brought in reports that the Germans were beating, robbing, and killing them, and were compelling all able-bodied men to serve as porters. It is significant that in every part of Africa where the German has attempted the task of colonisation—South-West Africa, the Cameroons, Togoland, and East Africa—he has invariably succeeded in making himself cordially hated by the native population.

In East Africa, as in the Cameroons, the German military authorities had to stop the fishing industry, because they were afraid that the fishermen would convey information to the British. For two years the Bagamoyans had been forbidden to fish when, on 18th August, Commander Watson gave them leave to resume this and other industries, which had been similarly interdicted, and to reopen the markets. The expression of joy among the whole population was loud and long. On the same day a military detachment arrived from Sadani, including some Zanzibar Rifles, whose beaming faces made quite an impression on the Askari deserters, suggesting to them that military service under the British Government must be quite a different affair from the military service they had known. Next day, another detachment of soldiers arrived, and took over garrison duty from the Navy, which was thus enabled to re-embark and proceed to its next job.

On 21st August 1916 a naval bombardment of Dar-es-Salaam was commenced, and was continued intermittently until 1st September, the gun positions and trenches, revealed by the aerial observers, being selected for special attention. It was during this period that the kite-balloon achieved what was a record in those days by remaining up for four and a half hours at a stretch, spotting for the flagship and reporting all enemy movements for the information of the intelligence officers. In the meantime the military were making their preparations to advance on Dar-es-Salaam, and on 31st August they got under way from Bagamoyo, to march for thirty-six miles through a barren and waterless district.

On 3rd September they approached their objective, whereat the Navy devoted half an hour's intense bombardment to the gun positions at the northern end of the town. Next morning, our troops being encamped on the outskirts and our squadron lying ready to renew the bombardment at a moment's notice, the *Challenger* hoisted a white flag, and proceeded towards the harbour with a letter demanding surrender. One of our small craft sent the letter ashore, and in a short while the answer came in the shape of the deputy *burgomaster*, accompanied by the bank manager and an interpreter. They were taken to the flagship, where they agreed to surrender the town unconditionally. Our troops then moved in to take possession, and by three o'clock that afternoon the Union Jack was floating over the Magistracy.

There remained a few smaller towns along the coast, which had to be taken to complete the Navy's task. On 7th September Kilwa Kivinje surrendered to the *Vengeance*, and Kilwa Kisiwani to the *Talbot*; on 13th September the squadron landed a military force at Mikindani, which offered no resistance; on 16th September the troops occupied Sudi, while the squadron proceeded to Lindi, and found the place deserted; and on 18th September two men-of-war and a transport proceeded to Kiswere, which was occupied without encountering any opposition. With the capture of Kiswere the whole coast of the country, once known as German East Africa, passed into our hands, excepting only the Rufigi Delta— an uninviting swamp inhabited mainly by mosquitoes, crocodiles, and alligators. We bombarded enemy camps there from time to time, but made no attempt to land there until we had thoroughly reconnoitred the ground by aircraft. The story of one of these reconnaissances, in which Commander Bridgeman lost his life, and Flight Lieutenant Moon was taken prisoner, has been told in the account of the Navy in East Africa.

While the flagship was lying off Bagamoyo, Admiral Charlton conceived the idea that he would like to make an ascent in the kite-balloon. It was fortunate that the sea was fairly calm, for I have heard of an occasion when an admiral went up in a kite-balloon, and, on descending again to his quarterdeck, was obliged to beat a precipitate retreat into his cabin. It is a curious fact that the motion of a ship, when communicated to the kite-balloon she is towing, becomes accentuated to such a degree that only an extra hardy mariner can hope to escape the effects of it. Admiral Charlton, however, was quite pleased with his experience, and later on he made a signal to the *Manica*.

I am very much pleased with the efficiency of the Kite-Balloon Section, and the smart handling of the balloon. I wish to assure them that they are doing good and useful work.

The tribute was much appreciated, for it is often the misfortune of those who labour with a new device to receive more criticism than encouragement. That it was also well deserved I hope that this record may afford ample evidence.

The best tribute, however, to the efficiency of the kite-balloon, and to the accuracy of its control over gunfire, has been paid by the enemy himself, both in East Africa and at Gallipoli. If the *Manica* came within range of the German guns with her kite-balloon down, they invariably opened fire, but, if the kite-balloon was up, the Germans in East Africa, like the Turks at Gallipoli, preserved a dignified silence. Experience had taught them wisdom.

The Navy in the Persian Gulf

Chapter 21

The Tangistani Raids

Judged by the standard to which the war has accustomed us, the whole thing was a very small affair, so small that even in peace-time it would not have occupied more than three columns in the morning newspapers. In war-time it could not be expected to occupy more than half a dozen lines, tucked away in a corner where no one would notice them. It happened to turn out all right, and of course that makes a difference. If a small colony of Englishmen, women, and children had been murdered by Arab cut-throats, Fleet Street in peace-time would have found enough material to fill a whole page, and even in war-time would have produced some artistic effects in headlines. But by the grace of God, and the efforts of British soldiers and seamen, the tragedy was averted.

In order to understand how the affair came about one must go back a few years in the history of the Persian Gulf. Great Britain had been policing the waters and shores of the Gulf for 300 years before it occurred to Germany that her designs upon the Middle East were severely inconvenienced by the British paramountcy in Arabia and Western Persia, and with Teutonic perseverance she set about the task of undermining that paramountcy. It is not my purpose to relate the adventures of Herr Wonckhaus, the modest trader in mother-of-pearl, who built most palatial edifices round the shores of the Gulf out of mysterious funds, which certainly did not arise from the profits of his small trade; nor the advent of the Hamburg-America liner dispensing champagne dinners up and down the Gulf, while the stewards' band discoursed sweet music, nor the long tale of intrigue whereby Turkey, in her role of Germany's vassal, made several attempts to acquire territory round the Gulf, but was happily frustrated by British vigilance.

Suffice it to say that the attitude of our Foreign Office was clear and precise throughout the course of all this scheming.

We had managed very nicely for 300 years to keep the Gulf open to the traders of all races without discrimination; we had suppressed the activities of Arab pirates, and our political residents had acted as arbitrators between the various Arab tribes whenever they became disputatious with one another, and had won the confidence and respect of them all. For doing this work we sought no remuneration or *quid pro quo*; we made no attempt to secure territory for ourselves, beyond a small island which we leased to house a telegraph station; we did not even claim any advantage in trading facilities for British merchants. But, on the other hand, we were quite determined that we wanted no assistance with the work, and that no other nation should step in and rob any of the Arab chiefs of an inch of territory.

In fact, we postulated the right to establish a kind of Monroe Doctrine in the Gulf. Our object, of course, was that we did not want any European Power to be able to use the Persian Gulf as a base for warships, which would be able to threaten a flank attack on our line of communication with India. Germany knew our object, and knew the value of defeating it, and that is why she spent many years and much money in assiduously trying to establish an influence over the natives of Persia and Arabia.

The most important character in this little drama first appears on the scene in 1910 in the shape of the German consul at Bushire, Herr Wassmus. Bushire lies on the east side of the Gulf, near the northern end of it, and is important mainly because it is the only place on that side which can boast a harbour, or anything like a harbour. Vessels of small draught can make their way into the port, but any ship drawing twenty feet or more must lie outside, a prey to the strong *shamals* which blow from the west across the Arabian desert. Here is the end of the caravan trade route, which leads from central Persia through Shiraz, bringing dates, raw cotton, oriental carpets, silks, and other merchandise for export to Europe, India, and China, as well as goods for the Persian Gulf trade which are transported in native sailing vessels, called *dhows*.

Here the great Wassmuss arrived in 1910, ostensibly to safeguard the interests of German traders. At that time he was a portly gentleman with grey hair, but I am told that he has grown thinner since then, and that his hair has turned white, which is not altogether surprising, for Bushire is no health resort. He left it for a while, but was back again in 1913, and upon his return he found it necessary to spend the worst of the hot weather at Shiraz, which again is not surprising, for Shiraz, standing .5,000 feet above the sea-level, is a good deal more habitable than Bushire in the summer.

There were, however, other points about Shiraz which recommended it to Herr Wassmuss, and these must be mentioned in order to explain the part he plays in the story. This ancient centre of Persia's civilisation happens to be the headquarters of the *gendarmerie* of the province of Fars. The force consists of about 1,760 officers and men, the officers being partly Persian and partly Swedish, Their duties are to patrol the caravan routes, restrict the activities of Arab brigands, and collect the revenue of the country. How much of the money collected finds its way into the Exchequer I do not know, for the Gendarmerie always had a substantial claim against the Persian Government for arrears of pay. This circumstance proved useful to Herr Wassmuss, who was always well supplied with funds, and found that a judicious distribution of them went a long way towards securing the good-will both of officers and men. Travitz, the Swedish commandant at Shiraz, became a confirmed Wassmussian, and through him the subordinate officers were influenced in the same direction.

Another influential friend of Wassmuss was the Governor-General of Fars, Mukhbir-us-Sultaneh. He had spent some years in Germany, where he had imbibed the national belief that the Germans are the chosen people of the earth. He gave himself body and soul to the new propaganda, and wrote letters to all the local khans (Arab chiefs) expatiating on the virtues of the Teuton and the vices of the British. It must be understood that all this was happening in peace time, in the days when we innocently believed that we could make friends with the Germans, when Herr Wassmuss himself was a member of the English clubs at Shiraz and Bushire, and was treated with all that spirit of *camaraderie*, of which the Englishman abroad is capable.

The intrigues of Herr Wassmuss extended beyond the borders of Persia to the Trucial Coast and right round to Muscat, but for the moment we are concerned only with his activities so far as they affected Bushire. In July 1913 an incident occurred, which had an important bearing on subsequent events, and threw another valuable friend into the arms of the German consul. This was Rais Ali, the chief of the Tangistani tribe, who lived at Dilwar, a coastal village about twenty miles south-east of the town of Bushire. The trade, profession, or occupation of Rais Ali is not easy to define.

He was not a pirate himself—nothing so vulgar—but he was a kind of officer commanding piracy, and he derived his income, I suppose, partly by trading in pirated goods, and partly by blackmailing the pirates. He made Dilwar a pirates' nest, and organised pirates' expeditions to the pearl fisheries. In July 1913 we happened to be looking for a notorious pirate, and at last traced him to his lair at Dilwar. There a British man-of-war demanded that he should be handed over, but Rais Ali, who, it must be said, showed commendable loyalty to his friends, refused point blank to do anything of the kind. Whereat the man-of-war proceeded to argue the point with the aid of naval guns, and in a few hours Dilwar was looking very sorry for itself, while the assortment of pirate *dhows* anchored there was soon floating about in the form of match-wood. Then Rais Ali gnashed his teeth, and swore eternal enmity against the British. Herr Wassmuss heard of the incident, and said to himself that really Rais Ali must be a very nice man, whom it would be a pleasure to know. So he opened his arms wide to the Arab chief, hugged him to his breast, and poured words of consolation into his ear.

A year later, in July 1914, Herr Wassmuss had news from Germany which caused him to leave Bushire in a hurry. He had not reached home when war was declared, and consequently he was delayed *en route*, but eventually he found his way to Berlin. He did not stay there long, however, for the German Government knew where he was likely to make himself most useful to them, and packed him off again back to Persia *via* Constantinople. His mission, as revealed by papers in his possession, was definite enough. He was to raise Persia and Afghanistan against the British, and to tamper with the loyalty of the troops in our Indian Army. They sent with him another German, called Linders, but his career was soon cut short. He was captured by Haidar Khan, one of the friends of the British, was handed over to us, and sent to India to be interned.

One of the first persons that Herr Wassmuss approached on his return to Persia was Rais Ali, the pirates' friend. In December 1916 the two were busy formulating plans for a general anti-British rising in Persia. In his house at Shiraz the great Wassmuss, clad in the garb of a Persian gentleman, received the Arab chief in state. With Teutonic thoroughness he had not only discarded his European clothes, but he had thrown off his European religion at the same time, and declared himself a convert to the faith of Islam.

He greeted Rais Ali with Eastern salutations, refreshed him with

Eastern sweetmeats, and got to business. The outcome of the negotiations was an agreement that Rais Ali would lead his Tangistani tribesmen against Bushire, and massacre every English man, woman, and child in the place. If Herr Wassmuss was at any time troubled with scruples about the ethics of conspiring with an Arab cut-throat to murder defenceless civilians, his new religion would be invoked to quiet them.

So Rais Ali's share in the proceedings was definitely settled. Of the tasks allotted to Mukhbir-us-Sultaneh, the governor-general, to Pravitz, the *commandant* of *gendarmerie*, and to the various other friends of Wassmuss, I have no definite knowledge. Suffice it to say that a blood feud between two of the local *khans* was turned to account, that one of the disputants, the Khan of Borasjan on the road between Bushire and Shiraz, was joined by two other *khans*, to form an anti-British alliance, while the other disputant, Ismail Khan, was joined by our friend Haidar Khan, to form an anti-German alliance.

But where the anti-British *khans* secured an advantage was in the reinforcements they received from deserters of the *gendarmerie*, who had good German money rattling in their purses, and had been promised that there was more to come. They were also presented with good German rifles, so that they had every reason to feel pleased with their prospects.

There followed a delay of six months, possibly caused by the necessity of waiting for further consignments of rifles, and it was not until July 1915 that word was passed to Rais Ali that the time had come for him to fulfil his compact. On the 12th of that month the first Tangistani raid was made on Bushire, and, though the attack was repulsed, two British officers and one *sepoy* lost their lives, and two *sepoys* were wounded. It seems fairly evident that this attack was made prematurely and without adequate preparation, for the defending force at that time was very small.

Finding that we could obtain no reparation from the Persian Government, we immediately took steps to secure the safety of the inhabitants of Bushire. We sent a naval and military force to take possession of the port and town, and set to work upon a system of defences. We also took steps to punish the Tangistanis, by sending a naval squadron commanded by Captain (later Rear-Admiral) Wake, to Dilwar, where we landed a small detachment of Indian troops and a party of seamen. The naval guns drove the Tangistanis inland, but during the next two days (14th and 15th August) they returned several times to the attack, only to be driven off by rifles, machine-guns, and the shell-fire from the ships. The fort and village of Dilwar were destroyed, and the casualties to the enemy were heavy.

Our own casualties were slight, but unfortunately included the commander and one of the lieutenants of the *Juno*. On the night of the 15th the force was re-embarked, partly because the heat was too intense to allow of the operations being protracted, and partly because there was a danger that Rais Ali might adopt the offensive defensive scheme, and make another attack on Bushire during the absence of our ships and troops.

Some such idea must have been in his mind, for he soon began a series of night raids, which suggested the prelude to a more serious attack. Our line of outposts was provided with acetylene searchlights, but at first these proved very unsatisfactory because they had a mysterious way of refusing to work as soon as the first rifle-shot was fired. The probable explanation is that they were manned by Eurasians, who had no great liking for the sound of rifle-fire. The senior naval officer was requested to provide seamen to man these lights, and thenceforward they gave entire satisfaction. It was during one of these night raids that Wassmuss suffered a heavy blow in the loss of his cherished friend Rais Ali. The Tangistani chief had boasted that it was his own rifle which killed the two British officers on 12th July, and it is probable that all the crack shots defending Bushire were longing for the chance of revenge. When one of the searchlights illumined the features of Rais Ali, his doom was sealed. His faithful followers removed him from the battle-field, but he is said to have died of his wounds very shortly afterwards.

The town of Bushire stands on what would be an island, were it not for a low-lying tract of sand which joins it to the mainland. This causeway is known as the "Mashilah," and is from five to seven miles across. During high tides it is occasionally inundated, and at all times the area of firm dry sand is narrow. The presence of British warships made it impossible for the Tangistanis to approach Bushire by sea, and so the Mashilah offered the only possible line of advance. Its main drawback from the invader's point of view is that not an inch of cover can be found anywhere until the island of Bushire is reached. Round the edge of the island on the Mashilah side is a line of low cliffs, which form a kind of natural rampart. These cliffs, however, are intersected by numerous *nullahs*, or gullies, sloping down from the island to the Mashilah. At the top of them are loose rocks and boulders, and at the

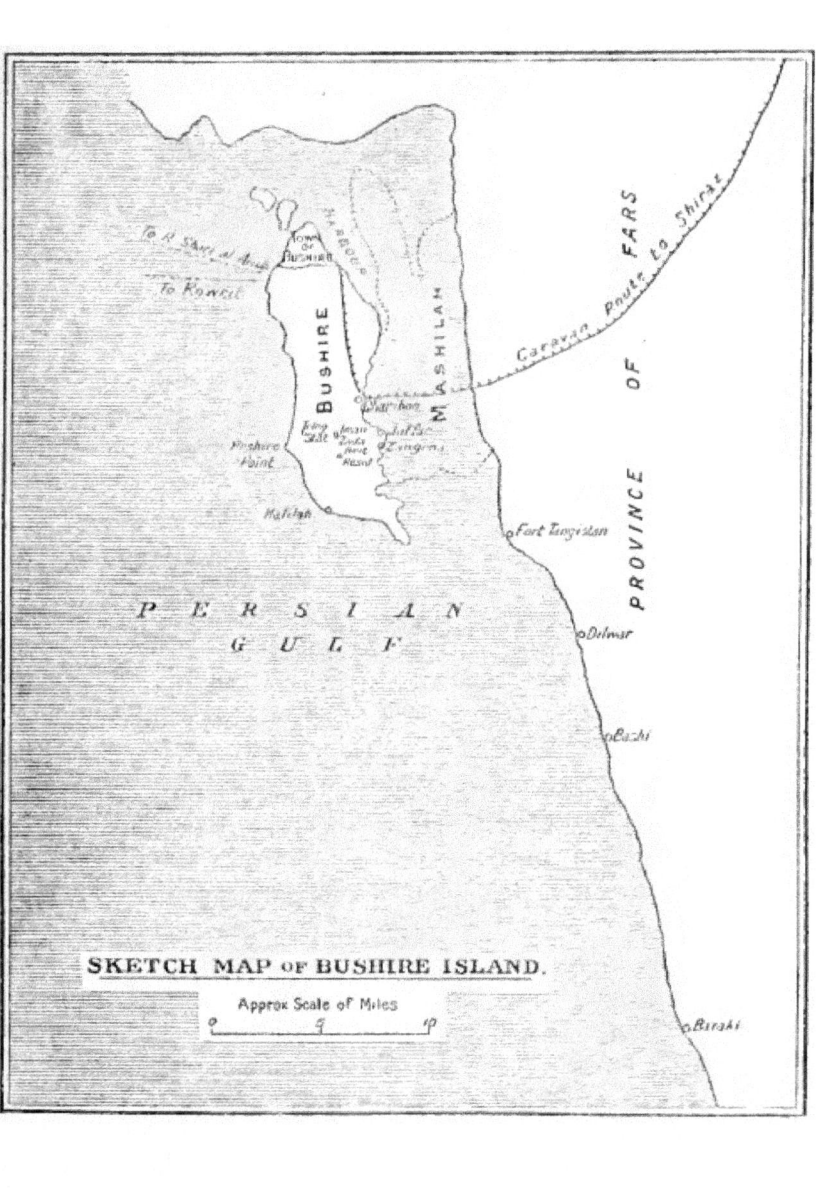

SKETCH MAP OF BUSHIRE ISLAND.

foot of them a belt of palm-trees extends for some distance. It the Tangistanis could contrive to cross the Mashilah under cover of darkness, they would be able to take up a strong position on the edge of the island, and to find shelter from our fire by dodging behind the rocks and palm-trees. And this is exactly what they did.

The ships lying off Reshire Point were the *Juno*, *Pyramus*, and *Lawrence*. It would be idle to pretend that they were enjoying life, for no one does that at Bushire during the hot weather. The shade temperature was always hovering in the vicinity of 100° Fahrenheit, and the atmosphere was always damp and sticky. Their routine was largely made up of rehearsals for the Tangistani performance, which they knew to be imminent. Parties were landed on the beach, and in the comparatively cool hours of the early morning they went through their field exercises, practised the art of bringing a machinegun into action rapidly, and received instructions about the handling of it under fire. The rehearsals were conducted by Captain George Carpenter, R.M.L.I., of H.M.S. *Juno*, in conjunction with the gunnery lieutenant of that ship. By tapping the resources of the three ships the navy managed to provide a field force of seven officers, 153 men, and four maxims, as well as supplying to the Russian Consulate a guard of twenty men and a maxim, and a further six men to work the searchlights.

On the night of 8th September Captain Carpenter landed with three officers and sixty men of H.M.S. *Pyramus*, spent the night at the base camp near the Telegraph Station, and at six o'clock next morning was busily engaged in putting them through their exercises. When they returned to the camp for breakfast they found that a message had just come in from Brigadier-General Brooking, who was in command of the troops at Bushire, ordering them to proceed to the reserves' camp at Imam Zada. This suggested that something must be happening, so they sent for their transport carts, swallowed their breakfast, and got under way.

In that region the sun begins to get hot at six in the morning, by seven it has become unpleasant, and by eight it is beyond the pale of printable language. The glare of it strikes against the white dust on the track, so that the most capacious sun-helmet does not avail to shield the eyes. Here and there relief is found in a cluster of green palms, such as shade the British Residency and a few other European dwellings, but the general aspect at this season is of a parched and dreary land, unredeemed by God or man. I remember the first time I landed at Bushire I had just been re-reading Omar Khayyam's ecstasies about his Persian garden, and my hopes ran high at the prospect of setting foot in Persia. But I landed at the wrong place. If I had gone to Shiraz, there, perhaps, I might have seen the real thing, and might even have feasted my eyes upon a *"moon of my delight who knows no wane."* That is one of our misfortunes in the Navy—we seldom have the chance of seeing the best of the countries we visit.

The men of H.M.S. *Pyramus* trudged on steadily, while the perspiration dripped from their faces and soaked through their cotton clothes, until they reached the camp at Imam Zada. Here they found another message from the G.O.C. ordering them to advance farther east to a tower near the village of Zangena, and there take up the best position they could find, in order to command the two gullies leading down to the Mashilah at that point, the British outposts were situated at intervals along the edge of the Mashilah as far as a point south of Zangena, and then stretched across the island to the sea on the west side. The village of Halilah was suspected of harbouring enemy agents, and was therefore shut out beyond our line of defences. To man these outposts and to provide supports and reserves, we had only two small detachments of Indian troops—Rajputs and Ghurkhas. The latter had been on duty all night, and consequently the general did not want to use them if it could be avoided. We had, however, a big pull over the enemy in the possession of artillery, consisting of field and mountain guns, and we had also a small body of cavalry ready to move out on the Mashilah as soon as the Tangistanis showed signs of retreating.

The general had seen at once that the troops holding the outposts were insufficient to drive off the enemy, who were over 600 strong, and that he must call up his reserves from Reshire, including the naval party. It took an hour or so to bring them up, and in the meantime the Rajputs at the outposts clung on grimly, for they knew well enough that they were not likely to receive quarter if the Tangistanis once got in among them. The batteries were also busily engaged, though there was always a danger that an enterprising rush on the part of the enemy would sweep right over them, or that a flank attack might get in behind them.

The men of the *Pyramus*, now painfully conscious that each one of them was carrying his rifle and equipment, while some of them had the additional burden of machine-guns and ammunition-boxes, had reached within 800 yards of the objective when they came under heavy rifle-fire from Tangistanis hidden behind rocks 300 yards away. They were ordered to lie down and take breath, and then the advance was continued by means of short rushes in the orthodox style. It is an exhilarating exercise when carried out on the fields of good old England, but the effect is very different when a tropical sun is beating down on one's head, and a choking dust is filling the mouth and nostrils. It is no disparagement of Tangistani marksmanship to record that our casualties from heat stroke exceeded those caused by bullets.

They got to the tower at last, and mounted a maxim there. Another maxim was got into position at the left end of the line, but the gun on the right could not find cover of any kind, and was subjected to a tornado of bullets from the enemy.

The gun's crew had to fall back from it, but Captain Carpenter called for volunteers to bring it into action, and Lieutenant-Commander Dorman and Yeoman of Signals Wood immediately went forward to it. Wood was mortally wounded as soon as he reached it, and fell right across the gun. Carpenter then saw that the enemy's fire was too accurate, and that he could not afford to risk further casualties in his small force, so he called to Dorman to come back. There was no danger of the enemy capturing the gun, for the two other maxims completely covered their line of advance. So there the little force remained, taking what cover they could find, and seizing every chance to pot a Tangistani when he was rash enough to show himself. Carpenter sent a message to the G.O.C. informing him of the position of affairs, and asking for a stretcher-party to remove the wounded and heat-stroke cases. The G.O.C. sent back word telling him to hang on until the reserve infantry arrived to clear up the situation, and that medical assistance would be sent as soon as possible.

Soon after ten o'clock Lieutenant-Colonel Lane came up with the reserve infantry, and charged right into the enemy, who promptly broke and fled, and that was virtually the end of the business. The naval party moved forward with their machine-guns to hold the gullies, and proceeded to deal with any stray Tangistanis found lurking among the palm-trees. The cavalry moved on to the Mashilah and got right into the fleeing tribesmen, while the artillery lengthened their range and played havoc with them all the way across. The Arabs brought up donkeys to remove most of their dead and wounded, but we collected between fifty and sixty of them near the edge of the Mashilah.

So ended the great coup which Wassmuss had been planning for months beforehand. Its failure must have been a serious blow to his prestige, for, although there were plenty of alarums and excursions during the succeeding months, and various tribesmen showed a good deal of unrest, there was no other concerted effort against Bushire. The little colony of British subjects went about their vocations with untroubled minds, and slept peacefully in their beds. Captain Carpenter was awarded the D.S.C. for his services at Dilwar and Bushire, and was shortly afterwards promoted.

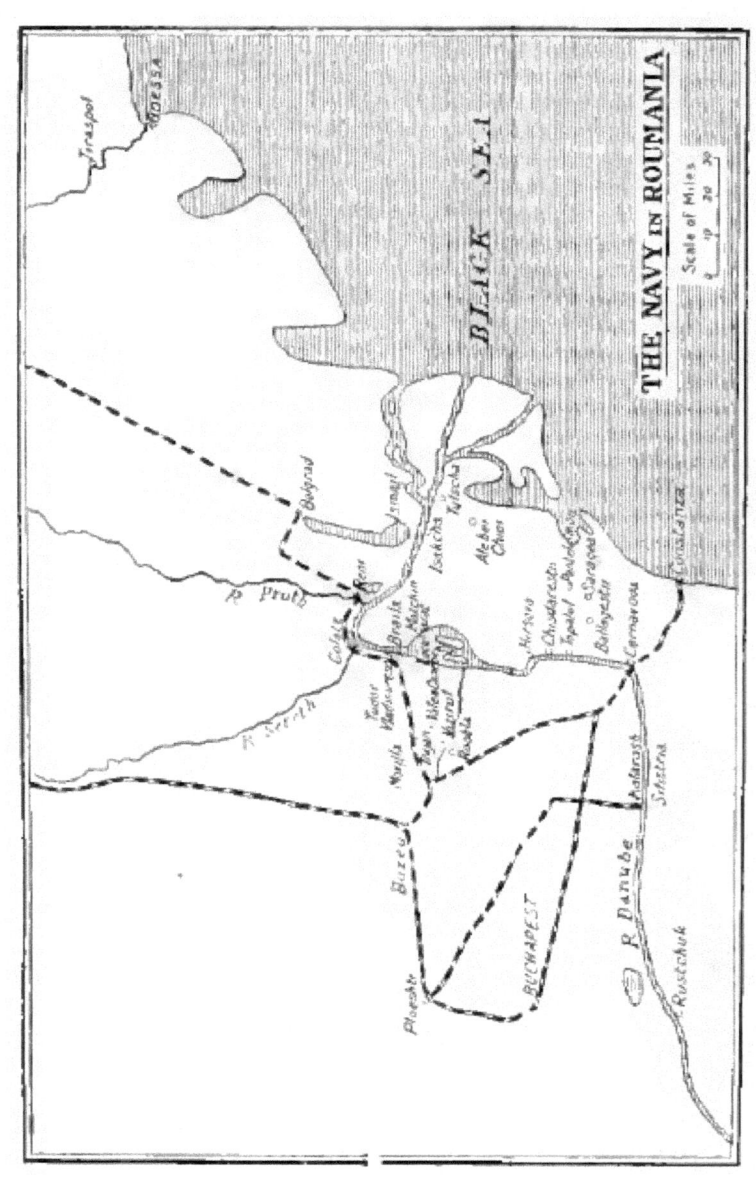

CHAPTER 22

The Battle Near Topalul

The British Armoured Car Force of the Royal Naval Air Service had seen quite a lot of the world before they found their way to Roumania. They had done their bit in Belgium, they had wandered thence to Russia, and they had sampled the roads of Persia; in fact, a kind of supernatural instinct seems to have led them to all the best places for a lively scrap, and, as soon as the liveliness was at an end in one quarter of the globe, they were off to another.

In the late autumn of 1916 they had abandoned Persia, having come to the conclusion that it was completely played out as a theatre of war, and they had assembled at Odessa, wondering where they should go next. They definitely belonged to the Russian Army, and they made up their minds that it was up to the Russian Army to keep them supplied with jobs. Roumania had just entered the lists, and for a time things seemed to be going well with her, until General Mackensen began his great push in the Dobrudsha, and then the British armoured cars said to themselves, "Here is a job for us," So they appealed to the powers that governed the Russian Army at that time, and obtained permission to transfer themselves to Roumania, and there attach themselves to the Russian forces operating in that country.

Of course they knew in their hearts that an armoured car is not really the same thing as a ship, but when the white ensign is fluttering above it, they think and talk of it as though it were a ship. The man who said that R.N.A.S. means Really Not A Sailor was no psychologist, and failed altogether to appreciate the psychological effect of the white ensign. When an officer in command of a car receives his instructions, he calls them his Sailing Orders, and sometimes the officer who writes them out in his best official language, heads them with the words "Sailing Orders" in black and white. But, on the whole, they are very careful with their official reports, and all such expressions as "Put the helm hard over to starboard," or "Proceed full speed astern," have been translated into the lingo of the motor garage.

Towards the end of November 1916 they found themselves at Hirsova on the Dobrudsha side of the Danube, where General Sirelius of the 4th Siberian Army Corps told them that they were just in time for a big battle, and that he wanted them to take an important part in it. Things had been going badly of late, for General Mackensen had been mopping up Roumanian divisions on a wholesale scale, and walking through the Dobrudsha as though it were the *Unter den Linden*. But there was just a possibility that the advance had been too rapid, and that a counter-attack might find the enemy unprepared, and with his supply columns many miles to the rear. A Russian force, sweeping down between the Danube and the Black Sea, might be able to cut off the enemy's forces, which had crossed the river and were operating against Bucharest, and cheery optimists among the Russians even contemplated the recapture of Cernavoda bridge and of the port of Constanza.

The push was timed to start on 29th November, and the force of armoured cars was ordered to be in readiness to lead the attack. But when the day arrived all these orders were cancelled unceremoniously, and the cars were told to proceed across the Danube to a destination near Bucharest. The truth of the matter was, that the Roumanian Army defending Bucharest had failed to hold their positions, and the capital was in imminent danger. The general in command of the Russian forces co-operating with the Roumanians had at once sent out an S.O.S. signal, of which the effect was, "For Heaven's sake send us the British armoured cars." Commander Gregory, in charge of the force, at once sent scouts to examine the state of the roads, for it is one thing for a general at Bucharest to say he wants armoured cars, and another thing for the people in the cars to get them to him. The scouts all reported that the roads leading to the pontoon bridge across the Danube were too bad for any parliamentary language, and quite unfit for motor traffic. So Commander Gregory went to the Chief of Staff of the 4th Siberian Corps, and told him that it was beyond human possibility to comply with the latest order that the force had received. Incidentally he relieved his mind by pointing out that he had been given nothing but contradictory orders, one on top of another, for the past six weeks.

Now, when General Sirelius heard from his chief of staff what Commander Gregory had been saying, he smiled blandly, for the truth of the matter was that he did not want to part with the British armoured cars. Already the Bucharest army was taking from him all the best of his reserve battalions, which were to have enabled him to carry out the great push through the Dobrudsha, and was transferring them across the Danube to the defence of Bucharest. The result was that the great push had to be postponed, and the general intended to wait until fresh reserves could be sent up to him. But here again his intentions were frustrated, for it was not many hours before another S.O.S. signal came from Bucharest. "For Heaven's sake make your push, or do something to cause a diversion." This was rather hard on the general, first to take away his reserves, and then to tell him to make his push; but such things are liable to happen when things are going badly, and he consoled himself with the thought that, at all events, they had not succeeded in robbing him of the armoured cars. So he ordered that the push should commence next day—30th November.

The British armoured cars were divided into three squadrons, two of them to operate from the village of Topalul towards Ballagestii and a third from the village of Panteleimon towards Saragea. The morning broke dull and misty, and the artillery soon found that they were quite unable to observe the effect of their shells; but soon after noon it cleared up, as Lieutenant-Commander Belt, in command of Number One Squadron, was ordered into action along the road running from Topalul to Ballagestii. He found that the enemy was leaving nothing to chance; first there was a forest of barbed wire entanglements, then another forest fifty yards behind the first, then the first line trenches fifty yards behind that, and then the second line trenches fifty yards behind the first line.

The road along which the cars had to advance to the attack was no road at all, but just an unmetalled track running through cultivated fields. The ground on either side of the track was soft and uneven, for, though it had not received any recent ploughing, it was equally unprepared as a terrain for fighting cars. Two Russian cars of powerful build, carrying two maxim guns each, had joined the British squadron, and when they were ordered to attack the enemy's trenches, they went full speed along the track right up to the barbed wire. They then conceived the idea of turning off the track and running along the barbed wire, so as to enfilade the trenches all along the sector. It was a bold scheme, but it failed to take into account the factor of specific gravity. An armoured car is no fairy with light fantastic toes to trip nimbly over arable land. They had no sooner left the track than they found themselves firmly embedded in the soft ground, with their flanks almost touching the barbed wire, and infuriated Bulgarians expressing their indignation by means of a hot fusillade.

Then came a telephone message from the Russian observation post, ordering one of our light "Lanchester" cars to go in to support the Russian cars, and incidentally to assist the Russian infantry in launching an attack. Lieutenant-Commander Belt sent Sub-Lieutenant Lefroy, accompanied as usual by a motor cyclist, whose job it was to watch the progress of events, and bring back reports from time to time. Now, the ordinary practice when going into action is to turn the car at a respectful distance from the enemy's lines, reverse the engine, and approach stern first towards the enemy. This is a fairly simple operation on a metalled road, but when there is no road worthy of the name, the whole science of fighting an armoured car has to be reconsidered. Unfortunately, there was no time to work out the problem, for the Russian infantry were waiting to advance, and Lefroy's main purpose was to lead the way for them. He proceeded up the track to the enemy's first line, the Russian infantry followed, and the great push had begun.

When he had approached within a few yards of the barbed wire, he decided that it was high time to carry out the ordinary manoeuvre of reversing the engine, and advancing stern first. But, first of all, he had to turn the car round. Turning a heavy car on a narrow farm-track is no easy operation under the best of circumstances, and when rifles, machine-guns, and artillery are devoting the main share of their attention to frustrating the effort, it becomes a decidedly ticklish job. He had put the lever over to the lowest speed when, as ill luck would have it, a shell exploded underneath the car and jammed the speed-gear, so that he was doomed to stick to his lowest speed until he could get back to the repair shop. Meanwhile his wheels were steadily subsiding into the soft earth, and the enemy was making things so uncomfortably warm for him that he had no alternative but to try and get out of his tight corner. Luckily, he managed to extricate his wheels, but he did not enjoy the journey home at the speed of a perambulator pushed by a superannuated nursemaid suffering from rheumatism, and with high explosive shells following him steadily all the way.

Next, Lieutenant Walford was sent into action with another light

"Lanchester." By this time the enemy had made up their minds that they did not like armoured cars, and had become obsessed with the idea that if their rifles and machine-guns could only pour enough lead into the brutes, they would become discouraged and retire gracefully from the action. This theory suited the Russian infantry admirably, for it enabled them to advance under far pleasanter conditions than they had anticipated. When Walford got within forty yards of the stranded Russian cars, the patter of the bullets on his armour plating grew louder and louder; but an armoured car does not worry much about bullets, so long as they do not come through the loopholes.

The trouble was that they split into fragments, and the fragments caused a kind of mist, so that the driver of the car could not see the track in front of him. In trying to turn he did just the same thing as Lefroy had already done before him—got his wheels stuck in the soft earth at the side of the track. He succeeded, however, eventually in getting round, and then the maxim in the car opened fire on the enemy, doing considerable damage at that close range, until a bullet came through a loophole and punctured the maxim's water-casing, which keeps the gun cool. This effectually put the gun out of action, and there was nothing for it but to take the car back to safety. It is regrettable to have to record that the personal beauty of Lieutenant Walford and of the driver of his car were completely spoiled for the time being by the nickel splashes of the enemy's bullets. These had found their way into the car, and dug themselves into the faces of its occupants, until they looked like the masterpieces of a post-impressionist artist.

Meanwhile the two Russian cars were hopelessly stuck, and were being subjected to a terrible fire from rifles, machine-guns, and artillery, so Lieutenant-Commander Belt himself went to the rescue. He had exactly the same experience as his predecessors when he tried to turn his car, and for nearly a quarter of an hour he remained with the front wheels of his car deeply embedded in the mud.

"If I was to tighten up the gears a bit," suggested the driver, "I think we might get her to move."

So he got to work with a screw-driver, while the enemy got to work with artillery, maxims, and rifles, and concentrated everything they could bring to bear on the car. At last, with a series of protesting snorts and vigorous jerks, she began to move. By this time it was quite dark, and moreover the road had become pitted with shell-holes, so that the journey home promised plenty of excitement. But there were the two derelict Russian cars lying a few yards away, shrouded in gloom, and the thought of leaving them to their fate was not an easy one. There are times when it requires more courage to avoid a danger than to run into one, and this was just one of those occasions. Lieutenant-Commander Belt knew that the result of any further attempt to rescue the Russian cars would be that the enemy would be able to rejoice over three derelicts instead of two, so he braced himself up to the decision that there was no alternative but to cut the loss.

On his way back through the dark he met another "Lanchester," coming to the rescue, but this too he ordered to return, for he knew it could do no good. It afterwards transpired that three of the crew of the first Russian car were killed by a shell, and that the remainder were badly wounded, but managed to escape in the dark, as also did the crew of the second Russian car. The two cars had to be destroyed by the Russian artillery.

Such is the record of the first day's fighting, so far as the armoured cars were concerned in it. It must be put to their credit that, by causing the enemy to concentrate his fire upon them, they had enabled the Russian infantry to capture a hill on the left flank, and to get a footing on another hill on the right flank near the river. This was something to the good, but it was already becoming painfully obvious that the enemy were fully prepared, and that ground could only be gained from them by means of a ding-dong struggle. All through the night the Russian infantry pressed forward the attack, but only at the cost of heavy losses, which made General Sirelius parody the great Augustus, exclaiming, "*Varus, Varus, give me back my reserves.*" The truth of the matter was that the breakdown of the Roumanian forces defending Bucharest had placed the Russian Army in the Dobrudsha in a most unenviable position, and had completely ruined the chances of a successful counter-attack against Mackensen.

All next day (1st December) the fighting continued, and again the armoured cars did valuable work. No more Russian cars were available, but the British cars kept on running through heavy fire right up to the enemy's trenches, pouring a hot fusillade into them, and running back again before the artillery could get their range correctly. For two solid miles each way they had to run the gauntlet of bullets and shells, and the enemy never left them in any doubt as to the opinions he entertained about them, for he devoted all the best of his energies in their direction. On one occasion, when Lieutenant Crossing had brought his car within 300 yards of the enemy, he noticed that a Russian shell had made a neat gap through the parapet, exposing to view a large number of fleeing Bulgarians. He immediately switched his machine-gun on to them, and got through two belts of ammunition before the high explosive shells began to fall uncomfortably close to him.

So far the attack had been pressed mainly from Topalul in the direction of Ballagestii, and, though the Russian infantry had advanced without hesitation, they had gained but little ground, and that little had been very expensive in casualties. In fact, what reserves had been left to General Sirelius were now all used up, and by the end of the second day's fighting the whole Corps was so thoroughly worn out that there was a grave danger that a counterattack on the part of the enemy might prove too strong to be resisted by tired and dispirited troops. When day dawned on 2nd December the situation had become critical.

At 9 o'clock in the morning Commander Gregory was requested by the Russian Staff to send two cars into action, and he promptly complied with the request. But the cars went into action alone, unsupported by the Russian infantry, who made no attempt to advance. The bitter truth was that they were in no fit condition to advance, and the sending of the cars into action was merely a device to deceive the enemy into thinking that the push was still in progress. It was a vital necessity to conceal the fact that the Russian troops were so badly in need of rest and recuperation that a counter-attack on the enemy's part would find them incapable of adequate resistance. For nearly two hours the cars of Lieutenant Walford and Sub-Lieutenant Gawler carried on this pseudo-attack against General Mackensen's army, dodging up and down the road to keep the hostile artillery from finding the correct range, and pouring many hundred rounds of ammunition into the Bulgarian trenches.

The notion of two armoured cars fighting an army has something of the farcical about it, which must have appealed strongly to the British sense of humour. The strange part of it is that the ruse succeeded, and on that part of the line the enemy attempted no counter-attack, but patiently waited to see what was going to happen next.

It was in the direction of Panteleimon that the counter-attack was made, and there Lieutenant-Commander Wells Hood with his squadron had been standing by for orders during the past two days. On 2nd December the enemy commenced an attack in strong force, and immediately the cars were ordered to proceed along the road between Panteleimon and Saragea to meet the attack. There were three of them, and they went into action at intervals of 150 yards along the road, Lieutenant-Commander Wells Hood leading. They soon came under heavy shellfire, and when they were about halfway to Saragea the rifles and machine-guns opened fire on them. The leading car was only 60 yards from the Bulgarian trenches when the enemy were seen to be advancing in open formation—a long line of Bulgarian infantry coming forward at the double.

The range was 400 yards, and the maxim in the car soon began to make appreciable gaps in the line. But the moral effect of an armoured car is even greater than the material damage it can inflict; it is always a nasty job to attack an object which is impervious to rifle-fire, while it is pumping out hot lead faster than a street-corner orator can pump out hot air. The Bulgarian infantry dropped back into their trenches, and the maxim pumped another 500 rounds into them there, just to show them that there was no scarcity of ammunition, in case they should care to make another effort.

The next manoeuvre was to turn the car round, and to reverse towards the enemy, so as to get near enough to enfilade the trenches. There was an ulterior object in this manoeuvre, for the hostile artillery had found the range of the ear, and shells were falling too close to be pleasant. If the car could only get close enough to the Bulgarian trenches, the artillery would be forced to discontinue their attack, for fear of hitting their own men. Such at least was the theory, but in practice it did not prove successful. The artillery shortened their range, pursuing the car relentlessly, until it became obvious that the new position was untenable. When the car started forward again the engine suddenly stopped, and it was discovered that the pressure petrol tank had been pierced in two places by bullets.

This was an awkward predicament at such a juncture, when the car was within a few yards of the enemy's trenches. But the driver treated it as though it was all in the day's work, and promptly switched on to his gravity spare tank. The next problem was how to start her up again, and this was solved by the gunner. Chief Petty Officer Vaughan, who, without a moment's hesitation, jumped out of the car, started her up, and jumped in again, before any Bulgarian sniper had time to realise his chance. So they successfully got back to Panteleimon, where they filled up with water, repaired the petrol tank, and took a fresh supply of ammunition aboard.

Meanwhile the two other cars were not enjoying life quite so whole-heartedly. Lieutenant Mitchell's car was about 40 yards from the road on the left-hand side, and there it seemed to be stuck. It had been noticed that the gun was at its extreme elevation, and that three of the crew were outside the car, but what they were doing, or trying to do, was not clear. The third car, commanded by Lieutenant Ingle, was also on the left hand side of the road, about 400 yards from it, and only a few yards from the Bulgarian trenches. This car also seemed to be stuck. The history of its exploits was not known until the next day, but it will be convenient to relate them here.

The car had run very nicely until it was traversing No Man's Land, when the soft wet earth clogged the wheels badly, with the result that the engine stopped at a spot uncomfortably close to the enemy. Lieutenant Ingle jumped out, and started her up, but after a few yards she stopped again. Again Lieutenant Ingle risked the chance of stopping a bullet, and started her up once more, but the result was just the same; she stopped after a few spasms. Lieutenant Ingle was indefatigable; for the third time he tried to start her up, and, in doing so, became a handy target for some Bulgarian sniper. A bullet struck him just above the knee, breaking his leg, and at the same moment the enemy's artillery began to drop shells in the vicinity. He rolled into a trench close to the car, and ordered his men to do the same. It was a lucky chance that he did so, for immediately afterwards a shell hit the car, twisting the turret beyond recognition, and carrying away the water-jacket of the maxim. Strangely enough, however, it did very little damage to the engine.

So there were the whole of the crew hiding in a trench on the wrong side of No Man's Land, and the next thing to happen was a Bulgarian advance which swept right over them, Some Bulgarian soldiers presently came up to them, and intimated that they were prisoners, and must march to the rear of the Bulgarian lines. Then they grasped the fact that Lieutenant Ingle was wounded, and could not march, so they solemnly went through the motions of carrying a man on a stretcher, to indicate that they were going back to fetch one. By this time it was quite dark, and when Lieutenant Ingle was left alone to think things out, he came to the conclusion that he did not want to become a prisoner of war.

Slowly and painfully he started to crawl out of the trench towards the Russian lines. He knew that many hours of darkness lay before him, and that if he could only traverse the distance before his strength failed, he ran a very good chance of getting through without being detected. That crawl lasted exactly twelve hours—twelve weary hours on all fours with one of them broken. At daybreak some Russian soldiers in their trenches saw a British naval officer lying on the other side of the parapet, and dragged him into safety. Then they got a stretcher and took him to the hospital at Panteleimon.

In the meantime things had been happening all round Lieutenant Ingle, in which he would have been keenly interested under happier circumstances. As soon as night had fallen the Russians had counter-attacked, and had succeeded in driving back the Bulgarians for 300 yards. This again brought our cars within the Russian lines, and it only remained to send a party of men and horses to tow them out of the mud. It was not an easy operation in the dark, especially when Bulgarian snipers discovered what was happening; but both cars were successfully recovered, and those who worked hard and risked much to recover them had their reward, when they saw an enemy *communiqué* reporting the capture of two British armoured cars. It was the main feature in the *communiqué*, for both Germans and Bulgarians had an unreasoning prejudice against the cars, and hailed their capture in grandiloquent phrases; nor did they take the trouble to issue an amended statement, when they found that they had been counting unhatched chickens.

Of the crews of these two cars it is regrettable that all except Lieutenant Ingle were taken prisoners, but it is some consolation to know that the work of the three cars between Panteleimon and Saragea had most important results, and that official information was forwarded to the commanding officer of the Armoured Car Force to the effect that, had it not been for the three cars operating at this point, the Russian trenches would have been captured, and the line broken. General Sirelius took the trouble to write an autograph letter of thanks to the officers and men of the force, in which he referred to their "brave and unselfish work during the battle," and regretted that it had entailed such heavy losses upon them.

The battle was over, and the result was profoundly unsatisfactory. It may have produced a diversion, which for the moment relieved the pressure on Bucharest, but the original objective of a sweep through the Dobrudsha between the Danube and the Black Sea down to Cernavoda had faded away like a dream, leaving only the consciousness of a heavy casualty list, and a general feeling of depression. The cars returned to Hirsova, where the repair staff got to work on them at once, anticipating that it would not be long before they were wanted again. In fact, the general had applied for permission to retain them with his division, and had intimated that he hoped shortly to renew the operations.

No account of the battle of Topalul would be complete without mentioning the work of the medical staff attached to the British armoured cars. Staff-Surgeon G. B. Scott was in command of them, and at once placed all his resources at the disposal of the Russian Senior Medical Officer. He sent Surgeon Glegg with two sick berth ratings and an ambulance to Panteleimon, while he and Surgeon Maitland Scott, with the rest of the staff, attached themselves to the hospital at Topalul. At six o'clock in the evening of 30th November the Russian wounded began to arrive, and continued in a steady stream until three o'clock the next morning. There was only one Russian officer capable of performing operations, and before many hours he was completely worn out. He appealed to the two British doctors to take over all the operating work, and this they did cheerfully, carrying on until 4 a.m., when they finished for the night and turned in.

On 1st December Staff-Surgeon Scott was aroused early in the morning by the Russian S.M.O., who had a new problem to present. One day's fighting had filled the hospital, and the battle was to continue. The question was, how to get the cases removed to a place of safety. The only medical transport the Russians possessed was a lot of horse-drawn carts, which were very slow and of small capacity. The only possible solution of the problem was to borrow some of the transport lorries of the Armoured Car Force, and convert them into ambulances. Commander Gregory agreed to lend the lorries for this purpose, and in a very short time some of the ratings belonging to the force were busy fitting them up with naval cots and spare stretchers, and covering the floor with loose straw. By eight o'clock in the morning the fleet of improvised ambulances was not only ready for service but was loaded up with 116 wounded men, and off they went on the road to Chisdarestii, where the cases were to be placed on barges and taken down the river to the base.

It is astonishing to find how little sleep a man requires when necessity compels him to keep awake. The two naval doctors had been busy with operations until 4 a.m., but at 8 a.m. they were on their way to Chisdarestii with the new British medical transport section that had been improvised within the last hour. It is equally astonishing to find what versatility there is in the average man, when occasion calls for it. Before long Staff-Surgeon Scott and his staff found themselves playing the role of road-makers, for there was one spot between Topalul and Chisdarestii where the road was quite impassable by motor traffic. Fortunately Staff-Surgeon Scott had anticipated this, and had armed all the drivers and spare drivers with picks and spades.

By picking away the road in places where there was more than enough of it, and transferring it to places where there was a great deal too little, they made quite a decent road, and all in the space of half an hour. At Chisdarestii they put all the wounded men safely on board the barges, and then went back for another load. The second trip removed 84 men to safety, making a total of 200 for the morning's work. And then the two doctors went back to the hospital, starting in again at 10 a.m. with the routine work.

On this day (1st December) they were able to get to bed at midnight, and it requires no great effort to believe that they slept soundly. But they were up again early next morning for more transport work, and they took another 300 cases to Chisdarestii before they resumed the professional work at the hospital—again at 10 a.m. Three o'clock had struck on the morning of 3rd December before they were able to turn in, but they did so with thankfulness in their hearts, for they knew that the fighting was over for the time being, and they had been able to get through three days of stress without any breakdown or serious hitch in the medical organisation.

On turning out they performed an abdominal operation on a case, who had been brought in during the small hours, and then accompanied the heavy lorries with another batch of cases to Chisdarestii, taking fifty of them all the way to Hirsova to relieve the pressure on the barges. The lighter lorries could no longer be used because the road had become too bad. At Hirsova they found Lieutenant Ingle, sent there from Panteleimon, and they set his broken leg. In spite of the assistance rendered by the British motor-lorries, it was found impossible to provide all the wounded Russians with transport, and large numbers of lightly wounded men had to tramp the ten miles to Chisdarestii.

Staff-Surgeon Scott mentions that at Topalul he and his staff were treated with the utmost kindness by the Russian senior medical officers and staff. The modesty of this statement is admirable, but one is left wondering where the Russian medical arrangements would have been without the fortuitous assistance of the medical unit provided by the British Navy. During the whole period of the battle the two doctors and their staff of sick berth ratings had worked almost day and night, and by their energy and resource in making use of the transport lorries they had averted the catastrophe of a hopeless congestion at the field hospital. It had been a period of gloom and depression for the allied forces, but the devotion to duty of these officers and men, and the unflinching courage of the combatants, both Russian and English, endow the battle of Topalul with a shining ray of light. It is the courage which "*mounteth with occasion*" that is the best brand of all.

CHAPTER 23

The Retreat from the Dobrudsha

Those were dark days for Roumania in December 1916, when Mackensen's giant strides had rushed an army through the Dobrudsha, while on the other side of the Danube the Austro-German forces were steadily closing on Bucharest. It is not for me to try and fix the responsibility for her misfortunes, even if it were possible to do so from the mass of conflicting accounts which have emanated from various eyewitnesses; but a warning may not be amiss that all such accounts must be received with caution. When things are going wrong, everybody blames everybody else; such is human nature. A distraught staff officer eases his mind with a few forcible expressions about the regimental officers, while the regimental officers are equally eloquent about the staff officers; and the general sends for his chief of staff in order to blow off steam about the War Office and the Government—all in the strictest confidence. When two nations, very wide apart in race and national characteristics, join hands for the purpose of waging war, and when, moreover, the alliance is based, not upon an old-established friendship, but upon political expediency, it would be strange if, in the hour of disaster, each did not ascribe the chief share of the blame to the other.

In the Dobrudsha a Russian army had been striving to stem the tide of Mackensen's onslaught, and had even attempted a counter-attack to push him back beyond the Cernavoda Bridge. But on the eve of that counter-attack all the reserves had been hastily snatched away from General Sirelius, and thrust across the Danube in a desperate effort to save the Roumanian Army which was defending Bucharest. The counter-attack was a failure in all except the spirit shown by the Russian troops, who throughout the Battle of Topalul were faced by greatly superior artillery, and except the courageous efforts made by the British armoured cars. If bravery alone could win battles, Mackensen's army would have suffered a heavy defeat that day, but unfortunately in modern warfare a great deal more than the soldiers' heroism is required to gain success. The fighting quality of every individual man may count in the long run, but, however brilliant it may be, it is of no avail if the great machine behind it is faulty.

So the Russian Army in the Dobrudsha, denuded of its reserves, failed to drive back the enemy, and was on the point of sitting down to recover its breath, when the news came through that Bucharest had fallen. It was a staggering blow, not only on account of its political aspect, but also because it exposed the flank of the Dobrudsha army. It must be remembered that General Sirelius had been asked to make his great effort at Topalul before fresh reserves had had time to reach him, in order to cause a diversion, and so relieve the pressure on the Roumanian army before Bucharest. The fall of the capital, therefore, added another failure to the list of those objectives which he had attempted to secure. Moreover, it placed his army in serious jeopardy. The general, however, had no such word as "panic" in his vocabulary; he immediately sought some means of putting heart into his dispirited troops, and his mind, surveying the events of the past few days, lingered over the work of the British armoured cars.

"Give me the list of those Englishmen in the cars who have been recommended for decorations," he said to his *aide-de-camp*. The list was handed to him, and he ran his eye down the sheet. "Tell the Chief of Staff that I want a full parade of the division tomorrow morning," he said, "and send a note to Commander Gregory to tell him that I want to see these men there."

On 7th December 1916 the general presented the crosses and medals of St. George to the men of the British armoured cars before a full muster of his troops, and when the presentation was over he made a little speech to thank them for what they had done. Then he turned to his troops and told them about the work of the armoured cars.

> On 2nd December, the enemy's forces made a strong counter-attack on our left flank at Panteleimon. It was a critical moment, for I had no reserves available, and if the enemy had broken through our line, it is impossible to say what might not have happened. It was then that the squadron of British armoured cars, under Lieutenant-Commander Wells Hood, went right beyond our first line and poured into the advancing infantry of

the Bulgarians such a heavy fire that they were obliged to get back into their trenches. Their counter-attack was broken up, and our lines were saved. That was at Panteleimon. At Topalul our English comrades were performing similar feats. Bulgarian prisoners who have been brought in declare that no less than half their casualties have been due to the fire of the armoured cars.

This parade was held near Braila, on the left bank of the Danube, where the railway from Bucharest into Southern Russia begins to skirt the river. The place was in a state of hopeless confusion, for Roumanian fugitives, both soldiers and civilians, were streaming through it, so that the railway and the roads were blocked by them, and only the river was left to the Russians as a line of communication. Here Commander Gregory received orders from the staff that the armoured cars were to cover the right flank of the army during its retreat from the Dobrudsha, and with these orders he hastened back to Hirsova, where his force was carrying out a hurried refit.

During his absence at Braila he had left Lieutenant-Commander Belt in charge, and this officer had been informed by General Sirelius that Hirsova was liable to be attacked by the enemy at any moment, and that he had better make all preparations for removing the cars and their gear down the river. The advice was doubtless excellent, but how to act upon it was a problem. The quay was in a state of indescribable chaos; all the barges alongside it were thronged with soldiers and civilians, every man of them bent upon his own aims; the soldiers were loading up military stores, and the civilians were struggling to evacuate as much as they could of their household furniture and stock-in-trade. There was no one in authority to procure any semblance of order, and consequently every one was getting in every one else's way, so that none were making much progress with the work.

Lieutenant-Commander Belt saw at once that drastic measures were necessary, if the property of the Armoured Car Force was to be saved. He obtained the necessary sanction to commandeer a couple of barges, and, accompanied by an armed guard, he went down to the quay and commenced to load up all the heavier cars, the damaged cars, transport cars, spare stores and ammunition, and finally the sick men and those of the force who would not immediately be required. This left a squadron of light fighting cars, a few transport cars for supply, and a sufficient number of men for present needs.

The mobile force, which was thus reserved, was intended for the defence of Hirsova. There was some danger that Austrian monitors might come down the Danube and attack the town during the evacuation, and in that case the armoured cars would offer the best form of rear-guard on account of their mobility. As things turned out, however, the monitors neglected their opportunity, and, when all the inhabitants and all the troops had made good their retreat, the armoured cars received orders that they could leave the place to its fate.

Rain had been falling steadily for several days past, and consequently the roads were in a more horrible condition than usual. Commander Gregory had taken the precaution of reconnoitring them, in order to ascertain which of them offered some possibility of escape, and the result of the reconnaissance was that they had all been placed upon the black list with the exception of the road running eastwards to Alebei Chioi. Thither they started oil at daybreak on 14th December, and a tedious journey they found it. Every now and then they came across a hole in the road big enough to swallow a pantechnicon, and covered over with an unappetising mixture of mud and water about as thick as pea soup.

The forty odd miles occupied the whole of the day, and some strong language was heard on the road from Hirsova to Alebei Chioi. By the time they reached their destination they all felt quite ready for a nice hot supper followed by bed; but when the sailor goes a-soldiering he learns, among other things, that nice hot suppers and beds are not always to be picked up when they are wanted. It is no longer a case of going below to the mess deck and sitting down at a nice clean table, while the mess cook brings something fragrant and steaming from the galley; but he has to suffer an introduction to the mysteries of the commissariat and the field kitchen, and the hunt for billets.

At Alebei Chioi the village was under Roumanian control, and, to make matters worse, it was full of Austrian prisoners. For some time the men of the armoured cars could find no accommodation at all, and when at last they tumbled into some kind of a place with a roof to it—well, it is best not to go into details. Suffice it to say. that previous occupants had negligently left a few little things behind them. Of course it was inevitable that one of these desirable residences should be christened the Ritz, and another should become known as the Carlton. That is where the Britisher scores every time over the Hun and most of the other tribes of the earth—his sense of humour never fails him.

In such quarters they spent the next two days, and then came an order from General Sirelius that they should proceed at once to Braila, there to fill in an ugly gap in the Russian lines, which was threatening to grow wider at any moment. Just as they were about to start in the early morning, the clattering of a horse's hoofs was heard coming up the road, and a mounted orderly drew rein in front of them. He had ridden in hot haste with an urgent message from the general: "The enemy has broken through the lines in two places during the night. Dobrudsha army in full retreat. Cancel all previous orders, and proceed without delay to Tulscha. Two barges will be sent there to meet you, and bring you up the river."

So the Dobrudsha was to be resigned to the enemy, and the last flickering hope that it might be held until sufficient force could be collected to drive Mackensen southward, had died out. At Tulscha they found another scene of wild confusion, consequent upon an order to evacuate the place within forty-eight hours. There were no other means of retreat than by boat or barge up the Danube, or by road to Isakcha, where there was a pontoon bridge across the river. Needless to say, the more favoured of these two routes was the river, and consequently all floating craft was in great demand. The two barges referred to in the general's despatch were either mythical, or had been commandeered long ago by some distraught army officer, who was not likely to have made particular enquiries as to whether they were intended for some one else. After many hours, Commander Gregory succeeded in securing the whole of one barge to take the armoured cars to Reni, and half of another to take the lorries, stores, ammunition, and provisions to Ismail. He had just completed this arrangement, when a new problem was suddenly brought to his notice.

"How about the nurses of the Scottish Women's Hospital?"

This hospital had sent a unit to accompany a Serbian division fighting in Roumania. The division had been badly cut up, and very little was left of it, but the ladies of the Scottish Hospital had remained to carry on their good work, and found more than enough occupation in ministering to the soldiers of the Russian Army. They had recently been stationed at Braila, where some 8,000 wounded soldiers had been collected from the scenes of fighting on the Bucharest side of the Danube. And now they were lending their aid to the Russian medical units attached to the Dobrudsha army.

The problem of their evacuation from Tulscha was solved by invoking the aid of Sub-Lieutenant Turner, who proudly escorted his charge on board a barge, and, having signed a receipt for them and for the heavy transport lorries, which were also placed under his charge, he shoved off *en route* for Ismail, whence they were to proceed to Bolgrad. The light transport cars were taken by Lieutenant-Commander Belt along the road to Isakcha, and over the pontoon bridge to Bolgrad. The fighting cars went by barge with Commander Gregory to Reni. Thus, by a process of devolving his responsibilities, the commanding officer succeeded in shaking the chaotic dust of Tulscha from his feet.

The story of the fighting cars is the one which most concerns us at the moment, for the adventures of the transport lorries and the nurses belong to other realms than those of naval operations. When the cars reached Reni, they were so badly shaken by the rough roads they had traversed in the Dobrudsha that they had to be handed over to the repair stall for a hurried refit. It was fortunate that just at this time some extra cars arrived by train from Archangel, brand new from England. For the 4th Siberian Corps at Braila were sending S.O.S. signals, of which the burden ran:

For Heaven's sake send us some of the British armoured cars.

Now there was a liaison officer attached to the force, and there was also at Reni an officer belonging to the Russian armoured cars. With these Commander Gregory consulted as to the prospects of armoured car operations in the vicinity of Braila. Their advice was the same as that of *Punch* to young persons about to get married—"Don't."

> The roads round Braila are quite impossible for armoured cars. If you send those nice new cars of yours there you will lose them. The best thing you can do is to take the whole of your force to Odessa, and there wait upon events. That is what the Russian armoured cars are going to do.

But Commander Gregory was as obdurate as are most of the young people to whom *Punch* offered his advice.

> You see, it's this way. We were sent out here as a fighting force, and the first duty of a fighting force is to fight. I say nothing against Odessa as a delectable place for a rest cure, but it is not the kind of place for a fighting force, not at present. And if all the Russian armoured cars are going there, that seems to me an excellent reason why the British cars should stay within easy reach of the firing-line.

Of course he put it more politely than this, but he left no doubt as to the state of his mind on the subject. So the Russian cars went to Odessa, and the British cars remained at Reni, except a special flying squadron which was sent under the command of Lieutenant Smiles to Braila. The story of the achievements of this squadron is told in another chapter.

On 21st December the town of Tulscha fell into the hands of the enemy, and from that moment the Danube Army ceased to exist. In its stead a new army was formed under the title of the Sixth Army, and to this the British armoured cars were now attached. Commander Gregory, after conferring with Headquarters, decided to collect all the remainder of his force at Galatz, where they would be within call of the army based on Braila if any urgent need for their assistance should arise. In making this decision he knew that he was incurring considerable risk, for, in the event of a sudden retreat, it was very doubtful whether he would be able to extricate his force. There were no adequate roads behind Galatz leading to the rear; the railway was blocked with Roumanian refugees, while the stretch of river between Galatz and Reni was likely to be commanded before long by the enemy's artillery. On the other hand, there was the prestige of British arms to be considered, and this consideration was enough in itself to determine him to remain near the firing-line up to the last possible moment.

The repair staff, by working night and day, had made every one of the lighting cars lit for immediate service, when they were placed on a barge and taken up to Galatz. There they were joined by the light transport cars, brought from Bolgrad by Lieutenant Commander Belt, after some minor adventures with an Austrian aeroplane near the demolished pontoon bridge at Isakcha. The heavy transport lorries also found their way to Galatz, and so did the doctors and nurses of the Scottish Women's Hospital. In fact, none of the British contingent found the charms of Odessa powerful enough to entice them from the vicinity of the firing-line.

Of the formation of a second special squadron under Lieutenant-Commander Wells Hood, to operate in the neighbourhood of Tudor Vladimirescu, not much need be said, for the roads there were found to be quite impossible for armoured cars. The squadron left Galatz in a blinding blizzard, lost their way several times, eventually arriving at Tudor, where they reconnoitred the roads in several directions, but were obliged to condemn them all. They had considerable difficulty in getting back to Galatz again, for the main road was being continually cut up by heavy artillery retreating eastwards.

The next event was the decision to evacuate Braila, the base from which Lieutenant Smiles's squadron was operating, and Commander Gregory therefore sent a telegram to recall him. But late in the evening of New Year's Day an urgent message came through from General Sirelius, begging that the squadron might remain with him, and undertaking to place at their disposal a special train to take them from Braila to Galatz at the last moment.

> The cars have established such an ascendency over the enemy that he never attacks when they are present, knowing that he is sure to suffer heavy losses by doing so, and, moreover, the cars produce a great moral effect upon my own men, which is invaluable to me at this critical juncture.

So Commander Gregory cancelled the order recalling Lieutenant Smiles, sent him two new cars to take the place of two which had been damaged in the fighting, gave him a fresh supply of ammunition, and wired to the general that the squadron was to remain at his service.

From the quayside at Galatz they could see a fierce battle raging in the Dobrudsha—the last desperate effort to contest Mackensen's advance. Far and wide across the long stretch of flat country great fountains of smoke kept on shooting up into the sky, and mingling with the river mists, while the bursts of the shells gave a lurid tinge of red to the overhanging pall. As a spectacle it was magnificent, but to the watchers at Galatz it was all too evident that the Russian artillery was no match for that of the enemy, and that the Russian infantry was everywhere being driven back by superior numbers. In the evening of 2nd January Matchin—the last town in the Dobrudsha—fell into the enemy's hands, and nothing now remained but to extricate the Russian troops by withdrawing them across the river.

It is a curious illustration of the uncertainties of war that on that very morning the general commanding in the Dobrudsha had actually been contemplating an offensive, and three cars belonging to Lieutenant Smiles's squadron had been sent across the Danube in the afternoon to assist the attack. When they arrived, however, the whole situation had changed; the Russians had been shelled out of their positions, and, instead of expecting to advance, the general was now wondering whether he could get his forces out of the tight corner in which they were placed. The three cars proceeded to a position 400 yards in advance of the Russian lines, and did not drop back until the evening.

One car developed engine trouble, and had to be towed home, while another was ordered to return, as it was a heavy car with a 3-pounder gun, which could not be used advantageously after dark. This left Sub-Lieutenant Kidd in a light Ford car abreast of the Russian first-line trenches, where he remained after the commanding officer of the Cossacks had announced his intention of retiring the whole force from the trenches.

For another quarter of an hour he kept up an intermittent fire on the enemy, while the Russian infantry made good their retreat, and then he slowly followed them—the sole barrier between the Russian forces and Mackensen's advancing army. A small body of cavalry were just ahead of him, and he followed them slowly towards the pontoon bridge, until he came to the last line of Russian trenches, where he found some infantry in possession but on the point of retiring. He had no definite orders, but he considered that it was his job to see the whole of the Russian Army off the premises and over the river before he himself left the Dobrudsha.

So he waited for twenty minutes to let the infantry get away, keeping his machine-gun rattling away from time to time at the unseen foe. It was very dark and very foggy, and he could not help speculating upon the chances of running his car into a shell-hole, and so losing it. At last he moved on again, picking his way very cautiously through a thick bank of fog. Presently a voice hailed him through the darkness. It was the Cossack commander, who wanted to thank him for what he had done.

"They're all over the bridge," he said, "cavalry and all."

"Where is the bridge? "

"Here, you've just come to it; and we must hurry up and get across, for our fellows are going to blow it up."

So Sub-Lieutenant Kidd splashed through the mud on to the pontoon bridge—the very last unit of the allied forces to leave the Dobrudsha. Less than an hour later the bridge was no more.

At Galatz there was a scene of bustle and activity, for it was obvious that in a few hours the town would be subjected to bombardment, and all the available barges were being loaded up with stores, ammunition, and everything not immediately required by the defending force. The army from the Dobrudsha had brought with them a large number of sick and wounded, and it was fortunate for these men that the nurses of the Scottish Women's Hospital were at Galatz to receive them. There was also a unit of the British Red Cross Society under Dr. Clemow and Mr. Berry. The former is an English doctor who has spent many years of his life at Constantinople, and whose intimate knowledge of the Near East and its inhabitants made him a very valuable asset to the medical forces in Roumania. All the nurses stoutly refused to leave Galatz until the last possible moment, and the Russian staff, finding that neither argument nor entreaty produced the least impression, besought Commander Gregory to intervene. He effected a compromise by persuading them to transfer their hospital to a big barge, where they could carry on with their work, and then shove off at once when the first shells began to fall on the town.

Here are a few extracts from letters received from some of the nurses.

> Commander Gregory of the British Armoured Car Corps sent down a message to say that in the last resort he would see us out, so we were able to work with quiet minds. We owe a great debt to Mr. Scott, surgeon to the British Armoured Car Corps, who asked us if he could be of any use. I sent back a message to say that we should be most grateful, and he worked with us without a break until we evacuated. He has just pointed out to me that we operated for thirty-six hours on end the first day, with three hours break in the early hours of the morning, and, as we had been working twenty-four hours before that—admitting patients, bathing, and dressing them—you can imagine what a time we had. Dr. Corbett has also been calculating, and she says we worked sixty-five hours on end with two breaks of three hours' sleep. We came out of it very fit—thanks to the kitchen.
>
> A Roumanian officer talked to me about Glasgow, where he had once been, and had been 'invited out to dinner, so he had seen the English custims.' It was good to feel those 'English custims' were still going quietly on, whatever was happening here—breakfasts coming regularly, and hot water for baths, and everything as it should be. It was probably absurd, but it came like a great wave of comfort to feel that England was there—quiet, strong, and invincible behind everything and everybody.

Yes, England was there, to stand by Roumania in her hour of trial, even as she had stood by Serbia; even as she had shared in the retreat from Mons, and more recently in the retreat from the Isonzo. Since the war began England has always been there, in every part of the world where fighting was to be done—in the conquest of the Cameroons, of East Africa, of South-West Africa, in the advance across the plains of Mesopotamia, and over the hills of Palestine. Sometimes alone and sometimes aided by her Allies, wherever the guns have been fired in anger, by sea or by land, England has been there.

CHAPTER 24

The Battle of Vizirul

When Lieutenant Smiles left Reni on 21st December 1916, with a party of eight officers, five chief petty officers, and thirty-seven petty officers, forming a special service squadron of armoured cars to assist the 4th Siberian Corps at Braila, the situation had already become critical. Bucharest had fallen, and the Russian Army in the Dobrudsha was being steadily driven back by superior forces, while its right flank was all the time exposed to attack from across the Danube. In fact, it had already been decided that the Dobrudsha must be evacuated, and the next problem was how to extricate the Russian troops on the other side of the river, and bring them back to the line of the Sereth, or any other line which it was possible to hold. One of the virtues of the armoured car is that it can be as serviceable for a retreat as for an attack, its mobility enabling it to harass the advancing enemy up to the last moment, and then make good its escape.

Lieutenant Smiles is an Irishman by birth, and has the Irish gift of quick intuition, which is invaluable to one whose responsibilities continually call for promptness of decision. He had served with the armoured cars in France, Belgium, and Persia, and had just recovered from a wound received in the Dobrudsha, but this did not deter him from volunteering to lead the special squadron, which was sent off in a hurry to Braila upon receipt of a message from General Sirelius earnestly soliciting their assistance, he took with him two heavy cars and six light Ford cars, as well as lorries for the transport of ammunition and stores. These all proceeded by barge to Braila, where they were unloaded and prepared for immediate action. The force was then divided into two sections, one going to Movila under the command of Lieutenant Hunter and the other, under Lieutenant Smiles, proceeding to Valea Canepei. It was not long, however, before the squadron was united again, for the roads in the direction of Movila were found to be unfit for armoured cars, and Lieutenant Hunter returned to Braila, proceeding thence to Valea Canepei to rejoin the rest of the squadron.

At Valea Canepei General Sirelius greeted the British officers by inviting them all to lunch with him, for he had a warm place in his heart for the armoured cars. The next business was the inspection of the front, which was carried out the same afternoon by Lieutenant Smiles, in company with Lieutenant Edwards and Chief Petty Officer MacFarlane. The Huns must have scented trouble in store for them, for they greeted the trio with an extra dose of shells. Colonel Bolgramo, who was in command of the brigade at that point, conducted the party and showed them all the beauties of the place, including the village of Roobla in the distance, where enemy troops were said to be billeted in large numbers.

Lieutenant Smiles called to mind a similar scene somewhere in France, and remembered how the heavy cars there used to wander up towards the enemy's trenches, blaze away with 3-pounder guns at certain objects behind their lines, and then, when the Hun artillery began to find the range of them, used to dodge back to safety. He saw a glowing prospect of playing the same kind of game on the road to Roobla.

Next day at dawn, Lieutenant Lucas-Shadwell went into action with the "Ulster" heavy car, and started to demolish the village of Roobla. On the east side of the road the houses were stoutly built, and it was said that the enemy had a battery there hidden behind two of the houses, Lucas-Shadwell found the range at 1,200 yards, and blew those two houses into little chunks. Then he turned his attention to the west side of the road, where the houses were more flimsy, and where the troops were supposed to be billeted, and he felt his way systematically up and down the village, firing deliberately and taking careful observation of the fall of the shells. He spent just a quarter of an hour at it, and then, according to orders, brought his car out of action. It was not until he was on his way back that the Hun artillery woke up and started to speed him on his journey. The scouts at the advanced base reported that he had done good execution.

Next morning another heavy car, a "Londonderry," commanded by Sub-Lieutenant Henderson, went into action, while the "Ulster" was held in reserve. The "Londonderry" is a bit top-heavy, and consequently difficult to steer. Lieutenant Smiles anticipating that there might be trouble with it, came up behind on an ordinary bicycle, which he had borrowed from a Russian officer, and ordered the "Pierce Arrow" lorry to stand by with a couple of tow-ropes in case of accidents. His orders to Henderson were to bombard Roobla and the roads round about it, not to remain in action more than fifteen minutes, not to attempt to go beyond a certain shell-crater in the road, and, if he got stuck, to fire three rifle-shots in quick succession. The anticipation of trouble was an intelligent one, for the "Londonderry" had no sooner reached the Russian advance post than it slid gracefully into a ditch. Smiles at once cycled back to Vizirul for the "Pierce Arrow" lorry, at the same time ordering Sub-Lieutenant MacDowall to take the "Ulster" into action.

Then came the job of pulling the "Londonderry" out of the ditch. It was rather a long job, and it was not rendered any easier by the enemy's artillery, which always showed a marked partiality for a stationary target in the shape of an armoured car. It should, however, be observed that the artillery was very inferior to that brought against us in the Dobrudsha. The truth of the matter was that the enemy forces closing on Bucharest had moved so rapidly that their heavier pieces were still many miles to the rear. The tow-ropes were attached to the stranded "Londonderry," and the "Pierce Arrow" began to haul, but at first no visible impression was produced.

Then various devices were tried to ease the path of the sunken wheels. The workers were so much absorbed in their task that they had no time to look round towards the enemy's lines, and worked on in blissful ignorance of the fact that the Bulgarian troops had climbed over their parapet and were advancing steadily towards them. At last, with a squelching sound, as the wheels were drawn out of the mud, the "Londonderry" began to move, and in a few minutes was on her way along the road towards Vizirul. Less than half an hour later the enemy were in possession of the spot where she had been lying.

The "Ulster" returned about the same time, and Lieutenant Smiles called at Colonel Bolgramo's headquarters for further orders.

"Do you see that long line of infantry?" said the colonel, waving his hand towards the enemy. "They are advancing on Vizirul, and, if they take it, Heaven only knows how we shall extricate ourselves. I want you to go at once to the general, and ask leave to send all your cars up to the front lines, for I honestly believe that is the only way of beating off the attack."

To the general he went, and the order to send up all the cars was confirmed. Henderson, MacDowall, and Lucas-Shadwell were sent off post-haste, and Smiles himself followed in a Ford. On his way he saw Colonel Bolgramo at the field telephone, and the colonel signalled to him to stop.

"My fellows have lost terribly," he said. "They cannot stand much more of it. I want you to go right beyond our barbed wire, and do what you can to check the advance."

The Ford car used by Lieutenant Smiles was in the nature of an improvisation. The ordinary armoured car had often proved too heavy for its purpose in districts where the so-called roads were little more than cart-tracks. When the force was in Persia they found endless difficulties in getting over the ground where dust a foot deep lay on the tracks, and it was soon driven home to their minds that some lighter form of car was essential in the East. They conceived the idea of converting an ordinary Ford car into an armoured car by rigging steel plates round it, and mounting in it a maxim with a gun-shield. Thus the Ford armoured car came into being, and proved very useful for skirmishing, though of course it could not take the same risks as a "Lanchester" or any of the heavier cars. It was usually manned by an officer, a driver, and a gunner—sometimes only by driver and gunner, and the latter very often lay on his back, so as to get shelter from the steel plates, and worked his gun in that position.

Smiles found that he could not get his car to reverse, and therefore had to go into action forwards. The disadvantage of this is that the car has to be turned round in order to get back again, and on a narrow road turning is not an easy process under any circumstances, and is quite impossible if the car refuses to reverse. There was, however, no choice in the matter, so he went full steam ahead past the line of barbed wire, and was 500 yards beyond it before he stopped. Then he opened fire with his maxim at the advancing Bulgarians and played havoc with them.

It is a queer sensation to be stuck out in the midst of No Man's Land, unsupported by friends, and a conspicuous target for foes. It seems that all the rifles, all the machine-guns, and all the artillery the enemy can muster are directed at you and no one else. You seem to be such a landmark for miles round that you start wondering how the Hun's big guns can possibly contrive to miss you. At the same time you experience a kind of exhilaration from the sense of fighting an army single-handed, and the sight of enemy infantry dropping one after another, accompanied by the sound of shells bursting all round you, and the strident ha-ha-ha-ha of your own machine-gun, has a curiously stimulating effect.

Life is so full of crowded moments then that you lose count of the passage of time, or rather, you exaggerate the count, and imagine that the space of a few minutes has sent the clock round many hours, for those few minutes contain as much excitement as the majority of people find in a whole life-time. All the same, the officer in command of an armoured car has little opportunity to study these psychological effects, for he has sooner or later to make up his mind upon the chances of receiving a direct hit by a shell. When the artillery has crept up closer and closer, so that the shells begin to straddle him, he knows that the moment has come to get a move on.

Now Lieutenant Smiles had gone into action nose forward because he could not get his car to reverse. When he wanted to come out of action, he found that the road was too narrow to turn in, and was bordered on either side by a ditch. But hope springs eternal in the human breast, and he had a vague notion that the old car, which had thrown its hand in when asked to reverse into action, would be so jolly glad to get out of it that it would not only reverse, but would stand on its head if necessary. So he told the driver to try the reversing gear. There was a grunt, a groan, and a squeak; and then silence. The engine had stopped. The silence, of course, was only inside the car; outside it there was plenty of noise, for bullets were whistling and shells were bursting incessantly. Lieutenant Smiles, however, showed no hesitation; he jumped out of the car, seized the handle, started up the engine, and jumped in again.

There was just a moment of extreme suspense, when every one inside the car was wondering would she go, or would she not, and then she began to move, slowly and protestingly, but still she moved, and moved backwards. For fifty yards she floundered along the road, with about as much grace as an old sow being pushed through the gate of its sty, and then the engine again stopped dead. Smiles was outside the car in a moment, and was turning the handle vigorously; but the engine made no response to his efforts, and just as the unwelcome truth dawned on him that the car had an unreasonable prejudice against progressing backwards, a bullet caught him in the leg just above the knee. He rolled into the ditch by the side of the road to do a little quiet thinking. Petty Officer Classey put his head out and shouted to him:

"Shall I have a try, sir?"

Leading Petty Officer Graham also put his head out.

"I think I might be able to manage it, sir."

But Lieutenant Smiles was firm. It was quite useless to start the engine up because it would only stop again; it had consistently refused to work when the reversing gear was applied, and, being an inanimate thing, it could not realise the extreme necessity of overcoming its prejudice. In extenuation of its behaviour it must be observed that all four tyres had been punctured by bullets, and consequently the strain on the engine was considerable even when the car was going forwards. The process of quiet contemplation was not aided by the persistent attentions of the enemy's artillery, which became all the more persistent when it was realised that the car was stuck.

"You fellows had better come and join me in the ditch," said Lieutenant Smiles; "they'll be scoring a direct hit before long, if they have a decent gun-layer among them."

The two men jumped out of the car and dropped into the ditch,

"Look here, Graham," said the officer, "the chances are that some of those Russian sportsmen will be thinking of coming to the rescue. I want you to crawl back along this ditch, get hold of their commanding officer, and ask him, as a special favour, not to let a single Russian soldier risk his life on our account. Tell him that we are all right, and can look out for ourselves."

So Graham started off towards the Russian lines, keeping himself under cover as far as the depth of the ditch would allow.

"As a matter of fact," said Smiles, "I see no reason why we shouldn't get out of this mess after dark."

"If we could get space enough," said Classey, "to turn round without reversing."

"There's only one way, and that is to run her off the road across this ditch, turn round in the field, and then run her back again on to the road."

"I don't see why we shouldn't be able to do it after dark. But, bless my soul, sir, you're bleeding."

"So I am. I stopped one when I was trying to start up the engine— just above the knee. For Heaven's sake, man, keep your head down."

Petty Officer Classey was too busy rendering first aid to worry about the bullets whistling over his head, and Lieutenant Smiles had to remind him constantly not to expose himself. But he made quite a neat job of the bandage, and when he had finished it the pair of them began a long weary wait for nightfall.

The reaction after the excitement of the last quarter of an hour was painful; nothing to do but wait all through the day, remaining in a cramped position in order to secure the shelter of the ditch. At times the artillery did their best to hit the abandoned car, but fortunately they never scored a direct hit. While their efforts lasted, however, they made life very uncomfortable for the two in the ditch, and during the lulls it quite astonished them to find how little a man heeds a perfect tornado of rifle and machine-gun bullets, when he has successfully passed through the ordeal of shell-fire. When darkness had fallen they crawled out of the ditch and into the car, Classey having started up the engine. She bounded forward with a mighty jerk, as though eager to show what she really could do when people did not play silly tricks with the reversing gear. With a mighty lunge she waddled across the ditch by the side of the road, took a short tour round the adjacent field, and then tried to waddle back across the ditch on to the road. The second waddle, however, was not so successful, and it required a good deal of hard shoving to help her up the slope of the ditch. Once on the firm road she was off in a twinkling, and was soon safely back in the village of Vizirul.

Meanwhile the other cars of the squadron had been having little adventures all on their own. Lieutenant Shadwell had experienced the same trouble as his leader in getting his car to reverse, but he had taken her right up to the enemy's barbed wire, and done some good execution with his machine-gun. Just as he was withdrawing, a bullet caught him in the neck, causing a nasty wound, which put an end to his activities for the day. MacDowall with his "Ulster" was one of the first to go into action in the early morning, when there was a heavy mist, which obscured his view of the enemy. Chief Petty Officer Mac-Farlane and Petty Officer Fear went up the road as scouts, and presently came back with a report that a body of Bulgarian infantry were creeping up towards the car.

The crew in the car waited until the Bulgarians were about 150 yards off, and then let drive at them with machine-gun and rifles. This had the effect of thinning the ranks, but not of stopping the rush, and it soon became obvious that they intended to capture the car by storm. Possibly they were not sufficiently conversant with the various breeds of armoured car to know a heavy one from a light one, for when MacFarlane and Fear dropped their rifles and got to work with the 3-pounder, the Bulgarians were completely dismayed. They turned and fled, some of them dropping into a shell-crater about 50 yards up the road from where the car stood, and here the 3-pounder dropped two or three shells into them just to make sure that they would try no more of their storming tactics. The supply of shells was then finished off on the village of Roobla, the road leading to it, and finally into the trenches 1,000 yards away, and then the car came out of action, having suffered no casualties.

After a short interval MacDowell went into action again. The enemy were then advancing in rushes against our advanced posts, and at times it looked as though they stood an unpleasantly good chance of breaking through the Russian lines. The car ran up to within 700 yards of the advancing Bulgarians and started pumping lead into them as hard as it could, which had the effect of checking the advance for the time being, and of compelling the enemy to dig themselves in. Unfortunately it is not possible for an armoured car to carry any large stock of 3-pounder ammunition, and so it behoves its occupants to use their shells sparingly, reserving fire until they see a group of three or four of the enemy together.

After two hours steady pummelling of the Bulgarian infantry, the car had to withdraw for more ammunition, but it went back into action almost immediately and contrived to remain in action for the next five hours until darkness began to fall. To the enemy it must have been a constant source of annoyance, for the troops had no inclination to advance against shell-fire at point-blank range, and wherever the armoured cars were operating the enemy's offensive was completely held up.

Lieutenant Henderson had the "Londonderry" car in which he took up his station near the entrance to Vizirul village, and steadily shelled the enemy from half-past nine in the morning until two o'clock in the afternoon. He had some trouble with his turret, which refused to budge until Chief Petty Officer Common and Petty Officer Wildbore got out of the car under heavy fire to swing the turret round by means of the gun. Then the "Londonderry" played its old trick of sliding into a ditch, where it sat patiently for some time, and was finally rescued by the "Ulster."

Just before nightfall the enemy drew off his infantry and commenced another artillery bombardment, which only ceased when darkness fell. That night the Russian scouts were busy collecting rifles from Bulgarians who had fallen in the fight. In one spot, where the armoured cars had been busy, 380 rifles were collected. Colonel Bolgramo had many appreciative words to offer Lieutenant Smiles upon the work done by the armoured cars during the day. The outstanding fact, which eclipsed all others, was that at that point in the Russian line the enemy had been completely repulsed. Unfortunately, however, it was the only point of which this could be said, and before long there were messages coming through showing that both flanks to right and left of Vizirul had been driven back.

The next morning dawned with the usual thick fog clinging to the valley of the Danube and the marshes on either side. It was impossible to see more than 100 yards ahead, and, though a fresh attack was expected at any moment, it was not likely to materialise under such conditions. At eleven o'clock the fog had abated, and the scouts reported that the Bulgarians were advancing in great numbers on the road from Roobla to Vizirul. Lieutenant Smiles at once went into action with the "Ulster;" he was 300 yards beyond the Russian trenches before he saw any sign of the enemy, and then he was greeted by a storm of bullets from rifles and machine-guns. He had to drop back a bit, but he kept his maxim searching up and down the Bulgarian trenches, while his 3-pounder, at a range of 1,500 yards, was peppering one of the enemy's observation posts. All the time he moved his car backwards and forwards to baffle the enemy's artillery, and by this means contrived to keep in action all day until half-past five in the evening.

The enemy was still held at bay between Roobla and Vizirul, but this did not compensate for the fact that he had been successful everywhere else, and had advanced so far on either flank that the Russian forces at Vizirul were in danger of being surrounded. On the evening of 28th December the colonel received orders to evacuate Vizirul during the night, and, with a view to making a demonstration. Lieutenant Hunter and Sub-Lieutenant Kidd were sent with a couple of cars up to the Russian first-fine trenches. There they stopped their engines, and the Russian infantry silently pushed them into No Man's Land.

At midnight the Russians crept out of their trenches, and the retreat began, while the two cars kept up a merry tattoo with their maxims, to give the enemy the impression that they were about to receive a furious onslaught. For three-quarters of an hour they blazed away, and then began slowly to follow the Russian troops. Kidd led the way, and, as ill luck would have it, missed the line of the road in the darkness and slid into a ditch. Hunter came up behind and found that Kidd's car was damaged sufficiently to make its extrication a matter of impossibility under the circumstances, so there was nothing for it but to salve the gun, demolish the engine, radiator, petrol-tank and coils, and abandon the wreck to the enemy.

Some of the crew managed to get into Hunter's car, and some had to walk, but all of them managed to overtake the Russian rearguard, and reached Locul Sarat at five o'clock in the morning. They had the satisfaction of knowing that the retreat had been completely successful, and that out of the whole Russian force at Vizirul, only one man had been wounded during the evacuation.

The battle of Vizirul was over, and, though the arms of the Allies had suffered another reverse, the defeat reflected as much credit upon the armoured cars of the Royal Naval Air Service as if they had participated in a glorious victory. The bare recital of the facts is sufficient to indicate how invaluable were the services of these cars to the Russian army at a very critical juncture, and if further testimony were needed it can be found in the words addressed by the General Commanding the 6th Army to Commander Gregory on New Year's Day—three days after the battle ended.

> I am proud to have under my command such a brave and splendid force as the British Armoured Car Division, and I thank our British comrades very much for their help in all these fights of the last few days, and in the Dobrudsha.... The squadron of cars commanded by Lieutenant Smiles saved the left flank of my army twice in forty-eight hours at Vizirul. It is an achievement for which I can find no adequate words of praise. I wish you all a happy New Year, and I want to take an early opportunity of rewarding the gallantry of the men under your command by conferring on them the Crosses and Medals of St. George.

The reader will probably have observed that Lieutenant Smiles went into action on the day following that on which he was wounded, he himself speaks lightly of his wound, but others have expressed a different opinion. The fact is that he persuaded Petty Officer Classey to join in a conspiracy of silence about it until the battle was over, for the Irish blood in him revolted from the prospect of being cooped up in a hospital when there was real fighting to be enjoyed. Some days later the story reached the headquarters staff at Galatz, and the chief of staff sent for Commander Gregory and asked him for the name of the British officer who went on fighting after he was wounded. For his share in upholding the highest traditions of the British Navy and the prestige of British arms in Russia and Roumania, Lieutenant-Commander Smiles has been awarded the Distinguished Service Order.

THE ADEN PATROL

CHAPTER 25

An Outpost of Empire in Somaliland

On 9th May 1916 some Somalis belonging to the Warsangli tribe arrived at Aden with a report that their tribe was being attacked at Las Khorai by some of the Mullah's dervishes. Now Las Khorai lies on the northern coast of Somaliland not far from the boundary between British and Italian territory. It is not linked by telegraph wire nor by wireless station with the civilised world; it has no regular mail service; its sole means of communication is the sailing *dhow*, which may take as much as a fortnight to reach Aden or Berbera, if the wind happens to be unfavourable. Fortunately for its inhabitants, the wind on this occasion was favourable, so that the news of the dervish attack reached Aden within three days of its commencement.

On Saturday evening 6th May 1916, some 2,000 *dervishes* swooped down from the mountains and surrounded the little village, with the intention of completely annihilating it and all its inhabitants. They set about the work deliberately and systematically, believing that they had plenty of time in front of them. On the morning of Wednesday 10th May up came H.M.S. *Northbrook*, like a bolt from the blue, and the inhabitants of Las Khorai were saved.

The genesis of this incident can only be explained by going back a few years, and giving a brief summary of the history of British Somaliland. At the end of 1869 the Suez Canal was declared open, and the high road to India and the Far East thenceforward lay through the Red Sea and the Gulf of Aden. At that time the Khedive of Egypt claimed sovereignty over Berbera and the villages along the coast of Somaliland, and kept garrisons in them as a token of his sovereign rights. But in 1884 the *khedive* was confronted with a mighty problem consequent upon the rise of the *Mahdi* in the Sudan, and therefore the

Egyptian garrisons were withdrawn from Somaliland, and the country was, metaphorically speaking, put under the hammer.

As a country it was not a desirable purchase for anybody, but it happened to be situated on the flank of one of the narrow parts of the high road to India, and consequently the British Government felt that they had no option in the matter; the creation of a British Protectorate in Somaliland was inevitable. So in 1884 we occupied Zeila, Bulbar, and Berbera; in 1888 we settled a boundary between British and French Somaliland; in 1894 we made an agreement with Italy, and in 1897 one with Abyssinia, to settle the other boundaries; and so British Somaliland became an accomplished fact. But it was not long before our troubles began.

Of the early history of the "Mad" Mullah very little is definitely known. He was born in the Dolbahanta country about 1865, spent some of his boyhood at Berbera and Aden, and as a youth is supposed to have found employment in one of the ocean liners plying between Europe and the East. According to Mr. Drake-Brockman (in his book on British Somaliland) it was the life on board ship which first impressed on the mind of the young Mahomed bin Abdillah the value of discipline in dealing with large bodies of men, and very probably gave him an insight into human nature such as the ordinary shore-goer does not often acquire.

His wanderings took him to many cities unknown to the Somali peasant, and threw him into contact with many different races professing the Mahomedan faith. While still a young man he conceived a desire to make a pilgrimage to Mecca, and there he came under the influence of Mahomed Saleh, the head of a sect which enjoins a strict adherence to the laws of the Prophet. Many of these laws were unknown to the Somali s until they were introduced by Mahomed bin Abdillah, who, after his return to his native country, embarked on the career of a *mullah*— a wandering preacher—and started to preach the doctrines he had learnt at Mecca.

It is noteworthy that one of the principles of the sect is total abstinence from *kat*. The practice of taking this drug is widespread among the Arabs, and in Arabia, where the plant is grown extensively, the tender leaves are eaten as though they were an ordinary food. The effect of them is said to be stimulating, as well as intoxicating, with the result that the Arab is content with remarkably little sleep, and is able to spend most of the night in sociable conversation. One would suppose that in course of time Nature must assert herself and demand full pay-

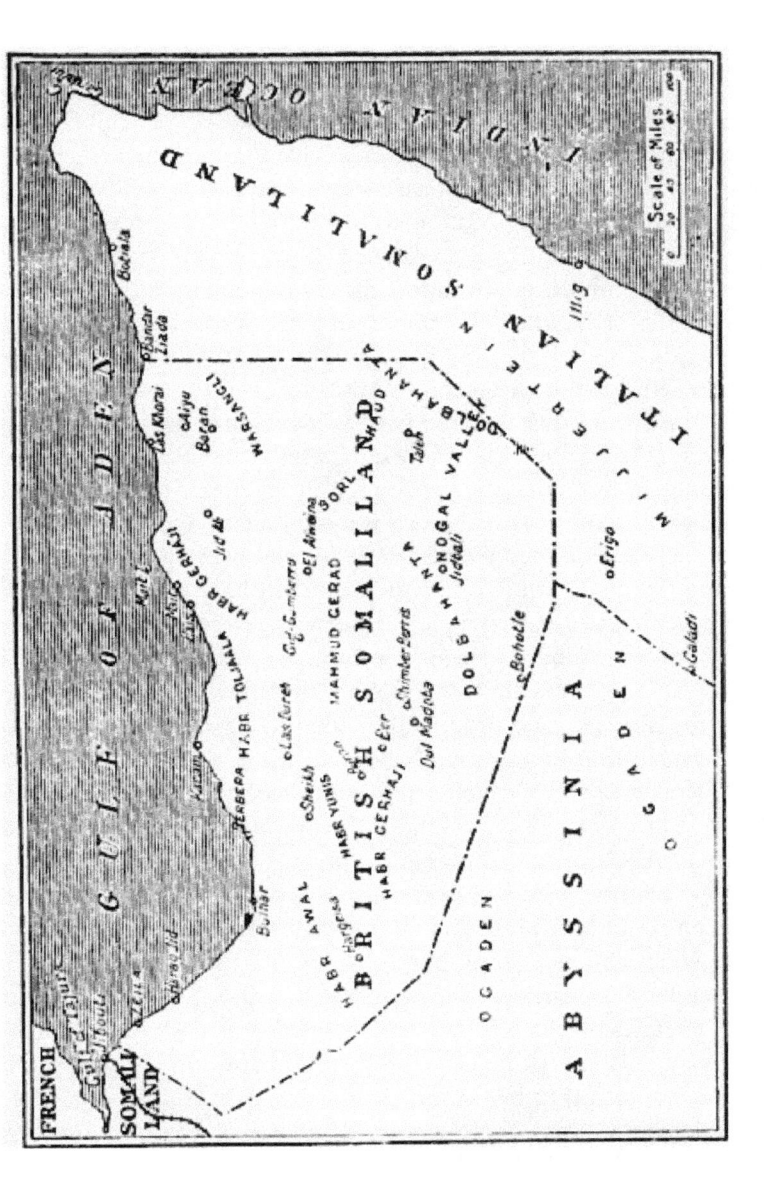

ment for this encroachment upon the hours of sleep; but, according to Paul Emile Botta, the French naturalist who visited the Yemen about the middle of the nineteenth century, this is not the case. He says that the *kat*-eaters live to a ripe old age, and that their health does not seem to suffer in the least. He cites the example of the despatch runners who can keep on the move for several days and nights continuously with no other nourishment than a bundle of *kat*-leaves. But the plant is none the less a drug, and appears to have some of the properties of opium in that it is said to induce pleasant dreams.

If the puritanism of Mahomed bin Abdillah had ended in a crusade against the use of *kat* the British Government would have had no cause of complaint, but unfortunately it went a good deal further. Among the laws which he imported into Somaliland was a penal code against theft—the loss of the right hand for the first offence, and the left foot for the second. Mutilation and torture for the most trivial misdemeanours became part of his regime, for he soon found that terrorising gained him more adherents than could be secured by preaching. It is said that the penalty for disobedience to his commands on the part of one of his followers is instant death, and that sometimes this penalty is extended to the whole of the man's family, presumably on the principle that the disobedience might have been infectious.

The epithet "Mad" which has been assigned by the Somalis to Mahomed bin Abdillah, is supposed to have originated from certain disagreeable eccentricities of the man. For instance, he would wake up in the morning and order 300 women to be put to death, because he had been told in a dream that they had refused to pray. There are many stories of this character, and, if they are true, they suggest that the Mullah was seeking a method of working upon the superstitious nature of the Somalis. In this he was quite successful, for he was soon credited with superhuman powers, and all sorts of legends have been invented about him. He wears round his neck an amulet, which is said to contain a complete copy of the Koran, and the natives believe that this amulet is a charm which preserves him from death at the hands of his enemies.

It was in 1899 that he gave the first intimation to the government that he was going to be a thorn in their side. In August of that year he collected a strong force, marched to Burao, occupied the town, and declared himself the *Mahdi*. He used Burao as a convenient centre from which he could carry out raids against the various tribes, murdering them without discrimination, and looting their livestock.

Here was a vocation which always makes a strong appeal to the Somali character, and so it was not long before the *mullah's* band of followers was largely augmented, and became a formidable force. Those of the natives who felt no longing for a career of brigandage and murder, but preferred to seek their livelihood by the more humdrum method of breeding sheep and cattle, naturally resented these raids upon their property, and appealed to the British Government for protection. It was then that we realised that the establishment of a protectorate in Somaliland, which we had undertaken so light-heartedly, promised to give us plenty of food for thought.

In May 1901 Colonel Sir E. J. Swayne was sent with native levies to drive the *mullah* out of Burao, and, heavily defeating him three times, forced him to flee across the Sorl Haud into Italian territory, to take refuge among the Mijjertein tribe. Six months later, however, he was back again at Burao, raiding the friendly tribes as happily as ever, and reducing them to a state of destitution by the wholesale capture of their sheep, cattle, and camels. In May 1902 Colonel Swayne made another effort, this time supplementing his Somali levies with a detachment of King's African Rifles, recruited from the Yoas of Nyassaland. Again the *mullah* fled across the Sorl Haud into Italian territory. Permission was obtained from the Italian Government to follow him, but on 6th October 1902 one of our detachments fell into an ambush, which the *mullah* had prepared for them at Erigo, and, though after a hot fight we put the *dervishes* to flight, we lost 101 killed and 85 wounded, with the result that we were unable to follow up the *mullah* when he retired to Galadi, on the borders of Abyssinia and Italian Somaliland.

The following year Major-General Manning took charge of the operations, having a combined force of British and Boer Mounted Infantry, Indian troops, and African troops. He pushed right across Italian Somaliland from the sea, and finally concentrated his various detachments at Bohottle; but he never managed to get to close grips with the *mullah*, Our force was raised to 7,000 men, and Major-General Sir C. C Egerton took command; but the game of hide and seek went on as before. The *mullah* had established himself in the Nogal Valley, and we had made all preparations to meet him there, when we heard that he had seized and occupied the Italian coast town of Illig. In January 1904, however, we did manage to secure a pitched battle at Jidbali; where we routed the *dervishes*, killing over 1,000 of them. Unfortunately, however, the *mullah* was not present at the battle. By May 1904 he was again a refugee among the Mijjertein tribe, and, as there was no prospect of being able to catch him, it was decided to leave him there. Though the operations had lasted intermittently for over three years, we were really no nearer to our goal at the end of them than we had been at the beginning.

During the next few years the *mullah* remained very quiet, and we had serious hopes that we had heard the last of him. But in 1908 he quarrelled with his friends the Mijjerteins— possibly because they had grown weary of feeding him and his followers gratuitously—and in 1909 he was at his old games again, raiding the friendly tribes in British Somaliland. It was then that we seriously considered the question whether we could undertake the task of protecting and administering the interior of the country. It must be borne in mind that our imperial aims in Somaliland extended no farther than the sea littoral; that, so long as the coast was secured to us, the rest of the country was of very little concern to us. To protect the coastal tribes was a simple matter, but to afford adequate protection to the tribes in the interior would necessitate building a railway, making roads, and keeping military garrisons at strategic points throughout the country. At that time (1909) the revenue of the protectorate was £30, 000, and the expenditure had crept up steadily until it had reached £134,000, so that we were dropping £104,000 a year on the venture.

Nor was there any prospect at that time of commercial developments which would raise the revenue. A railway from Berbera to Harrar in Abyssinia was suggested as a means of bringing the interior of the protectorate within easy access, and at the same time of catering for the trade of Abyssinia; but it was vetoed on the ground that to compete with the French railway from Jibouti to Adis Ababa would be poor policy at a time when the *entente cordiale* had just been firmly cemented. The final result of our deliberations was that we decided that we could not undertake the responsibility of safeguarding the tribes in the interior, and that the best we could do for them was to provide them with rifles and ammunition, so that they could protect themselves, if they chose to do so, from the *mullah's* incursions.

In 1910 we withdrew all our outposts, and restricted British administration to the coastal towns. Doubtless the theory that by arming the natives we should enable them to defend themselves was sound enough as a theory, but in practice it was found to be full of complications. For rifles can be used as weapons of attack as well as of defence, and no sooner were the British garrisons withdrawn from the interior than the tribes were blazing away at each other as hard as they could go. Some of them had ancient feuds, which had been quietly smouldering during the past few years; others unashamedly took up the brigandage business as being the most lucrative of all trades in Somaliland. The Somali has an acquisitive nature, and when he sees a Somali of another tribe in possession of a fine flock of sheep, he loads his rifle and gets to work without waste of time. The best hunting-ground was afforded by the caravan routes, where all sorts of useful articles were to be picked up from the caravans, in addition to the sheep, cattle, and camels accompanying them—all by the simple process of murdering the owners. One tribe showed more than usual enterprise by crossing the border into Abyssinia, and raiding the Ogaden tribe in that country. In fact, they all became so busy that they almost forgot their troubles with the *mullah* and his *dervishes*.

The government tried various measures to save the country from this state of chaos. They invited the headmen of the various tribes to Berbera, and spent wearisome days in examining their respective claims, and in arbitrating thereon. They persuaded them to shake hands with each other, settle their differences, and promise to be good children for the future. But within a week or two they were going for each other again as vigorously as ever. To solve the caravan problem, the government tried an old expedient—making each caravan pay a small fee for an escort to be provided by the tribe through whose country it was passing. It promised well at first, but escorts are but human after all, and when one of them made the discovery that by expending a few rounds of ammunition they could get not only the fee but the caravan as well, the system suffered a severe blow to its prestige.

Finally, in 1912, the *mullah* himself became active, and raided the Dolbahanta tribe so effectively that they were reduced to starvation, and came in large parties to the coast towns begging the government to give them food. Then it was realised that the policy of non-intervention in the interior was not altogether satisfactory, and that something must be done to remedy the anarchic condition of the country.

The device adopted was the establishment of a small striking force, to be based on the coast, but to be capable of moving quickly into the interior in order to impress upon the friendly tribes that intertribal fighting and raiding caravan routes were not regarded with favour by the government. It must be understood that the Camel Constabulary were never intended to be a military force in any sense; they were commanded, not by military officers, but by civilians; their orders were to preserve the peace among the friendlies, and not to risk an engagement with the *mullah's dervishes*. If they received news at any time of any considerable dervish force in their vicinity, they were to retire immediately and fall back on the coast.

The Camelry Corps was a distinct success for the purpose for which it was intended, and within a few weeks after its inauguration it established such a peace and calm among the tribes as they had not known for the past two years. But it did nothing towards solving the dervish problem, which remained as before. The *mullah*, however, was not so powerful as he used to be; his force was being continually depleted by desertions, for he found that in this irreligious age the preaching of pious maxims was not so effective as it ought to be in securing the fidelity of his followers. Materialism was their besetting sin; what they wanted was a plentiful supply of good fat sheep, rather than a bunch of quotations from the *Koran*. About this time he opened negotiations with the commissioner, declaring an earnest desire for peace, doubtless because he had begun to have misgivings as to his ability to continue the struggle. His letters are picturesque examples of the epistolary art, but are rather too lengthy for full quotation:

> Praise be to God who created, who leads and misleads, who gives and withholds, who raises up and casts down, who gives life and death. Prayers and salutations to our Prophet Mahomed. Thereafter. This is an answer to the words sent by the British.

He says all this, while we should be saying, "Dear sir, I am in receipt of your communication, etc." Then he goes on to declare that his one and only desire is for settlement and peace, and to explain that recent regrettable incidents were due solely to some of his *dervishes* getting out of hand, and carrying out raids contrary to his orders. The commissioner, however, knows the man he has to deal with, and answers cautiously:

> You say that you desire peace, and again I inform you that the British Government is willing to talk of peace, if your words are not words of deceit. You know very well that on former occasions you have spoken words of peace, and afterwards you and your people made war without cause, and much evil was done in the war.

In January 1913 a letter was received from the *mullah*, complaining that his solicitations for peace were met with "bad answers and unsuitable words," and repeating that his *dervishes* had got beyond his control, so that he had been obliged to take from them their arms and their horses.

And I inform you that I am disposed to make peace and settlement, and I therefore have returned to you the cows which the *dervishes* have taken from your subjects.

(He did, as a matter of fact, return a small part of the looted stock.) At the same time he was writing a letter to the Gadwein tribe, which he did not intend the commissioner to see, but which happened to find its way to Government House. Here are a few extracts from it:

Thanks be to God, prayers and salutations to the Prophet.... The object of this letter is twofold. One is to give you *salaam*; may God's mercy, blessing and salaams be upon you; and the other is to inform you that you are oppressed from all sides.... I also inform you that it is no offence in you to fight the *infidels* and hypocrites, for fighting them is the duty of every Moslem. You are Moslems, and they are *infidels*.... I also inform you that I am a pilgrim and a holy fighter, and have no wish to gain power and greatness in this world.... And now, O my brothers, this is a time of patience, this is a time of oppression, this is a time in which corruption and adultery spread, this is a time in which the *infidels* defeat the Moslems.... This is the end of all things. May God guide us. May God prosper our ends, for the sake of the Prophet and his companions.... I also beg that I may be with you, and that you may be with me, and the first thing should be a visit between us.

And so, towards the end of his letter, he gets to business, and proposes an alliance between *dervishes* and Gadweins to fight those *infidels*, to whom he had just been writing a request for peace.

In August 1913 a bad disaster befell the Camel Corps, which was then based on Burao. A report was received that dervishes were raiding the friendlies between Idoweina and Burao, and the acting commissioner, Mr. Archer, ordered Mr. Corfield, the commandant, to make a reconnaissance in force. Mr. Corfield, accompanied by Mr. Dunn, his second in command, and by Captain Summers, a military officer, who was not placed in command because no military operations were anticipated, took with him 116 rank and file, and proceeded towards

Idoweina, where he heard that the dervishes were encamped. Having located them and discovered their overwhelming numbers, he should have fallen back to Burao, but he allowed his valour to outrun his discretion. His aim was to intercept the dervishes so that they could not drive their looted stock back to their own grazing grounds in the Nogal Valley; but his force was hopelessly inadequate for such a purpose. In the stilt fight which ensued he was killed by a bullet through the head, Captain Summers was wounded three times; and, of the 116 rank and file, 30 were killed and 21 wounded.

The *dervish* losses were 395 killed and an unknown number wounded. The fight lasted for five hours, and there is not the least doubt that the Camel Corps would have been utterly annihilated if it had not so happened that the dervishes ran short of ammunition. Their force was over 2,000 strong, and they fought with that utter disregard for death which always characterises them. The maxim gun belonging to the corps was put out of action by a bullet early in the fight; the heat was intense, the men had no water; and, while some of them behaved splendidly, others bolted into the bush at the first approach of the dreaded dervish. Mr. Dunn finally succeeded in withdrawing the remnant of his force and all the wounded to Burao. And so ended the battle of Dul Madoba. Its effect only served to emphasise the fact that we had no adequate force to protect the tribes of the interior from dervish raids, and that the Camel Corps could not be safely maintained so far from the coast. Burao was evacuated, and the Corps withdrawn to Sheikh. Meanwhile the dervishes had walked off with 5,000 camels and 30,000 sheep.

As a result of the Battle of Dul Madoba the strength of the Camel Corps was increased to 350 men, and the Indian troops in the country were gradually increased to 700. But, in spite of these measures, the dervishes continued their depredations, and in March 1914 actually made a flying raid on Berbera, firing into the town, and withdrawing before there was time to realise what had happened. The object was doubtless to terrorise the friendlies, and impress their minds with the idea that the British were quite impotent before the mighty hosts of the *mullah*. To some extent this object was successfully attained. At all events, the dervish problem had to be considered anew, for it had become very evident that at the end of fifteen years no real progress had been made towards its solution.

Then someone had an inspiration. Here was a country in which ordinary military operations were severely handicapped by the absence of all means of communications. Why not attack the Mad Mullah with aircraft? The proposal was to send out two or three airships of the Parseval type, drop bombs on dervishes, stampede their cattle, and prevent them from gaining access to the wells. The Admiralty were approached on the subject, and finally decided to send out Lieutenants Boothby and Davis to reconnoitre and report as to the possibilities of aircraft work in Somaliland. These officers left London in May 1914, the intention being that, if they reported favourably, the erection of sheds for the airships would be commenced in September at the end of the hot weather. But before this intention could be carried out an event occurred in Europe, which completely upset many of the best-laid schemes of mice and men.

The outbreak of war necessarily relegated the problems of Somaliland to the lumber-room of unconsidered trifles. It was natural, therefore, that the *Mullah* should seize the golden opportunity for making himself more cantankerous than ever. Finding that the supply of rifles and ammunition from Abyssinia was not always satisfactory, he began to intrigue with the coastal tribes with a view to securing an alternative source of supply by means of *dhows* from Arabia to one of the coastal villages, and thence overland to his *haroun*. Thus he wrote to the Musa Arreh on the coast, inviting them to join in the crusade against the infidels, and salting his letter with many little homilies to improve their minds:

> This letter is sent to the followers of Islam. Salaams to you all, and to all believers. Further, I let you know that your deeds have spoiled my life and also yours; and you have broken the oath that was between us. You have forsaken the true religion and done evil before *Allah*. By going to the English you forsake Islam and become *infidels*. . . . I advise you to return to the true God, and to the Mahomedan religion, and the Shariat. . . . Do not join the British Government and the religion of the unbelievers, for, if you do, and if you forsake your religion before you die, you will go to hell.

And so on.

One imagines a tall, stately man, with a commanding presence, thin, clear-cut features, resolute mouth and chin, eyes glowing with the fire of religious fanaticism. It comes as a shock to us to hear that the *mullah* is not in the least like this. I cannot give a faithful portrait of him, for I have never had the pleasure of meeting him, and apparently he does not encourage photographers at his Court. But there is one fact which completely dispels all our preconceived notions of what he ought to be like. The horrible truth is that he has grown too fat. This may be mere vulgar obesity caused by overfeeding, but, according to another report, it is the outcome of a peculiar disease, reported to be fairly common among the Dolbahanta tribe, which results in an abnormal swelling of the flesh, beginning at the ankles and gradually extending to the whole body.

Whatever may be the cause, the *mullah* has been afflicted with a superfluity of girth for several years past, and is said to require six men to lift him on to his horse. Probably this is the reason why he has changed his tactics, and decided that he can no longer rely upon a policy of elusiveness, but must be prepared to resist capture by other means. He is reported to have built a mighty fortress round his *haroun* at Taleh, with walls twelve feet thick, and there it is surmised that he would stand his ground if an expedition were sent against him.

Though he himself is no longer agile, his dervishes are as active as ever, and early in 1915 they occupied Jid Ali, only twenty-five miles from the coast, and established a fort there. This manoeuvre complicated the situation considerably, for it not only exposed the coastal tribes, such as the Warsangli, to periodic raids, but it also necessitated on our part a blockade of the whole coast to prevent the dervishes from obtaining supplies by swooping down upon the seaside villages. At the same time it was reported that the Gadwein tribe had been seduced by the *mullah's* allurements, and had gone over to the dervishes *en bloc*. The Warsangli, fearing that *dervishes* and Gadweins might combine in a vigorous attack upon them, besought the commissioner for assistance. For the moment no more could be done than to keep them well supplied with ammunition, but the commissioner took an early opportunity of recommending that the fort of Jid Ali should be destroyed by a military force.

The first proposal was to land 1,000 men on the coast north of Jid Ali, together with two or three naval guns, and march them inland through a pass in the chain of mountains which separates Jid Ali from the sea. But upon more mature consideration it was decided that the escarpment was too steep for heavy transport, and that the only method of attacking Jid Ali would be by marching a force to Las Dureh, and thence to an advanced base at El Afweina. H.M.S. *Philomel* was sent to patrol the coast, taking on board the commissioner to make a reconnaissance.

The effect of this was excellent, for the presence of the warships put fresh heart into the Gadweins, and made them resolve to sever their allegiance with the *dervishes*. They proceeded to collect their livestock and to drive them along the coast westwards. The dervishes followed up, and attempted to persuade them to linger yet awhile in brotherly love, using their rifles as the most eloquent means of persuasion. But when H.M.S. *Philomel* dropped a few shells into them they realised that this is a hard, cruel world, in which brotherly love has but small influence over the actions of man. The Gadweins got away with most of their stock, and settled down in the vicinity of Las Dureh.

The next report upon the situation was to the effect that the dervishes had gone back to their *haroun* at Taleh, leaving only a small garrison at Jid Ali to hold the fort. To the commissioner and to the officer commanding troops in Somaliland this report suggested a new idea. They had proposed to invoke the aid of the Egyptian Army Camel Corps and two battalions of Indian infantry for the expedition against Jid Ali *via* Las Dureh and El Afweina. It now occurred to them that this would be making heavy weather of the destruction of a fort held by a mere handful of *dervishes*, and that they ought to go for a more ambitious scheme whose object should be the final solution of the *dervish* problem. El Afweina, the proposed site of the advanced base, is almost equidistant from Jid Ali and Taleh. Why not accumulate a substantial force there, send a small detachment against Jid Ali, and use the remainder for a bold stroke against Taleh—a surprise attack, which might very well catch the *mullah* napping.

It was a brilliant conception, but unfortunately there were too many other things going on in the world at the time. London received the suggestion without the least sign of emotion or enthusiasm, and sent back a wet blanket by return of post:

> You will be aware that at the present moment it would be an impossibility to obtain for Somaliland the men and material required for carrying out your proposals.

So matters had to remain in *statu quo* for the time being.

Then came reports that the *mullah* was negotiating with Prince Lij Yasu of Abyssinia, that the latter had embraced Islam, that two of his Mahomedan councillors were in high favour at Court, and that his envoys had twice been to Taleh from Adis Ababa. How far these negotiations proceeded I do not know; it is sufficient to say that in the early part of 1917 Prince Lij Yasu was deposed from the throne of

Abyssinia, and that the British Government accorded prompt recognition and friendship towards the queen chosen to reign in his stead. Meanwhile the dervish problem in Somaliland never allowed its rulers a dull moment, and in 1916 it reached another crisis, consequent upon the return of the dervishes to Jid Ali.

The Warsangli tribe, who had become emboldened by a few months' immunity from danger, suddenly conceived the idea that it would be rather fun to assume the offensive against the dervishes. So they organised a raid upon dervish cattle, and did fairly well out of it. But the *dervish* is not the kind of fellow to take that sort of thing lying down. Retribution followed surely and swiftly, and the only things which saved the Warsangli tribe from extermination were firstly their good fortune in getting a *dhow* through to Aden within three days, and secondly the promptness with which H.M.S. *Northbrook* responded to the call for help.

It was about 8 o'clock on the morning of 10th May 1916 when the *Northbrook* arrived off Las Khorai, and no sooner had she come up than several natives were seen to plunge into the water and start swimming as fast as they could towards the ship. They were in such a state of panic and excitement that it was difficult to get out of them a connected yarn when they arrived on board. For the moment, however, Commander Turton was mainly interested in the report that the dervishes, on seeing the approach of the *Northbrook*, had commenced to retreat in a westerly direction towards the mountain pass leading to Jid Ali. He promptly turned the *Northbrook's* head to westward, and followed the line of the coast, until he came up with a compact mass of men hurrying along the stretch of plain which divides the chain of mountains from the sea.

The range was just over 6,000 yards, and the shell was lyddite. After the first round the compact mass was compact no longer, but small groups showed themselves from time to time, each one of them receiving its dose of high explosive, until finally the pass was reached. Here the *Northbrook* hove to, and, as the rabble came together in that narrow neck, whose range was calculated to a nicety, so the shells dropped plumb on top of them. It was diabolically easy—so easy that the sporting instinct must have revolted from it, even as our men at Omdurman sickened at the sight of the havoc that their own machine-guns created. After twenty-four rounds the *Northbrook* ceased fire. The number of her victims will never be known, for many dead and wounded were carried off by their comrades; the only available evidence of the result of those few minutes of gunnery was afforded by the 171 corpses lying at the entrance to the pass. The *dervishes* paid a heavy price for their raid on Las Khorai.

The price, however, was not excessive, for they themselves had shown no mercy. When the *Northbrook* had returned to the village, parties were sent ashore to investigate the extent of the damage. The place had been completely surrounded by the *dervishes*, who had captured the western part of the village at once, and had proceeded deliberately to murder some 300 women and children, whom they found there. But the rest of the village had put up a stout defence, and had kept the enemy more or less at bay from Sunday morning until the warship brought deliverance on Wednesday morning. The fighting had been intermittent, so that the casualties were not heavy, considering the duration of it.

According to the Warsangli Sultan, his tribe had lost thirty-two men killed and had accounted for ninety-three *dervishes*, but he altogether ignored the wounded, as the Somali native usually does. What the condition of these wounded must have been may be gauged by the fact that the dervishes captured the only fresh-water well near the town, so that the Warsanglis had been practically without water for four days, and had had a very meagre supply of food.

The rest of the work of the *Northbrook* was necessarily of the nature of first aid. Water and food were landed to satisfy the immediate needs, and the ship's doctor with a reinforced staff made a tour of the village. The wounded had been utterly neglected, not the smallest attempt having been made to alleviate their suffering, with the inevitable result that all the wounds inflicted during the early part of the fight had become gangrenous. Stab wounds were more frequent than bullet wounds, and it is significant of the cheerful disposition of the dervish that as many as fifteen stabs were sometimes found in one person. For five hours Dr. McCowen laboured beneath a tropical sun, treating some sixty cases with dressings and antiseptics. It speaks well both for his skill and for the healthy constitutions of the Warsanglis, that, when he returned five days later, he found nearly all his patients doing well.

Sympathy with the Warsangli tribe over this affair may well be overdone by unsuspecting sentimentalists. The truth is that this tribe deserved a great deal of what they got, for there was a time when they were intriguing both with the *mullah* and with his friend Prince Lij Yasu of Abyssinia. In fact, their *sultan*, Mahmood Ali Sherri, was a brother-in-law of the *mullah*, and the pair of them were thick as thieves until the dervishes built the fort at Jid Ali. The fort was too close to Las Khorai to please the Warsanglis, for no Somali tribe has much faith in the good friendship of any other tribe, and least of all in that of the dervishes. Even so it was the height of stupidity on the part of Mahmood Ali Sherri to make an unprovoked assault upon the *dervishes*, and to raid their cattle, seeing that their forces were sufficiently numerous to overwhelm his own.

The slaughter of the women and children is revolting enough, but unfortunately it has always been a common feature of Somali warfare, and there is not the smallest doubt that the Warsanglis would have done the same to *dervish* women and children, if the tables had been reversed. The net result of the tragedy must be regarded as salutary, for the Warsanglis learnt that the less they had to do with the dervishes, either in fighting or in intriguing, the better, and the dervishes learnt that it was wiser to leave the coast tribes severely alone so long as there was any chance that the British Navy might be hovering in the vicinity.

A touch of comedy was added to the business by the receipt in London of a letter concocted jointly by the Sultan of the Warsangli and a learned member of his tribe living at Aden, by name Haji Aden Ali. The letter was addressed to the Secretary of Slaves, London, but eventually found its way to the Anti-Slavery Society. With all its quaint phraseology, it presents a very genuine expression of gratitude for the salvation of the tribe.

> Surely we have found in Commander Turton a saviour of our place and people. God may give him long life and prosperity to enhance such heroic works. . . . Praise and gratification have been in the mouth of us all since the success achieved by the genius and talents of Commander Turton, R.N, of H.M.S. *Northbrook*. The results of his success are truly colossal for us. . . . May God keep the British flag for ever and perpetual upon us, under whose shelter we are happy and thriving in content.

Three months after the raid on Las Khorai the new Sultan of the Warsanglis, Ina Ali Shirreh, came to Berbera with a report that the *dervishes* had now occupied Baran in force, and that the *mullah* was trying to compel the Warsangli tribe to join him, and begged that British troops might be stationed at Las Khorai. The request was granted, a double company of Indian infantry being sent to garrison the fort there. Although the dervishes had not attempted any second raid on the place, they had been active enough in other directions, and their occupation of Baran, which lies due south of Las Khorai across a range of mountains, was quite sufficient ground for alarm.

It was at the end of January 1917, some six months after the British garrison had been established at Las Khorai, that I visited the place. The navy's mission on that occasion was of a peaceful nature. An epidemic of scurvy had broken out among the Sikhs stationed in the fort, and their commanding officer had sent a dhow to Berbera asking for aid. We called at Berbera to pick up Dr. Whitehead (attached to the Colonial Office) and proceeded at once to the scene of the trouble. On arrival we found that the epidemic was fairly widespread, but not severe. Our ship's stock of lime-juice, of which we happened to have a plentiful supply, came in useful as a palliative for the lighter cases, while the more serious cases were taken on board and put into hospital at Berbera.

My impressions of Las Khorai remain fairly vivid in my mind. Groups of reed-huts dotted promiscuously over the plain, the ruins of some stone buildings whose history I never learnt, a whitewashed stone house politely known as the palace of the *sultan*, and a whitewashed tower in the centre of the fort. Between the sea and the long chain of mountains, which skirts the coast at varying distances from the shore, is a wide stretch of sand, almost bare of vegetation, affording a dreary foreground to the vista of mountain peaks. Upon such a landscape the square white tower of the fort, with the ensign floating at its mast-head, stands out conspicuously. Here indeed is an outpost of empire, many weary miles from everywhere, and unconnected by any of those links by which the progress of science has brought most of the distant places of the earth within call of civilisation.

As I stood on the poop gazing at that white tower, while the ship was being brought to anchor, my thoughts were of the white man's burdens, which seem to have a way of accumulating as soon as he undertakes the tasks of empire. Here were we plunged into the responsibility of administering the affairs of a most unpromising country, simply because it lies upon the high road to India. What were the possibilities of turning to good account this slice of North-East Africa, which circumstances have forced upon us? The commercial products are livestock, hides, frankincense, and myrrh.

The exports of livestock just suffice to supply the needs of Aden; the hides of the sheep and goats reach as far as the American market, where they are used for making glove-leather and glacé kid; the frankincense, myrrh, and other gums find their market in various countries. Recently there have been attempts to develop a trade in fibre from the *sansevieria* tree, which, it was hoped, would run a good second to Sisal hemp, but so far the exploitation of this product has not advanced very far. There is, however, a gleam of hope in another direction. When I was at Berbera I heard much talk of the discovery of oil-fields at Agagwein, twenty-eight miles south-east of Berbera. If this discovery proves to be of value, the whole economic situation may be changed, and Somaliland may be converted from a burden into a valuable asset of the British Empire. But to return to Las Khorai and its fort.

I landed in the evening, carried pickaback through the surf by a Somali native (for there is no pier), and found most of the villagers lined up on the beach, the arrival of a ship being naturally an event in local history. Thence I was escorted to the fort to view all the improvements which have been made in its defences and accommodation. A perimeter of sandbags had been built around the whole enclosure, with a wide ditch outside the perimeter, and barbed wire entanglements beyond the ditch. Within the perimeter are barracks constructed out of sandbags and beams of wood, and a special bungalow built of the same materials for the *subadar major,* and designed by himself. It has a verandah with real wooden steps leading up to it—quite a triumph in architecture, for to make something ornamental out of sandbags cannot be easy.

The two English officers live in the tower itself, on the first floor, where they have furnished their mess-room in a severely simple style, with a plain deal table, two plain deal stools, and two deck chairs. The walls arc surrounded with shelves to accommodate the library and a plentiful supply of groceries, for they may have to last out for three months without seeing a ship or any other emissary of civilisation. Fresh meat they can get at any time, for sheep are pastured on the mountain slopes to southward, while fresh milk is provided by three cows kept inside the fort. But the difficulty is to procure fresh vegetables, even potatoes presenting a serious problem, for they go bad very quickly in that climate. Hence the scurvy.

I was eager for information about the *mullah*, whose horde of dervishes seemed to be in uncomfortable proximity just across the mountain range. 1 gleaned a little gossip about German agents in Abyssinia providing him with ammunition, and had retailed to me a rumour that he had been provided with a piece of artillery and a German gun's crew to handle it. But the officers of the Las Khorai garrison seemed to take only a perfunctory interest in these matters. That the dervishes were within an easy day's march of the fort, that they could muster several thousand rifles if they chose, that Las Khorai is about a hundred miles from the next outpost, that there were no other means of communication than a sailing *dhow* which might take several days to carry a message, that these two young English officers were alone in their desert surroundings, far removed from other white men—these were matters to which apparently they gave no thought.

Their whole mental energies were directed to a subject which seemed to them of far mightier moment—the subject of horticulture. Their conversation was just the conversation which we used to hear from among our newly wed suburban dwellers in the days of peace, and in the days of war from among those patriots who abandoned golf in order to serve their country with spade and hoe upon the allotments.

With an air of loving pride they showed me their garden, explaining that I must not expect too much, for the soil was just sand mixed with a little goat manure, and irrigated with the brackish water of their well. The garden products could be divided roughly into two classes—the things which they had really persuaded to grow, or rather, to be dragged up, and the things which they looked upon as experiments, and which they still cherished, stimulated by that hope that springs eternal in the human breast. In the first class there were pumpkins, water-melons, radishes, and mustard and cress; in the second were potatoes, onions, lettuces, and dwarf French beans—the last-named being a present from one of the Sikhs, who had been given the seeds when he was serving in France.

Their optimism was magnificent, surpassing even that of the suburban amateur gardener, for they spoke of the future of their garden in the days when they would know it no longer, in the days when a generation yet unborn would be privileged to inhabit this Eden of Las Khorai. The spirit of our father Adam had fallen upon them, as it must fall upon all mankind, when the gaudy trappings of civilisation are far removed. For if only we probe deep enough into man's nature, if only we can disintegrate it from its artificial environments, we find that all men are made in the image of Adam, as he was in the beginning, before Eve told him that his hair needed cutting, and that his fig-leaf was beginning to look shabby.

Chapter 26

Scotching the Wolf's Cub

H.M.S. —— was engaged on the Aden patrol, which consisted in leaving harbour every afternoon, and spending the night in running up and down a regular beat of about thirty miles along the coast. From our camp beds on the poop we could enjoy the panorama of a moonlit sea, a cloudless sky, and either the Pole Star or the Southern Cross according to inclination. But it was horribly monotonous, and sometimes in the wardroom we indulged in a gentle grouse and a questioning of the why and wherefore of it all.

There had lately been a long series of reports from British harbours in the southern seas of mines dropped in their vicinity. At Cape Town a vessel had struck a mine and had been damaged rather badly; at Bombay a mine-field had been discovered; at Colombo a ship crawled into harbour with a big hole in her side. Then came a message from the Admiralty. A German raider at large in the Indian Ocean; had sunk some ships *en route*; had laid mines off Capetown; was disguised as a tramp and flew false colours, but was known to be well armed with guns of heavy calibre; and her name was the *Wolf*.

The southern Red Sea Patrol was not so happy over the news as one would have expected. The prospect of meeting a German raider certainly adds zest to life, but when the raider's fighting weight, according to all accounts, is about double your own, and you know that in all probability you would be at the bottom of the sea before you could get a salvo anywhere near her, the rosiness of the prospect is shaded with dark streaks here and there. At the Union Club, Aden, I ran into an old acquaintance, who was navigating officer of one of the armed auxiliaries on the patrol, and enquired how the world was treating him.

"Splendid. We're off tomorrow morning to find the *Wolf*."

"I love a cheery optimist," said I.

"There's one virtue about my old packet," he said. "She can run. The trouble is that the skipper has some kind of a notion in his head that she can also fight. He has a great idea that we ought to loose off our popguns, just to show Fritz that they are really made to go off. But Fritz will be so far off that he won't be able to hear them. The whole show will be wasted on him."

"What worries me," I said, "is that Fritz has called and left his cards at Cape Town, Bombay, and Colombo in quick succession; we know the approximate date of each of these visits; an exact description of him has been circulated; and yet we haven't the foggiest notion where he is at the present moment."

"The sea is a mighty big thing—bigger than the proverbial haystack when you are looking for a needle. You see, there's nothing to distinguish the *Wolf* from any other old tramp. Her guns are concealed; so is her minelaying gear. As for the official description, there is nothing very exceptional in it—might be the description of any old cargo ship between here and Melbourne. And of course she can fake herself up from time to time—a coat of paint to change the marks on her funnels, or the colour of her hull, laid on at night when there's no one to see her; a bogus funnel rigged one day and unshipped the next. You bet your life that Fritz is no fool at the game."

"But how about coal and provisions?" I hazarded.

"Cleans out her victims before she sinks them, just as the Emden did. Takes their crews aboard as prisoners until she gets too big an accumulation, and then she tells the next fellow she meets that she will let him off on condition that he will take all the prisoners. Oh, it's quite a clean game. None of this U-boat lousiness of leaving a lot of wretched beggars in open boats in mid-ocean and telling them to get home as best they can."

"But she can't take any prizes, because there is nowhere she can send them."

"Well, I wouldn't like to take an affidavit on that. Wolves have cubs, you know. What is to prevent her from collaring some tramp—a tramp, mind you, not a liner because a liner's progress from port to port is watched, and if she's an hour late there's a panic about her, but nobody worries much about a tramp. What's to prevent her from collaring a tramp, taking the crew aboard herself, shoving in a prize crew, loading her up with mines, and sending her off to carry on with the good work?"

That evening I was sitting in the wardroom reading when the captain strolled in and sat down at the table, ready to make a fourth at a rubber of bridge if any one should suggest it. The first lieutenant was on the point of turning in, as he had the morning watch and it was getting on for ten o'clock. The navigator was buried in a book, and the doctor was strumming on the wheezy old piano a selection from the musical comedies and revues of bygone days. A signalman appeared at the wardroom door.

"From the officer of the watch, sir. Ship on the starboard bow showing no lights."

"All right," said the captain, looking rather bored. "Probably some tramp scared out of his wits by these yarns about the Wolf," suggested the first lieutenant.

"All these merchantmen are going about without lights now," said the captain.

"Did he say 'starboard bow'?" asked the navigator.

"Yes, she must be fairly close inshore."

"Taking a short cut. Some of these old sports are rather fond of doing that."

The captain strolled out of the wardroom and up the poop ladder. The first lieutenant rose, stretched himself, and disappeared below to turn in. Presently the navigator put down his book, and followed the captain to the bridge. The doctor finished up his performance with a touching little lyric, entitled, "If you were the only girl in the world," gave vent to a loud and ostentatious yawn, and sauntered up to the poop. The moon was nearly full, casting a white track across the dark-blue carpet of the sea, and making the steep volcanic rocks of the Arabian shore look like so many giant ghosts assembled at a Sabaean prayer-meeting. It was the kind of night that we in England associate with Thames regattas, with lounging in a well-cushioned punt, and listening to a well-conducted band. To connect such a scene with a German raider, with guns, and mines, and torpedoes, was quite impossible; the whole setting was absolutely and entirely wrong.

The mysterious ship had crossed our bows, and was now on the port side of us, about three miles ahead. A thick volume of smoke was pouring from her funnel, suggesting that she was in a hurry. We had been steaming along leisurely at about eight knots, but now the order came from the bridge to whack her up to ten. As luck would have it, one of our boilers was open with a view to cleaning, and consequently we were incapable of showing our best speed if occasion should call for it. The captain had sent for the first lieutenant to join the council on the bridge, at which the navigator and the officer of the watch were also present.

"Make What ship is that?" said the captain to the leading signalman.

The signalman rattled the shutter of his signal-lamp, and we waited patiently for the answer. He had to repeat the question three times before he evoked any response. Then the dark outline of the unknown ship was lit up spasmodically by a scintillating light, and the signalman took down the message on his pad.

Toritella.

"Ask him, what nationality," said the captain.

Again the signalman played a tattoo with the shutter of his lamp, and the answer came back, "British."

"Ask him for his signal letters," said the captain.

"J.F.K.L." came the answer.

"You are sure you have got the name right? Ask him for it again."

"What is your name?" asked the signalman, and this time the mysterious stranger expanded volubly.

"*Turritella*, London. Runs for British Admiralty Port Said for orders."

"You are sure you have spelt the name correctly?" asked the captain of the signalman, as he handed the signal-pad to the first lieutenant.

"Well, sir, that's how they made it the second time. *Turritella*. A 'u' and two 'r's. The first time, sir, they spelt it *Toritella*. An 'o' and one 'r'."

What manner of ship was this who seemed uncertain how to spell her own name? And that expression, "Runs for British Admiralty." Would an English merchant skipper talk about the British Admiralty? Wouldn't he say "under Admiralty charter" or some such phrase?

The light from the unknown began to scintillate again.

"Who are you?" ran the simple message.

There was a directness about that anyhow, suggesting the English skipper.

"Make back, 'A British man-of-war.'"

"Shall I give our name, sir?"

"No, certainly not."

"The blighter would look us up in the Navy List," said one of the officers on the bridge, "and, if he's the *Wolf*, he would off with his camouflage and send us to perdition in about two shakes of a jiffy."

"I am going to tell him to stop," said the captain, and gave the order to the signalman. There was a long pause, and then the answer began to flicker back, not with the smooth rapidity shown by a well-trained signalman, but with just a trifle of hesitation. The signalman presently brought it on the pad,

"Why did you not stop me when I was passing Aden?—Meadows, master."

His meaning was plain enough. We could have ordered him to stop when we first sighted him, when we were within range of the shore batteries, and when there were British men-of-war lying just round the corner inside the harbour. When a German raider is known to be roaming the seas, our merchantmen very naturally acquire a habit of running as hard as they can if a strange ship orders them to stop, and in doing so they doubtless carry out the instructions they have received. By running away, therefore, this man would only be carrying out his orders, and it seemed pretty clear that we could not overhaul him.

The first lieutenant went down the ladder from the bridge to the poop, mindful of the fact that in little more than four hours he would have to be up there again to keep his watch. The navigator followed him, for the proceedings were beginning to become boresome. After a few minutes the captain came down from the bridge and went into the wardroom. A wild goose chase is an ignominious occupation for the chaser, and one which the ordinary man is studious to avoid. Only the officer of the watch was left on the bridge to exchange comments with the signalman. Small details are sometimes fraught with great issues, and even the technicalities of a flagwagger may have their importance. On the stroke of midnight the reliefs stepped on to the bridge, and both officer and signalman went below, the former to seek the solace of a cigarette in the wardroom before turning in.

"I should like," he said, as he lighted up, "to get hold of that merchant skipper, and give him a piece of my mind."

"The question is," said a voice coming from behind a book, "whether he would understand your language. The skippers of ships which would run away from a British man-of-war for two solid hours are not all good linguists."

The speaker laid the book down on his knee as an intimation that he was quite ready to argue the point. The captain turned towards him with an enquiring look.

"If you, sir, were under the impression that you were being chased by a German raider, would you expect him to go on chasing you for two hours without firing?"

Here the officer who had just come off watch struck in.

"There was something funny even about that signal asking us why we did not stop him at Aden. I have just been talking to the signal-man, and he tells me that they spelt Aden with a 't' at first, and then corrected it. It was a funny kind of mistake to make."

The captain looked thoughtful.

"From the officer of the watch, sir," said a messenger at the ward-room door. "The ship on the port bow seems to be drawing away from us."

"Tell him to put on another couple of knots."

"Aye, aye, sir."

"Is that the best we can do, sir?"

Again the captain looked thoughtful, and then he rang the bell for the quartermaster.

"Ask the engineer to speak to me, and take the temperature of the magazines."

The quartermaster presently reported that the magazines were down to 68, and behind him came the engineer.

"If you were to knock off the magazine cooling do you think you could squeeze another knot or two out of her?"

"Yes, sir, quite that."

"Do the best you can, then. Quartermaster! stand by for a message to the wireless room."

"Aye, aye, sir."

The middle watch was slipping by very quickly in the midst of these alarums and excursions, and by the time the captain had made out messages to various men-of-war of the Patrol, telling them the circumstances, and giving his position, course, and speed, it was getting on for six bells. Then he returned to the bridge to watch the progress of the chase. The unlighted ship was now silhouetted against the setting moon, and was about two points off our port bow, so that we could just distinguish the outline of her funnel and masts. She was still making plenty of smoke, but, beyond this indication that she wished to avoid us, there was nothing in her appearance to make her an object of suspicion.

The situation was not an easy one. No British man-of-war cares about firing upon a merchant-ship at any time, and after all this fellow was only doing what any other merchantman would do if he got it into his head that a German raider was chasing him. Of course, it was very stupid of him not to know that no raider would chase him for so many hours without firing, but then there are stupid men as well as clever men on the high seas. Moreover, there were other possibilities. Supposing the strange ship were the Wolf herself? Would she take the trouble to run, when she could send her pursuer to the bottom with a couple of salvoes? She might, for the simple reason that her job was not to fight men-of-war, but to destroy British commerce. She could not know what was the calibre of our guns, or that her own fighting weight was considerably greater than ours. But, if we were to force matters to a crisis, she would have to fight.

Only one thing seemed to be indisputable—that we ought to keep her in sight; so our little ship strained every nerve, until she shook from stem to stern with the vibration of her engines, and her funnel grew red-hot with the forced draught of the furnaces. Then the moon went down, and sudden darkness fell upon the face of the waters. But still the chase continued.

The first lieutenant had just arrived to take the morning watch, when there seemed to be some abatement of the smoke from the stranger's funnel. It was very dark, so that it was impossible to say whether she was easing down or not. She seemed to be just the same distance off as she had been all through the night, and if there was any difference between the speeds of the two ships, it could only be a fraction of a knot in our favour.

The captain was standing on the port side, leaning over the railing in front, and peering through the gloom. Presently he turned abruptly, and sang out for the signalman.

"Sir?"

"Make, 'If you do not stop, I shall fire,' and be quick about it."

"Aye, aye, sir."

"Fall in the port guns' crews, will you. Number One."

The first lieutenant gave the necessary orders down the voice-pipe.

"If-you-do-not-stop-I-shall-fire."

The signalman closed his shutter on the final word with a loud snap, as much as to say, "Now, you blighter, what are you going to do?" here followed a minute or two of suspense, and then came the answer.

"What does he say?" asked the captain.

"I-am-stopping-now." read the signalman.

"Tell them to stand by the searchlight, Number One."

"Aye, aye, sir," said the first lieutenant, and repeated the order down the voice-pipe.

"Signalman, tell him to place his navigation lights." Very promptly in response to the signal, the lights appeared upon the strange ship.

"Now make this to him. 'Remain where you are. I will board you at daylight.' Have you got it?"

"Aye, aye, sir."

The distance between the two ships now rapidly diminished, and when we had approached within a mile or so the order was given to switch on the searchlight. The great white streak stretched across the sea and lit up the mysterious unknown. In large white letters across her stern ran the legend "*Turritella*, London."

"I believe I have been fooled after all," said the captain to himself.

"There's a party shoving off in a boat," remarked the first lieutenant.

Just at this moment a strong voice came through a megaphone from the stranger's bridge.

"Switch off that damned searchlight."

"He seems to be a bit ratty," said the first lieutenant.

The order to switch off the light was given.

In that half-hour or so before the break of day the air strikes chill even in the tropics, and it is no imagery that has proclaimed it the darkest of the night. When the searchlight was turned off, the gloom was enhanced by the contrast, so that the navigation lights of the *Turritella* seemed like will-o'-the wisps twinkling across the barren space of murky blackness. And then the eastern sky began to glow, feebly at first, casting a kind of half-light over the face of the sea such as one sees on the stage when the actors are supposed to be in the dark. Out of this theatrical obscurity there arose such a babel of sound as brought us all to the ship's side, straining our eyes to see whence it proceeded. I listened for the guttural note of the Teuton, but there was not the least resemblance to it.

The language was quite unfamiliar to me; it might be the chattering of monkeys for all that I could make of it. The only thing it clearly betokened was an extreme slate of excitement among the crowded occupants of two boats, one lying on our port, and the other on our starboard hand. We shouted to them in English that we would come back, and pick them up presently; then we tried Hindustani, Somali, Swahili, and Arabic, with the aid of our interpreter. But the jabbering was only pitched in a higher key, and so we left them, for we had to keep under way until there was light enough to distinguish friend from foe.

No sooner had we come abeam of the strange ship than we saw a cloud of smoke shoot up from her, followed at once by the dull thud of a heavy explosion. Next moment there came another dull thud, and the *Turritella* began to sink by the head. We steamed on straight past her, for a ship which carries explosives on board is as likely as not to carry them in the form of torpedoes. Gradually the eastern sky began to flush red, and the hue was reflected by the sea, until one could have fancied that the ship which had just committed suicide was staining the waters with her blood.

And then we saw a third boat, rowing fast away from her in the direction of the other two. We swung round to return and pick them up. And now for the first time I realised why we could not understand a word of all that excited chatter. The first two boats were full of Chinamen. When the third boat reached our gangway two officers stepped briskly up the ladder, followed by 26 men, each wearing a round blue cap with two black ribbons falling down behind, and across the ribbon in front was written, in gold letters, "*Kaiserliche* Marine."

The story of the *Turritella* since the beginning of the war is eventful enough for any self-respecting ship. Originally she had been a German, but in the autumn of 1914 she was captured, and turned over to the Admiralty to serve as an oiler, though she carried other cargo in addition. Her last voyage commenced at Shanghai, where she picked up her Chinese crew; she put into Rangoon, and thence went on to Colombo, where she spent some days loading up. She left there on 23 February 1917, and four days later walked straight into the jaws of the *Wolf*. Her British officers and men were taken aboard the raider as prisoners, but the Chinese remained in her.

A German prize crew took possession of her; she was loaded up with mines, and was sent to Aden to lay a minefield outside the harbour. Her subsequent movements had all been carefully arranged, and were made to fit in with the programme revealed by the ship's papers. On 6th March she was due at Perim, where she intended to call, looking us innocent as a lamb, with her Chinese crew on the upper deck and her German ratings securely stowed below. And then she was to proceed into the Red Sea to lay more mines. At least that was the programme as told me by the German navigating officer, and he spoke confidently of the prospects of carrying it through without a hitch—if only we had not happened to come along at night, when we could not see the Chinese Tindal in all his glory at the wheel, and the Chinese crew coiling ropes on the deck.

"So you have destroyed your ship?" said our captain to Lieutenant-Kapitan Brandes, when the latter stepped on to the bridge and gravely saluted.

"Yes," said the German simply, and I noticed that he was trembling slightly, as though he were not quite sure what kind of reception awaited him. His navigator stood beside me on the poop.

"You have had a sleepless night of it," said I.

"That is not at all unusual," he said with a smile.

"You sleep in the daytime, I suppose?"

"Not much—very little. We shall sleep when the war is over."

"You will have plenty of leisure for sleep before then," I thought to myself, but I refrained from saying it. Besides, the fellow was not speaking for himself, but for his countrymen. "We shall sleep when the war is over." It was a fine piece of sentiment. The war was the only thing worth considering; sleep and all other luxuries must go by the board until it was won.

"You have done very well," I said, referring of course to the war as a whole and to Germany's achievements. But this time he was thinking of his own personal share in the business, and the question he put rather took me by surprise.

"Don't you think," he said, "that all is fair in war?"

Was this a searching of his own conscience? Had he been asking himself. Why should I be spending my time in laying these death-traps for merchant service seamen, regardless of their nationality, when they have never done me any harm? But I was feeling too hungry to discuss the ethics of war.

"Let's go and have some hot cocoa," I said.

At breakfast he told us that he had been eight years in the English merchant service, and had lived ashore in England besides. The effect was to give him a sense of humour such as one does not often find in a Hun. His captain was a far more typical specimen, taking life very seriously. He gravely apologised to us in broken English for not having put up a fight, explaining that the *Turritella's* gun was such a little one—a 6-pounder, I believe—and he had had it taken below with the idea of averting suspicion. He brought a dog with him, a small dachshund, to which he seemed much attached. When we got back to Aden, and handed our prisoners over to the military authorities, the last thing he said on leaving the ship was, "Thank you very much for all your kindness. And you will be good to the dog?" We assured him that the little beast would be well treated.

The part which I cannot get over is that signal, "Why did you not stop me when I was passing Aden?" It was more than clever; it was an inspiration. If he had elaborated it, if he had said, "You did not order me to stop at Aden, where there are shore batteries and British men-of-war," he would have spoilt the effect. In the form of a trite question, it had just the flavour of an old tarpaulin merchant skipper. And then his signalman went and spelt Aden with a "T." It really was hard lines on Fritz.

In the *Times* of 9th March 1918, and in the evening papers of the previous day, there appeared a telegram from Melbourne to the effect that the German officers of the *Turritella* had been tried at Bombay for murder, on the ground that some Chinamen were left in the stokehold when the ship was sunk. I have been unable to find any authority for this statement. Nothing is known officially of any such trial.

THE RED SEA PATROL

CHAPTER 27

The Taking of Salif

The purpose of the naval patrol in the Red Sea requires a few words of explanation, involving a brief survey of the political conditions of Western Arabia. The subject is not an easy one to compress, for it is complicated by the fact that it has never been quite clear who are the governing authorities in the various parts of the peninsula. Nominally the three *vilayets*, or provinces, of Hejaz, Asir, and Yemen were part and parcel of the Turkish Empire before the war, but it would be an abuse of terms to say that Turkey was their governing authority. The Turkish conquest of Arabia dates back to the middle of the sixteenth century, and no nation has ever disputed her possessions; it is one thing, however, to conquer a country by force of arms, and quite another thing to hold it and administer the affairs of its inhabitants.

At no time has Turkey ever been able to maintain any real control over the various tribes of the Arabian peninsula. In the seventeenth century she gave up the attempt, so far as the province of Yemen was concerned, leaving the country to the guidance of one, Mansur-al-Kasim, the first of the *imams*, or religious leaders. Ever since then there has been an Imam of Yemen, directly descended from the said Mansur-al Kasim, and the present descendant is virtually the ruler of Yemen today.

It was not until 1869, after the opening of the Suez Canal, that Turkey again tried to establish her authority in Yemen by sending an army to Hodeida, which in due course occupied Sanaa, the capital of the province. At first the people of Yemen were disposed to welcome the aggressor, for they were so utterly weary of fighting with each other, and of the general state of lawlessness throughout the land, that even the prospect of alien domination was preferable to the prevailing conditions. It was not long, however, before they became even more weary of Turkish officials than they had been of internecine strife. In 1891 a rebellion of the tribes was suppressed with some difficulty by the Turkish garrison; in 1904 another rising occurred, and proved equally troublesome; in 1911 the Imam rallied the tribes around him, laid siege to Sanaa, and persuaded the Turkish military governor that there was no alternative but to consent to the Imam's terms.

These terms virtually abrogated Turkish authority in Yemen, abolished Turkish laws from the province, and substituted the old Islamic code, known as the "*Sheria*." which mainly concerns itself with the religious exercises of the people, and makes them liable to pains and penalties if they fail to say their prayers before sunrise, or do any of those things which good Mahomedans are supposed to do. As the penalties usually took the form of stiff fines, and the fines went into the *imam's* pocket, he found it worth while to maintain an elaborate system of espionage, in order that he might adequately shepherd his flock, and safeguard their souls from straying into the paths of unrighteousness. Moreover, the terms demanded that the *imam* should receive, as the price of his alliance with the Sublime Porte, the sum of £.T. 1,000 every month, and that certain smaller sums should be paid by Constantinople to various tribal chieftains, who might become fractious if they did not receive some little solace of this kind.

So, for the last three years before the war, Turkish dominion in Yemen was maintained by means of good honest Turkish gold. It is difficult to see where Turkey's *quid pro quo* came in, for it was certainly not in the trade of the country, which is worth very little at present. There are splendid natural resources to be developed, but development is impossible so long as every Arab is a law unto himself, and the caravan routes between the interior and the coast are continually beset with marauding brigands. The farmers grow produce just sufficient for local needs, knowing that any surplus would be wasted, for there is no way of establishing an export trade under the present conditions.

Hides, skins, and coffee are exported to a very small extent, and with considerable risk to the traders, the coffee being sent through Aden for the most part, for the port of Hodeida in Yemen is wretchedly equipped for the shipment of any kind of goods. In justice to the Turks it must be mentioned that in 1911 they started a big scheme to build a harbour near Hodeida and link it up with Sanaa by a metre-gauge railway. A syndicate was formed in Paris to finance the scheme, and the work was placed in charge of an Italian engineer, who was

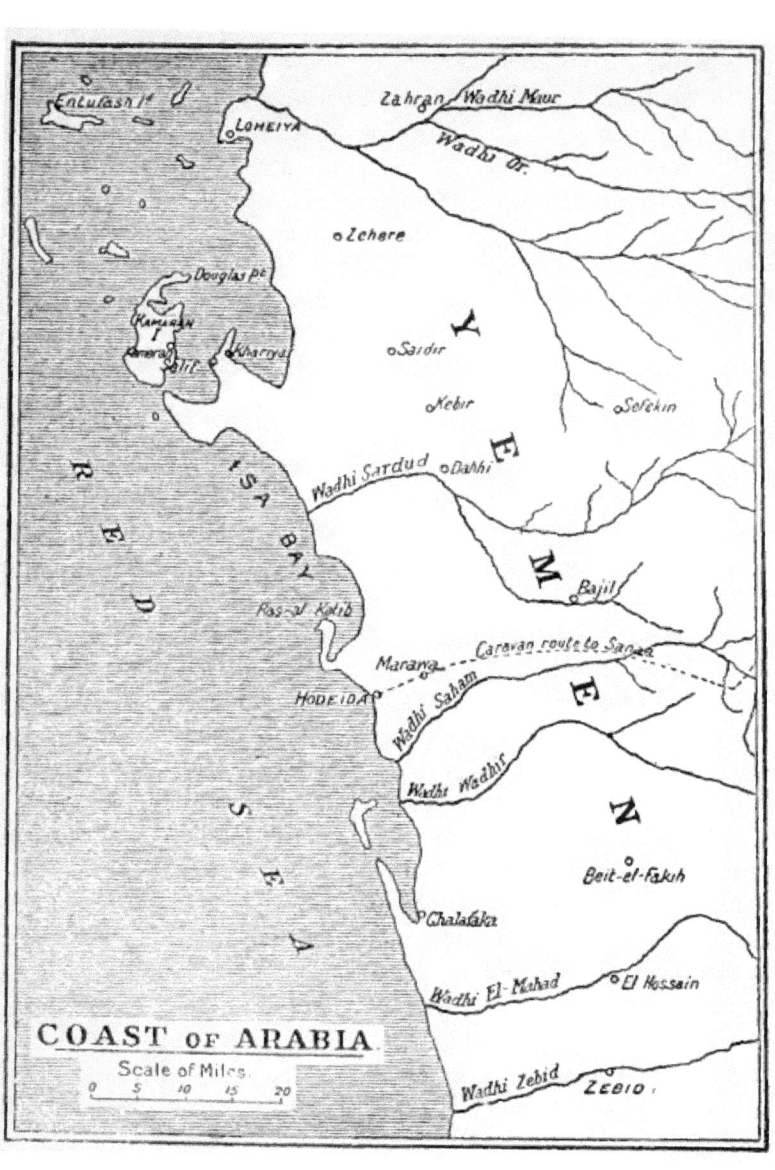

replaced by a French engineer in 1912, when the Turco-Italian War broke out. This change of engineers was unfortunate, for the Frenchman apparently had not mastered the art of dealing with Turkish officials, and the result was that very little progress was made with the undertaking

By the summer of 1913 some thousands of tons of railway material were lying on the beach and rusting, about five miles of single track had been laid, and another ten miles of embankment had been constructed; but towards the building of the harbour nothing had been done, beyond putting up a temporary jetty, and nobody seemed to be in the least interested in the subject. The Paris Syndicate resolved that they would be wise to cut their losses, rather than throw good money after bad. The Government of Constantinople, after having spent many thousands of pounds with no tangible result, shrugged its shoulders, and said "*Kismet*." And that is the story of the Sanaa Railway scheme.

The tragedy of Yemen is the tragedy of a fertile land run to waste. It is the same tragedy as that of Mesopotamia, where an empire, which had endured for 2,000 years and had been the centre of the world's civilisation, was converted by the blight of Turkish rule into a trackless desert, swamped for six months of the year by the ungoverned waters of two mighty rivers, and parched during the remaining six into a wilderness of barren dust. Yemen has not the potential wealth of Mesopotamia, but under wise administration it would become a prosperous country, contributing a substantial increment to the world's food stores. It has two distinct climates—that of the low-lying littoral belt, which stretches from north to south of the eastern side of the Red Sea and is known as the Tihama, and that of the mountains and high plateau which divide Western Arabia from the Great Red Desert.

Near the sea the Tihama is almost barren, for none of the mountain streams can find their way across the entire width of this plain, except when they are in flood, and consequently nothing can grow without the aid of artificial irrigation from wells. But farther inland towards the foot of the mountains the country is well watered, and the farmers grow millet, wheat, *dhurra*, sugar-canes, indigo, and sesame. The last-named, let me explain, has no connection whatever with lilies, as John Ruskin would have us suppose, but is an annual plant with oleaginous seeds, which the natives crush in a mill, formed of a large, hollow, conical stone, fixed base uppermost, and a smaller conical stone loosely fitting into the larger one. The smaller stone is turned by a camel, harnessed to a cross-bar, the seeds are dropped in at the top between the two stones, and the oil conies out at the bottom through a small hole. The oil is used by the natives for cooking, and the husks are used as cattle-fodder.

Behind the Tihama are the maritime ranges of hills. Here the husbandmen of bygone centuries have built terraces up the steep sides of the mountains, facing them with solid ramparts of stones, and shaping them to follow the contours of the ground, so that some of these terraces contain as much as a broad acre, while others are only a few feet wide. The soil is the alluvial deposit washed down by the streams. It grows wheat, barley, millet, and vegetables of various kinds, as well as fruits and spices both tropical and European, including bananas, plantains, cinnamon, grapes, apricots, peaches, apples, and quinces. The chief crop, however, is coffee, and for' this the soil provides excellent sustenance, while the highland mists, sometimes amounting to thick fogs, help to keep the plants irrigated. In spite of brigands and the absence of roads and railways in the country, the highland farmer contrives to export his coffee all over the world, and to make a comfortable living by his industry.

Beyond the maritime range is the great central plateau, which forms the watershed of western Arabia. Here the climate is almost temperate, and the vegetation changes accordingly. Towards the southern end of the plateau is Sanaa, the chief town of Yemen. Not far from Sanaa is the Mareb district, where the Queen of Sheba is supposed to have dwelt in the midst of pomp and luxury, though some commentators insist that her home was in Abyssinia, and that it was from Abyssinia that she drew the gold and rich spices that she presented to Solomon. However this may be, it is certain that the Mareb district is the site of a very ancient civilisation, of which traces may still be found in the remains of a vast dam, built by the Sabaeans to make a reservoir of water for the needs of their city and the irrigation of their land. It was through the bursting of this dam that the city of Sheba (or Saba) was washed out of existence, and the surrounding district reduced to a waterless waste.

Such in brief is the province of Yemen, the most fertile in Arabia. I have dealt with it first in the list because it is virtually the only part of Arabia which acknowledges any kind of allegiance to Turkey. Its ruler is the Imam, whose alliance with the Sublime Porte was maintained up to the beginning of the war at the price of £.T. 1,000 per month, plus the doles to the tribal chieftains, and w hose authority was propped up by keeping a small Turkish garrison in the province to supplement the native *gendarmerie*. Neither garrison nor *gendarmerie* have ever made any real attempt to establish law and order in the country, or to suppress the brigandage; nor can we blame them, for their wages and salaries were always many months in arrear. At one time the Turkish authorities used to try and collect taxes from the farmers, but they found that it was necessary to send a whole battalion to escort the tax-collectors, and so they gradually gave up the attempt.

As for the *Imam*, there is evidence that shortly before the armistice he was conspiring against the Turks, and the reason is not difficult to guess. The Turkish treasury at Sanaa was empty, communication with Constantinople was precarious, and so there can be little doubt that the payment of the *iman's* monthly honorarium was seriously behindhand. Moreover, he found that his authority over the tribes had suffered by reason of his alliance with the Sublime Porte, for the Arab does not love the Turk. Mr. Wyman Bury, who spent some years in Yemen upon zoological researches, and published his impressions in a book called *Arabia Infelix*, sums up the position as follows:

> The Turks entered Yemen at a time when any firm rule would have been welcome, and got control of a fertile country with a boundless water supply, if they had only been able to handle it. Yet they could not improve on the agricultural methods of the country, and cannot point to a single public work undertaken, completed, and maintained for the public weal. They have no continuity of purpose, and many schemes of theoretical excellence have been inaugurated in Yemen to die of inanition for lack of sustenance and support.... The Turkish authorities had the prestige of their race and the experience of former rule in Yemen to help them, yet they have even failed to gain the toleration of the people they have governed consecutively for the last forty years.

In a preface written shortly after the outbreak of the war, he adds:

> Turkey in Arabia will probably cease to exist—to the advantage of both parties, for her Arabian provinces are a constant drain on Turkey's resources, and Turkish rule is the curse of Arabia.

Of the other provinces of Arabia bordering the Red Sea it may be said unhesitatingly that they have ceased to have any truck with the Ottoman Government. To the south of Yemen is the British Protectorate of Aden, administered by the Indian Government. To the north of Yemen is the province of Asir, which is governed by a native chief called the *Idrisi*, so far as it can be said to have any government at all. He has always been consistent in his hostility to the Turkish Government, and when the Imam of Yemen became a *protégé* of Constantinople, the *Idrisi's* hostility was promptly extended towards him also. At no time has Turkish influence in Asir made any progress beyond the port of Kunfudah and its immediate vicinity, and even in this restricted area its existence has always been precarious. When the war began the *Idrisi* definitely declared himself the enemy of the Ottoman Government, and commenced active hostilities against the Turks.

North of Asir is the province of Hejaz—the largest and at the same time the least fertile of the western provinces of Arabia. Here the ruler is Hussein bin Ali, Emir of Mecca, now known as King Hussein of Hejaz, the acknowledged ally of the Entente Powers, whose troops cooperated with the British troops in the conquest of Palestine. Hussein spent many of his earlier years at Constantinople, and was regarded by the Ottoman Government as a man with a peaceable nature, who was likely to serve Turkish interests in Arabia faithfully and well. But in 1913 he showed very clearly that he had ideas of his own, which were distinctly contrary to Ottoman policy. At the outbreak of war he steadfastly refused to help the Turks to obtain recruits in Hejaz, and in the early part of 1916 he placed himself at the head of the tribes in a general insurrection against Turkish rule in Arabia.

Such, then, was the situation in Western Arabia at the beginning of 1917. On the extreme south a Turkish force, largely composed of Arab recruits, had invaded our Aden Protectorate, and occupied an entrenched position to the north of Aden harbour. It would have been a comparatively easy matter to drive them out of that position, but to follow them up into the interior through an inhospitable country would have required more energy, and have entailed more risk, than the object to be gained was worth. So we occupied a line of trenches defending Aden town and harbour, and there we sat and looked at the enemy, occasionally giving him a few rounds of shell, just to remind him that there was a war in progress.

It was quite clear that this force in the Aden Protectorate must derive its supplies from the interior. So far as food is concerned there was no mystery in this, for the Turkish soldier always manages to maintain existence on remarkably little, and that little would easily be obtained from the fertile country of Yemen. But the rifles and ammunition could only be replenished from outside sources, and there is not the least doubt that the traffic in small arms across the Red Sea, which the Turks had negligently allowed to go on without hindrance in peace time, was serving them in good stead in war time. It therefore became necessary for the British Navy to blockade the coast of Arabia.

From the description I have given of the operations in the vicinity of Aden it is not very obvious that it was a matter of much moment whether the enemy was kept supplied with munitions or not. There was, however, the possibility that, if he could succeed in equipping a sufficient force, he might be emboldened to try a raid on the town of Aden itself. (In fact, he did make one such attempt, but it was easily repulsed.) Moreover, there were other operations within the peninsula to be considered. In 1915 the Idrisi of Asir, with his tribesmen, made an attack on the Turkish garrison at the port of Loheiya, which failed mainly because the tribesmen showed a strong disinclination to face the Turkish artillery. In 1916 came the revolt in Hejaz, led by King Hussein and his sons, which eventually severed the Turkish garrisons in Arabia from the Turkish armies in Palestine by cutting the Hejaz Railway. Our blockade of the coast of Hejaz was intended to help King Hussein by persuading the Arabs that the Turk stood a very poor chance in Arabia, and there is no doubt that it has done much towards that end.

It must be borne in mind that the Arab, as a rule, is no student of international politics. He has a keen eye for the main chance, and a very human tendency to prefer to be on the winning side, but, until he is quite sure which side that is going to be, he is quite willing to turn an honest penny by making himself useful to either side. When I was stationed at Kurnah in Mesopotamia the Arabs there were employed by us to make a bund along the river banks to keep back the floods. Every night, about eleven o'clock, parties of Arabs would come sneaking down the river in canoes, presumably from the Turkish camp some six miles upstream, and would let drive at us with their rifles. Whereat we would sometimes turn on our searchlights and machine-guns, until the snipers had vanished as silently as they had come.

One night an Arab was shot, and was left behind by his companions by some oversight, for usually they were careful to carry their dead and wounded away with them. We found the body next morning, and in the pocket was a bright new *rupee*, which he must have received from our Field Treasure Chest officer the evening before he was killed. He was in the pay of the British Government for bunding the river in the daytime, and of the Turkish Government for sniping at the British by night. Such is the broad-minded impartiality of the Arab.

The question of money, prosaic as it sounds, was a very large factor in the political situation in Arabia, and afforded another cogent reason for a strict blockade of the coast. Intelligence reports told us that the Turkish treasury at Sanaa was empty, but that the merchants of Hodeida had been summoned to a conference, and had agreed to the imposition of a special war duty on imports to provide money for the Turkish force in Arabia. A Greek refugee, who had escaped from Hodeida, told us that the only money going into the Turkish treasury was derived from the customs dues collected at Hodeida, on goods coming from Massowa, Jibouti, and Aden, and he expressed surprise that we allowed so much to enter Hodeida.

The truth is that the navy was considerably handicapped in its work by the experts in diplomacy, who were all too conscious of the fact that many vested interests were involved, and feared to make Great Britain unpopular among the wealthy and influential Arabs. When, however, it became increasingly clear that the Turkish forces relied entirely on customs dues for their financial support, and that the pecuniary difficulties of the Turkish Government at Sanaa were alienating the sympathies of the Imam and other Arab notabilities, who looked in vain for their monthly "*douceurs*," even our experts in diplomacy were convinced that a rigorous blockade was the right policy.

So the British Navy in 1917 did what the Italian Navy had done during the Turco-Italian war of 1912—they carried the war into Arabia by blockading the coast. To attempt anything more ambitious, such as an invasion of the interior, would have required a substantial expeditionary force, which we could ill afford for such a purpose. It was obviously better suited to our means to aid the Arabs in their revolt against Turkish rule, by removing from the Turk his one and only means of retaining any influence in the country, than to provide an army to wrest it from him by force of arms. We did, however, take possession of the island of Kamaran off the coast of Yemen, where there is a quarantine station for pilgrims on their way to and from Mecca, consisting of a well-equipped hospital and some commodious residences for the quarantine officials. We also made an incursion to the mainland, opposite Kamaran Island, and, as this was entirely a naval operation, I propose to tell the story of it in detail.

On the coast which faces the island stands the small town of Salif, where large rock-salt works used to be carried on under the aegis of the Turkish Government. The main difficulty that the industry had to contend with was the inadequacy of the harbour, the only convenience for the loading of steamers being an old wooden pier, which was supposed to extend to the five-fathom line, though the depth of water at the end of it has probably been reduced by constant silting. Some time before the war the Turkish Government made a contract with Messrs. Sir John Jackson, Limited, to carry out certain improvements, and, as the work was still in progress when war was declared, the contractors had to take their departure in a hurry, leaving behind them a good deal of valuable plant.

It was this plant which caught the eye of the Commander-in-Chief, East Indies, when he was cruising down the Red Sea on his way to Aden, to discuss various matters with our political officer there. Having called at Kamaran Island, and learned there that the garrison of Salif was barely a hundred men, he proceeded on his way, and, on arriving at Aden, discussed the matter fully with the general officer commanding the troops. With this officer's concurrence he sent a telegram to the Government of India, asking that a company of Indian troops should be detailed to assist in the capture of Salif and its garrison, in order that the contractors' plant might be safely recovered .

The reason why the Government of India refused this request is unknown to me, but apparently they were nervous lest a landing of British forces on the mainland should have the effect of upsetting the friendly tribes in Arabia. Anyhow, the experts in diplomacy decided against the proposal of military co-operation, and the commander-in-chief was left to his own resources, which consisted of a small squadron of sloops and Royal Indian Marine vessels. The orders to Captain Boyle, the senior naval officer, were that, if no troops were placed at his disposal, he was merely to hold the enemy while the contractors' plant was being removed or destroyed, but that, in considering the further possibility of capturing the garrison of Salif, he must be guided by circumstances. With these orders Captain Boyle left Aden on the 10th June 1917 in the *Northbrook*, and, accompanied by the *Topaze*, *Odin*, *Espiegle*, and *Minto*, proceeded to Kamaran Island.

The village of Salif is situated on a peninsula, of which the northern end is merely a mud flat, covered by the sea at high tide. To the east of the village is a hunch-back of a hill, which is doubtless of volcanic formation, and in fact has a hollow in it suggesting the relics of a crater. It was in this hollow that the Turkish garrison had taken up their position when, at daybreak on 12th June 1917, our ships approached

Salif. The enemy's position was well chosen, for nothing could be seen of it from the sea, and only the high-angle fire of a howitzer could be expected to drop shells into it. Captain Boyle ordered the *Espiegle* to go northwards round the end of the peninsula, and enter the inlet between peninsula and mainland, possibly with the idea that the Turkish position might be more accessible from the eastern side of it. In any case the presence of a ship on that side would subject the enemy to a cross-fire, which is always disconcerting. The only danger to be avoided was that of the *Espiegle's* gun-layers, in an excess of enthusiasm, plumping shells right over the hill into the other ships; but fortunately no *contretemps* of this kind occurred.

The *Northbrook* anchored close inshore at the southern end of the peninsula, while *Minto*, *Topaze*, and *Odin* made a line to the north of her. They all kept as near to the shore as the depth of water would allow, in order that the landing parties might have as short a distance as possible to cover in the boats. As it turned out, the *Topaze* and *Odin* unconsciously followed the example of Lord Charles Beresford in the *Condor* at the bombardment of Alexandria, when he ran his ship in so close that the enemy ashore could not depress their guns sufficiently to hit him. The Turks in their hollow were in exactly the same predicament. They had two Krupp mountain-guns and three one-inch Nordenfeldts, with which they blazed away persistently, but their shells, in clearing the sides of the crater, also cleared our ships, and they did not score a single hit, though they occasionally dropped near enough to create an uncomfortable feeling on board.

The *Northbrook's* men landed at the south end of the peninsula, and took up a position near their ship to the right of the town. The others all landed at the pier, and extended themselves behind a ridge, flanked by a salt-mine at the south end, and by some houses at the north end. They then advanced cautiously to the foot of the hill, making a crescent-shaped line round it, with a party of Marines in the centre. The Odin's seamen remained behind in the village (where there were no signs of any Turks) and took possession of the condensing plant, the telegraph office, some mines, and one or two harems belonging to the Turkish officials. The last-named were transferred at the first opportunity to the *Northbrook*, which in due course took the women and children and the civilian males to Aden.

Commander A. R, W. Woods of the *Topaze* was in charge of the landing party, with Commander Salmond of the *Odin* as his second in command. His plan was to advance up the hill from three directions towards the Turkish position, and thus effectually surround it, for the fourth side was closed by the inlet from which the *Espiegle* was steadily plumping shells at the Turks. It is probable that the enemy, knowing that our force was a very small one, hoped to cause such havoc in it with their rifle-fire, while our men were coming up the hill, that we should be compelled to abandon the attack. If this was their calculation it failed to take into account the effectiveness of our gunnery.

An excellent system of signals had been arranged, and by means of this Commander Woods was able to turn on or off a barrage of fire as if it were a water-tap. The gun-layers were unfortunate in having the sun in their eyes, but, in spite of this, their shooting was so accurate that the men on shore could follow with confidence close behind the barrage. Under its cover they gradually crept towards the foot of the hill whereon the enemy were posted, and then, at a given signal, they made a rush forward and completely surrounded the Turks. The whole business lasted about three hours before the enemy surrendered. In justice to them, it must be said that they put up quite a good fight.

There are one or two amusing incidents to be recorded. Sergeant McLoughlin of the Royal Marines came across twelve Turkish soldiers, of whom one was wounded, decided that they were just about his own fighting weight, and went for them without a moment's hesitation. It was perhaps fortunate for him that Petty Officer Beaver was close behind him, for as a general rule the Turk does not allow estimates of this kind to be made with impunity. Between the pair of them they shot one of the twelve, took seven of them prisoners, while the rest retreated precipitately, but only to fall into other hands. Meanwhile Private Bartlett of the Royal Marines was having a little adventure of his own. He chanced upon a hut, and was prompted by curiosity to poke his head inside. There he discovered three Turks and three Arabs, all fully armed.

Some people might have been disconcerted and even embarrassed by such a discovery, but Private Bartlett regarded it as merely coming within the day's work. He was no great linguist, but he had his own methods of explaining to the assembled company that they were his prisoners, and he left not a shadow of doubt in their minds that he meant business. So they meekly handed over their rifles, and in due course Private Bartlett, wearing little more than a bland smile (for the sun was beating down hotly) handed them over to his commanding officer.

Having captured the whole garrison, together with their guns, ammunition, and stores, and having placed the prisoners aboard the *Topaze* for transport to Aden, the squadron moved off, leaving only the *Espiegle* behind to collect what was serviceable of Messrs. Sir John Jackson's plant, and to destroy the rest. Three days were spent in clearing up the place, during which time a company of Indian troops were sent over from Kamaran Island to do garrison duty. There was no idea of holding Salif permanently, for no object was to be gained by doing so.

The removal of the condensing plant made the place uninhabitable, since the only water supply is too brackish for ordinary consumption, and it was therefore most improbable that the Turks would attempt to reoccupy the village. Their removal made matters more comfortable for our small garrison at Kamaran, and we must also reckon on the credit side of the account the recovery of a certain amount of useful plant. On the other side we must place the death of Private Read of H.M.S. *Odin*, who had the misfortune to jump almost on top of a Turk, and to receive a rifle-bullet at point-blank range. It would seem that the Turk fired by accident rather than intent, for all his messmates were on the point of holding up their hands, realising that they were completely surrounded.

I have recorded this small affair at Salif, not because it was of any intrinsic importance, but because it is a fair sample of several small incidents, which have served to vary the monotonous routine of the Red Sea Patrol. There was another affair at Hodeida, which must, however, be written off as a failure, for it was an attempt to bluff the governor into releasing some British Indians interned there, and the governor showed very clearly that he did not belong to the race of those who are easily bluffed. There was also a small cutting-out expedition lower down the coast, when some blockade-running dhows were successfully captured; and more recently there were some bombardments of the coast, and the capture of the port of Loheiya. Take it on the whole, the Red Sea Patrol has had a fairly busy time of it.

This chronicle of naval operations during the Great War does not profess to be more than a collection of samples, which does not even include any mention of the main task devolving upon the navy. Yet I cannot refrain from winding up these stories by pointing a moral to them. There were occasions during the war when our cautious wiseacres spoke of a stalemate as the probable result, and our thoroughbred pessimists frankly contemplated defeat.

Even now, when victory has been achieved, there are many who cannot realise that this end was pre-ordained from the beginning; that, however the fortunes of the combatants might fluctuate, the ultimate issue was decreed from the very outset. They saw the transportation of the first Expeditionary Force across the Channel; they watched that small band of heroes expand into a mighty army; they know that that army was kept supplied with food and munitions, that large sections of it were transported overseas to the distant theatres of war, that, wherever British soldiers and British arms were needed, there they were sent with unfailing regularity; they have been told that some millions of men and some thousands of tons of munitions were brought from America to France; they saw the enemy's colonies snatched away from him one by one, while he was reduced to the role of a helpless spectator. All these things have been before their eyes, and yet there are some who cannot understand the true significance of what they have seen, who cannot realise that the result of the war was decided when Great Britain threw the weight of her navy into the scale.

What will be the verdict of posterity upon this Armageddon? How will the generations yet unborn sum up England's part in the conflict? I venture to hope that their verdict will be, firstly, that England's greatest pride was the quality of the officers and men who served her both ashore and afloat; secondly, that her greatest feat was the creation of a mighty army out of a small nucleus; and, thirdly, that her greatest good fortune was that victory was assured to her from the first moment of the war, because she had her Navy everywhere.

www.ingramcontent.com/pod-product-compliance
Lightning Source LLC
Chambersburg PA
CBHW031619160426
43196CB00006B/194